Famous Black Americans:
Folder Games for the Classroom

Curtis M. Graves
and
Jane A. Hodges

**Portraits by
Mauro Magellan**

Bartleby Press

Silver Spring, Maryland

This publication was made possible in part by a grant from the
American Association of University Women (AAUW)
Educational Foundation.

Copyright ©1986 by Curtis M. Graves and Jane A. Hodges.
All rights reserved. No part of this
book may be reproduced by any means, nor transmitted,
nor translated into a machine language, without permission.

Published and Distributed by:
Bartleby Press
11141 Georgia Avenue
Suite A-6
Silver Spring, Maryland 20902

The purchase of this book entitles the buyer to duplicate student activity
pages for non-sale classroom use only.
Any other use requires permission from the publisher.

ISBN: 0-910155-05-4

LIBRARY OF CONGRESS NO: 86-73090

Printed In The United States Of America

Contents

Acknowledgements	4
Foreword	5
Introduction	7

In Literature — 9

James Baldwin	10
Paul Lawrence Dunbar	12
Langston Hughes	16
James Weldon Johnson	20
Phillis Wheatley	24
Carter G. Woodson	27
Richard Wright	30

In Education — 33

Mary McLeod Bethune	34
Benjamin Mays	36
Samuel Nabrit	39
Booker T. Washington	43

In Politics — 46

Edward Brooke	47
Ralph Bunch	50
Shirley Chisholm	54
Richard Hatcher	58
Adam Clayton Powell, Jr.	61
Hiram Rhoades Revels	65
Robert Weaver	68
Andrew Young	72

In Science and Mathematics — 76

Benjamin Banneker	77
Guion S. Bluford, Jr.	81
George Washington Carver	85
Charles R. Drew	88
Garrett A. Morgan	90
Daniel Hale Williams	93

Civil Rights Leaders — 95

Frederick Douglass	96
W.E.B. Dubois	99
Marcus Garvey	102
Jesse Jackson	106
Martin Luther King, Jr.	109
Thurgood Marshal	112
Rosa Parks	115
Sojourner Truth	118

In the Military — 121

General Benjamin O. Davis, Jr.	122
Colonel Frederick Gregory	125
General Daniel James	129
Captain August Martin	131

In the Humanities — 134

Hector Hill	135
Marian Anderson	141
Louis Armstrong	145
Diahann Carroll	148
Nat King Cole	151
Bill Cosby	153
Sammy Davis, Jr.	155
Duke Ellington	158
Lena Horne	162
Ella Jenkins	165
Leontyne Price	169

In Sports — 173

Auther Ashe	174
Wilt Chamberlain	177
Ernie Davis	180
Althea Gibson	184
Joe Louis	187
Jesse Owens	190
Jackie Robinson	193

Card Game Matching Profiles and Mini-Biographies	196
Crossword Puzzles	206
Bibliography	214
Index	215

Acknowledgements

We would like to thank Tom Garmon, a teacher at Benjamin E. Mays High School in Atlanta, Georgia, for contributing various classroom activities and for field testing them with his students. Tom, a finalist in the Georgia Teacher in Space program, teaches aerospace education and Black History to his students.

We would also like to thank Laura Brown for typesetting this manuscript. Without her ambitious assistance, this book would not have been possible under the time frame allotted by the AAUW grant. Laura who is an adminstrative secretary at the Georgia Department of Education, received an AAUW grant to return to school to complete her degree in Business Administration.

We would also like to thank G. Anne Williams, Linda Pruitt-Hardie and J.D. Andrews for their editorial and artistic assistance and for their continued professional support.

Finally, we would like to thank Beth Harris for her contributions to the music sections. Beth was recently awarded a degree in Church Music and has been active in musical programs at her church in Independence, Missouri.

Foreword

Few Americans are aware of the extensive contributions of Blacks to every field of human endeavor. Few children have the experience of a hands-on learning activity that exposes them to prominent Black figures, past and present, in a variety of roles that range widely from the humanities to modern technological research. The selected sample in this book bears evidence that Blacks have invented and explored and discovered. Each new contribution makes us aware of the depth and uniqueness of the Black experience in contemporary American culture. Each new experience tantalizes us with a vision of what is yet to come.

A classroom activity book of selected Black Americans is intended to provide a guide for teachers and parents to help them introduce Black History to students at any grade or ability level. It is hoped that the brief biographical material will pique the student's particular interest and motivate him or her to delve further into little known aspects of Black contributions.

If we want our children to dream, to pursue, to discover, we must acquaint them with a full and comprehensive view of humanity. It is hoped that knowledge of their heritage will stimulate youngsters to greater curiosity about the world, to develop the confidence that encourages alert intelligence to ask "Why?" questions and to reject easy answers. Parents and teachers play a key role in shaping the direction of intelligence into the future.

We hope that this book compiled by my friends, Jane and Curtis, about a few prominent Black Americans will provide an example for each child who needs encouragement in his or her efforts at individual mastery. In the face of the new and challenging mysteries of the universe, our children need to develop the spontaneity, the curiosity and the freedom to look at the world in a new way. The Black Americans in this book share a common heritage. Despite whatever individual or social obstacles they had to overcome, they proceeded unfettered by traditional concepts to explore new ideas and new roles and to change the course of history.

Colonel Frederick Gregory
Space Shuttle Pilot
NASA Astronaut

Introduction

Famous Black Americans, Folder Games for the Classroom is designed as a classroom activity book that can be used as depicted on the minature file folders. It can also be varied according to the grade level and abilities of the students. The folder games can be made with blank file folders, watercolor marking pens, glue (glue sticks are ideal) and scissors. Color the profile of the person, then cut and glue it to the outside of the folder. Next cut the biographical data and glue it on the left side of the folder. (Questions about the biography, which should be placed under the data can be written by the teacher relating to student level. Next cut the activity page out and place it on the right side of the folder. Some folders may only require blank sheets of paper on this side, i.e. for library work, essays, etc. Other folders may have short additional activities that are to be placed on the bottom half of the back cover. Answers to the word search games should also be placed on the bottom half of the back cover. Next, cut out the directions and glue them to the top of the back cover. The miniature portraits may be glued onto index cards and kept for reference by the teacher.

During Black History Month students should prepare each folder for presentation. To honor Martin Luther King, Jr. students can also complete the section on him by the third Monday of January, designated as the National Holiday celebrating his birthday. (Parents can participate in this activity book by encouraging their children to make a folder each week for one of the fifty-two personalities featured. The projects in the book may be completed in one year. Since a laminator would not be available at home, clear contact paper may be used to cover and preserve the folders.

The teacher can use this activity book on all grade levels. Most activities are designed for middle grade students, however, since some of the biographical content may be new to students, the book can be adapted to fit various curriculum levels. Because the book is interdisciplinary it can be used in any classroom setting. Students who are motivated to learn when encouraged to add to this set of selected Black Americans can also make their own folders to commemorate other prominent Blacks.

Start creating your own learning center, varying the ideas in this book to reach your students' needs and interests!

James Baldwin

1924 -

Novelist, Essayist

James Baldwin was born in New York. He attended DeWitt Clinton High School. Three years later he won a fellowship that allowed him to write full time. His first novel, "Go Tell It on the Mountain," written in 1953, was given high critical notices, but it was his next novel, "Nobody Knows My Name," that brought him into the national spotlight. In 1962, Baldwin's third novel, "Another Country," was a big commercial success. The next year he wrote "The Fire Next Time," which became a best seller and is regarded as a brilliant history of Black protest against discrimination in America. Two of his plays have been produced on the New York stage: "Blues for Mister Charlie" and "The Amen Corner."

Name: James Baldwin

Skill: Language development

Procedure: Visit your library to find "Sonny's Blues," a short story by James Baldwin. His books should be explained to the students prior to reading.

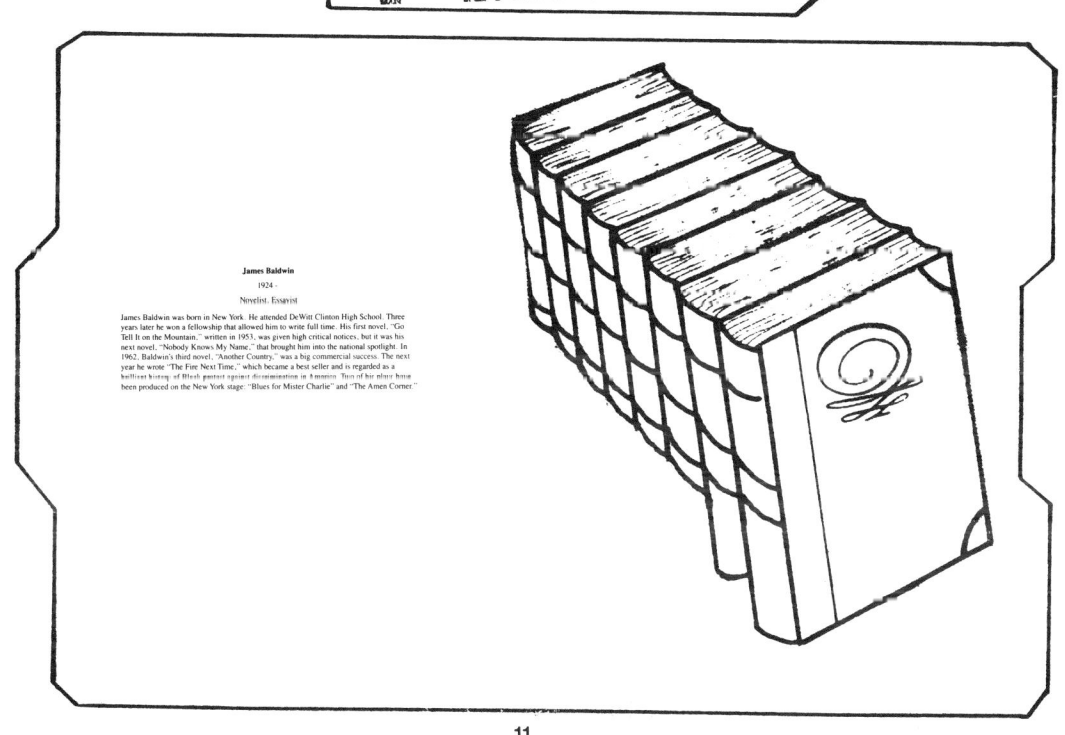

Paul Lawrence Dunbar

1872 - 1906

Poet

Paul Lawrence Dunbar was born in Dayton, Ohio, the only son of parents who had both been slaves. In high school he was the only Black in his class but was editor of the student newspaper. As a senior he composed his class's graduation song. He became an elevator operator for four dollars a week. His poems were first published individually in the Dayton newspaper and in 1893 he published at his own expense his first book of poems, "Oak and Ivy." He sold copies of his book on the elevator and in two weeks had paid his printing cost. After his second book was published, he received a full-page review in "Harper's Weekly." As a result of this article his books of fiction and poetry were bought out as soon as they were published. He lectured across the country as well as in England. When he returned to America, he took a job for an annual salary of $720.00. Dunbar married Alice Moore, an author and teacher, in New York City in 1898. He died of tuberculosis in 1906.

Name: Paul Lawrence Dunbar

Skill: Reading poetry

Procedure: 1. Read both versions of "When Malindy Sings," a poem by Paul Lawrence Dunbar. Discuss the grammatical differences between the two versions.

Variation: 1. Find other poems by Dunbar; memorize or read them to the class.
2. Find poems by Guendalyn Brooks, a contemporary dialetic poet, and compare her works to Dunbar's.

Paul Lawrence Dunbar
1872 – 1906
Poet

Paul Lawrence Dunbar was born in Dayton, Ohio, the only son of parents who had both been slaves. In high school he was the only Black in his class but was editor of the student newspaper. As a senior he composed his class's graduation song. He became an elevator operator for four dollars a week. His poems were first published individually in the Dayton newspaper and in 1893 he published at his own expense his first book of poems, "Oak and Ivy." He sold copies of his book on the elevator and in two weeks had paid his printing cost. After his second book was published, he received a full-page review in "Harper's Weekly." As a result of this article his books of fiction and poetry were bought out as soon as they were published. He lectured across the country as well as in England. When he returned to America, he took a job for an annual salary of $720.00. Dunbar married Alice Moore, an author and teacher, in New York City in 1898. He died of tuberculosis in 1906.

WHEN MALINDY SINGS
(Non-dialect Version)

Go away and quit that noise, Miss Lucy–
Put that music book away;
What's the use to keep on trying?
If you practise till you're gray
You can't start no notes a flying
Like the ones that rants and rings
From the kitchen to the big woods
When Malindy sings.

WHEN MALINDY SINGS
(Dialect Version)

G'way an' quit dat noise, Miss Lucy–
Put dat music book away;
What's de use to keep on tryin'?
Ef you practise twell you're gray,
You can't sta't no notes a-flyin'
Lak de ones dat rants and rings
F'om de kitchen to de big woods
When Malindy sings.

WHEN MALINDY SINGS

(Non-dialect Version)

Go way and quit that noise, Miss Lucy—
    Put that music book away;
What's the use to keep on trying?
    If you practise till you're gray,
You can't start no notes a-flying
    Like the ones that rants and rings
From the kitchen to the big woods
    When Malindy sings.

You ain't got the natural organs
    For to make the sound come right,
You ain't got the turns and twistings
    For to make it sweet and light.
Tell you one thing now, Miss Lucy,
    And I'm telling you for true,
When it comes to real right singing,
    It ain't no easy thing to do.

Easy enough for folks to holler,
    Looking at the lines and dots,
When there ain't no one can sense it,
    And the tune comes in, in spots;
But for real melodious music,
    That just strikes your heart and clings,
Just you stand and listen with me
    When Malindy sings.

Ain't you never heard Malindy?
    Blessed soul, take up the cross!
Look here, ain't you joking, honey?
    Well, you don't know what you lost.
You ought to hear that gal a-warbling,
    Robins, larks, and all them things,
Hush their mouths and hide their faces
    When Malindy sings.

Fiddling man just stops his fiddling,
    Lays his fiddle on the shelf;
Mocking-bird quits trying to whistle,
    'Cause he just so 'shamed his self.
Folks a-playing on the banjo
    Drop their fingers on the strings—
Bless your soul—forget to move 'em,
    When Malindy sings.

She just spreads her mouth and hollers,
    "Come to Jesus," till you hear
Sinners' trembling steps and voices,
    Timid-like a-drawing near;
Then she turns to "Rock of Ages,"
    Simply to the cross she clings,
And you find your tears a-dropping
    When Malindy sings.

Who's it that says that humble praises
    With the master never counts?
Hush your mouth, I hear that music,
    As it rises up and mounts—
Floating by the hills and valleys,
    Way above this burying sod,
As it makes its way in glory
    To the very gates of God!

Oh, it's sweeter than the music
    Of an educated band;
And it's dearer than the battle's
    Song of triumph in the land.
It seems holier than evening
    When the solemn church bell rings,
As I sit and calmly listen
    While Malindy sings.

Towsah, stop that barking, hear me!
    Mandy, make that child keep still;
Don't you hear the echoes calling
    From the valley to the hill?
Let me listen, I can hear it,
    Through the brush of angels' wings,
Soft and sweet, "Swing Low, Sweet Chariot,"
    As Malindy sings.

WHEN MALINDY SINGS

(Dialect Version)

G'way an' quit dat noise, Miss Lucy—
    Put dat music book away;
What's de use to keep on tryin'?
    Ef you practise twell you're gray,
You cain't sta't no notes a-flyin'
    Lak de ones dat rants and rings
F'om de kitchen to de big woods
    When Malindy sings.

You ain't got de nachel o'gans
    Fu' to make de soun' come right,
You ain't got de tu'ns an' twistin's
    Fu' to make it sweet an' light.
Tell you one thing now, Miss Lucy,
    An' I'm tellin' you fu' true,
When hit comes to raal right singin',
    'T ain't no easy thing to do.

Easy 'nough fu' folks to hollah,
    Lookin' at de lines an' dots,
When dey ain't no one kin sence it,
    An' de chune comes in, in spots;
But fu' real melojous music,
    Dat jes' strikes you' hea't and clings,
Jes' you stan' and listen wif me
    When Malindy sings.

Ain't you nevah hyeahd Malindy?
    Blessed soul, tek up de cross!
Look hyeah, ain't you jokin', honey?
    Well, you don't know whut you los'.
Y' ought to hyeah dat gal a-wa'blin',
    Robins, la'ks, an' all dem things,
Heish dey moufs an' hides dey faces
    When Malindy sings.

Fiddlin' man jes' stop his fiddlin',
    Lay his fiddle on de she'f;
Mockin'-bird quit tryin' to whistle,
    'Cause he jes' so shamed hisse'f.
Folks a-playin' on de banjo
    Draps dey fingahs on de strings—
Bless yo' soul—fu'gits to move 'em,
    When Malindy sings.

She jes' spreads huh mouf and hollahs,
    "Come to Jesus," twell you hyeah
Sinnahs' tremblin' steps and voices,
    Timid-lak a-drawin' neah;
Den she tu'ns to "Rock of Ages,"
    Simply to de cross she clings,
An' you fin' yo teahs a-drappin'
    When Malindy sings.

Who dat says dat humble praises
    Wif de Master nevah counts?
Heish yo' mouf, I hyeah dat music,
    Ez hit rises up an' mounts—
Floatin' by de hills an' valleys,
    Way above dis buryin' sod,
Ez hit makes its way in glory
    To de very gates of God!

Oh, hit's sweetah dan de music
    Of an edicated band;
An' hit's dearah dan de battle's
    Song o' triumph in de lan'.
It seems holier dan evenin'
    When de solemn chu'ch bell rings,
Ez I sit an' ca'mly listen
    While Malindy sings.

    Towsah, stop dat ba'kin', hyeah me!
        Mandy, mek dat chile keep still;
    Don't you hyeah de echoes callin'
        F'om de valley to de hill?
    Let me listen, I can hyeah it,
        Th'oo de bresh of angels' wings,
    Sof' an' sweet, "Swing Low, Sweet Chariot,"
        Ez Malindy sings.

Langston Hughes

1902 - 1967

Poet

Langston Hughes was known as the "Negro Poet Laureate." He was born in Joplin, Missouri in 1902. After high school Hughes spent a year in Mexico then later attended Columbia University in New York City. He became a seaman and traveled all over the world while doing some writing. After returning to the United States, he won the Witter Bynner Prize for undergraduate poetry while studying at Lincoln University. Some of his poems include "Not Without Laughter," "The Dream Keeper," "Shakespeare in Harlem," "One Way Ticket" and his autobiography, "The Big Sea." He edited several books to give exposure to Black authors. These include "An African Treasury" (1960), "New Negro Poets" (1964) and "The Best Short Stories by Negro Writers" (1967).

Name: Langston Hughes

Skill: Reading comprehension/Poetry

Procedure:
1. Read Hughes' poems. Discuss how the poems make you feel. How do you think Hughes felt when he wrote them?
2. Read "The Big Sea": An Autobiography by Hughes. Discuss events in his life and how they may have influenced his poetry.

Langston Hughes

1902 - 1967

Poet

Langston Hughes was known as the "Negro Poet Laureate." He was born in Joplin, Missouri in 1902. After high school Hughes spent a year in Mexico then later attended Columbia University in New York City. He became a seaman and traveled all over the world while doing some writing. After returning to the United States, he won the Witter Bynner Prize for undergraduate poetry while studying at Lincoln University. Some of his poems include "Not Without Laughter," "The Dream Keeper," "Shakespeare in Harlem," "One Way Ticket" and his autobiography, "The Big Sea." He edited several books to give exposure to black authors. These include "An African Treasury" (1960), "Poems from Negro Poets" (1964) and "The Best Short Stories by Negro Writers" (1967).

BALLAD OF THE LANDLORD

Langston Hughes

Landlord, landlord,
My roof has sprung a leak.
Don't you 'member I told you about it
Way last week?

Landlord, landlord,
These steps is broken down.
When you gonna fix them up yourself
It's a wonder you don't fall down.

Ten Bucks you say I owe you?
Ten Bucks you say is due?
Well, that's ten bucks more'n I'll pay you
Till you fix this house up new.

What? You gonna get eviction orders?
You gonna cut off my heat?
You gonna take my furniture and
Throw it in the street?

Um - huh! You talking high and mighty.
Talk on-till you get through.
You ain't gonna be able to say a word
If I land my fist on you.

Police! Police!
Come and get this man!
'He's trying to ruin the government
And overturn the land!

Copper's whistle!
Patrol bell!
Arrest.

Precinct Station.
Iron cell.
Headlines in Press:

Man Threatens Landlord

TENANT HELD NO BAIL

JUDGE GIVES NEGRO 90 DAYS IN COUNTY JAIL

BALLAD OF THE LANDLORD
Langston Hughes

Landlord, landlord,
My roof has sprung a leak.
Don't you 'member I told you about it
Way last week?

Landlord, landlord,
These steps is broken down.
When you come up yourself
It's a wonder you don't fall down.

Ten Bucks you say I owe you?
Ten Bucks you say is due?
Well, that's Ten Bucks more'n I'll pay you
Till you fix this house up new.

What? You gonna get eviction orders?
You gonna cut off my heat?
You gonna take my furniture and
Throw it in the street?

Um - huh! You talking high and mighty.
Talk on-till you get through.
You ain't gonna be able to say a word
If I land my fist on you.

Police! Police!
Come and get this man!
'He's trying to ruin the government
And overturn the land!

Copper's whistle!
Patrol bell!
Arrest.

Precinct Station.
Iron cell.
Headlines in Press:

Man Threatens Landlord

TENANT HELD NO BAIL

JUDGE GIVES NEGRO 90 DAYS IN COUNTY JAIL

The Negro Speaks of Rivers
(To W.E.B.) DuBois

I've known rivers:
I've known rivers ancient as the
 world and older than the flow
 of human blood in human veins.

My soul has grown deep like the rivers.

I bathed in the Euphrates when
 dawns were young
I built my hut near the Congo and
 it lulled me to sleep.
I looked upon the Nile and raised
 the pyramids above it.
I heard the singing of the
 Mississippi when Abe Lincoln
 went down to New Orleans, and
 I've seen its muddy bosom turn
 all golden in the sunset.

I've known rivers:
Ancient, dusky rivers.

My soul has grown deep like the
 rivers.

Mother To Son

Well, son, I'll tell you:
Life for me ain't been no crystal stair.
It's had tacks in it,
and splinters,
And boards torn up.
And places with no carpet on the floor.
Bare.
But all the time
I'se been a-climbing on,
And reachin' landin's,
And turning corners,
And sometimes goin' in the dark
Where there ain't been no light.
So boy, don't you turn back.
Don't you set down on the steps.
'Cause you finds it's kinder hard.
Don't you fall now—
For I'se still climbin'
And life for me ain't been no crystal stair.

James Weldon Johnson

1871 - 1938

Poet, Lyricist, Critic

James Weldon Johnson was born in Jacksonville, Florida in 1871. He was educated at Atlanta and Columbia Universities. He had many careers: he was a principal, a lawyer, a diplomat, the executive secretary of the NAACP, and the author of several books of poetry, as well as a collection of seven folk sermons in verse called "God's Trombones." His most famous work is the lyrics for the song, "Lift Every Voice and Sing." also known as the "Negro National Anthem."

Name: James Weldon Johnson

Skill: Reading/Music

Procedure: Read the biography aloud to class. Sing, "Lift Every Voice and Sing." Complete the word game that includes all of James Weldon Johnson's many jobs.

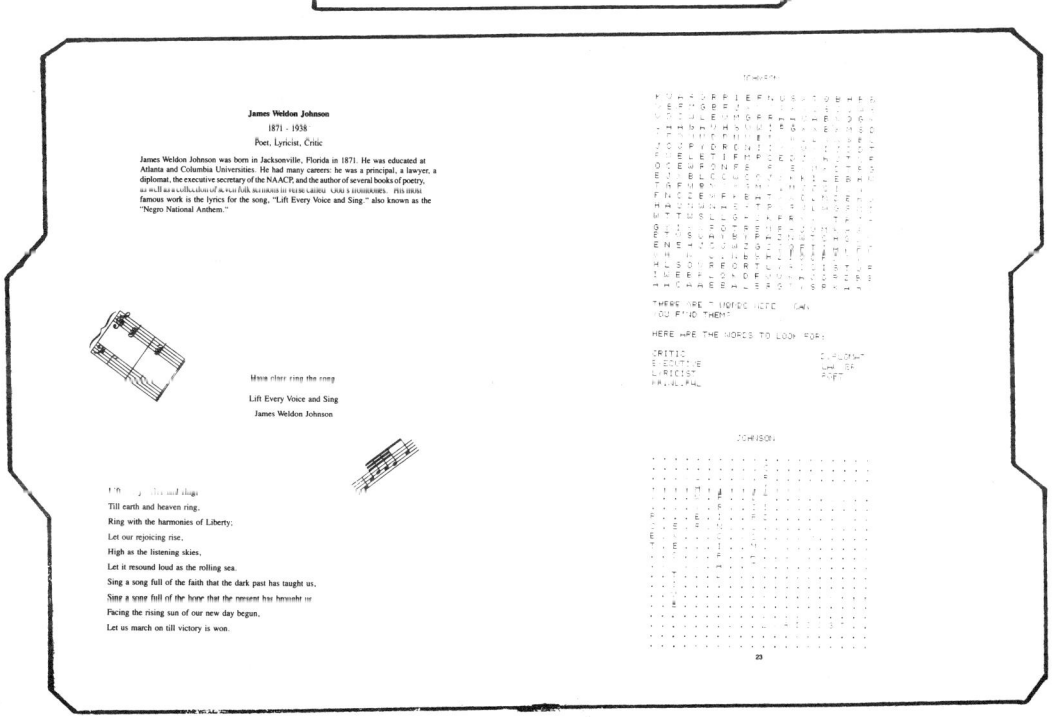

21

Have class sing the song.

Lift Every Voice and Sing
James Weldon Johnson

Lift every voice and sing,

Till earth and heaven ring,

Ring with the harmonies of Liberty;

Let our rejoicing rise,

High as the listening skies,

Let it resound loud as the rolling sea.

Sing a song full of the faith that the dark past has taught us,

Sing a song full of the hope that the present has brought us,

Facing the rising sun of our new day begun,

Let us march on till victory is won.

JOHNSON

```
K V A R Q R P I E F N U S X T Q B H E B
V B F M G B F J X V C I K X U S Q J W S
V D O W L E V M G P R A A U A B X Q G W
C A A G A V H S V W I P G K X B K M S D
D F D W W D P N V D T M R G Z X X S B L
J C J P Y D R D N I I X X V X I J D D T
P W E L E T I F M P C E D J X H U T L F
O O E W R O N F B L F V E K M K D T P G
E J X B L C C W C O J I K K I L E B H W
T G E W P N I X G M K U M J E G I G N V
F N C Z E W P K B A T X X C L M D E H U
H A U N W N A E F T P X R W L W G P M I
W T T W S L L G H Z K P R X Y X T R J H
G Y I K X P O T R E M P H J V M K H B Q
B T V S U A Y B Y P A Z N W T C H G D M
E N E H J C J W Z G Z O Q F T I A L F C
V H   N T C I N B S H Z I Q O F Z C Y Y
H L S O V R E O R T L Y R I C I S T U F
I W E B F L Q K D F V V K A J O R Z B S
A A C A A E B A L B R G I Y S P K A H V
```

THERE ARE 7 WORDS HERE - CAN
YOU FIND THEM?

HERE ARE THE WORDS TO LOOK FOR:

CRITIC   DIPLOMAT
EXECUTIVE   LAWYER
LYRICIST   POET
PRINCIPAL

JOHNSON

```
. . . . . . . . . . . . . . . . . . . .
. . . . . . . . . . . . C . . . . . . .
. . . . L . . . . . R . . . . . . . . .
. . . . A . . . . I . . . . . . . . . .
. . . . W . P . . D T . . . . . . . . .
. . . . Y . R . . I I . . . . . . . . .
P . . . E . I . . P C . . . . . . . . .
O . E . R . N . . L . . . . . . . . . .
E . X . . . C . . O . . . . . . . . . .
T . E . . . I . . M . . . . . . . . . .
. . C . . . P . . A . . . . . . . . . .
. . U . . . A . . T . . . . . . . . . .
. . T . . . L . . . . . . . . . . . . .
. . I . . . . . . . . . . . . . . . . .
. . V . . . . . . . . . . . . . . . . .
. . E . . . . . . . . . . . . . . . . .
. . . . . . . . . . . . L Y R I C I S T . .
. . . . . . . . . . . . . . . . . . . .
. . . . . . . . . . . . . . . . . . . .
```

23

Phillis Wheatley

1753 -1794

Poet

Phillis Wheatley, born in Senegal, West Africa, was brought to the United States as a slave. She was named Phillis by Susannah Wheatley, the wife of the Boston tailor who had bought her. She became interested in writing after reading the Bible and the classics under the guidance of the Wheatleys' daughter, Mary. Her first poem was published in 1770. It was called "A Poem by Phillis." George Washington was an admirer of her work. Her last poem, "Liberty and Peace," was published in 1794 shortly before her death.

Name: Phillis Wheatley

Skill: Reading comprehension

Variation: Have students recite Wheatley's last work, "Liberty and Peace." Discuss the poem with the class.

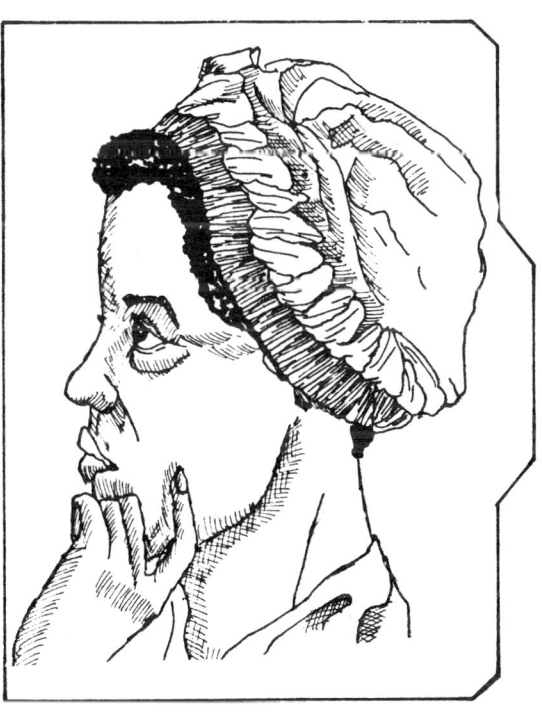

LIBERTY AND PEACE

Lo! freedom comes. Th' prescient muse foretold,
All eyes th' accomplish'd prophecy behold:
Her port describ'd, "She moves divinely fair,
Olive and laurel bind her golden hair."
She, the bright progeny of Heaven, descends,
And every grace her sovereign step attends;
For now kind Heaven, indulgent to our prayer,
In smiling peace resolves the din of war.
Fix'd in Columbia her illustrious line,
And bids in thee her future councils shine.
To every realm her portals open'd wide,
Receives from each the full commercial tide.
Each art and science now with rising charms,
Th' expanding heart with emulation warms.
E'en great Britannia sees with dread surprise,
And from the dazzling splendors turns her eyes.
Britain, whose navies swept th' Atlantic o'er,
And thunder sent to every distant shore;
E'en thou, in manners cruel as thou art,
The sword resign'd, resume the friendly part.
For Gallia's power espous'd Columbia's cause,
And new-born Rome shall give Britannia laws,
Nor unremember'd in the grateful strain,
Shall princely Louis' friendly deed remain;
The generous prince th' impending vengeance eyes,
Sees the fierce wrong and to the rescue flies.
Perish that thirst of boundless power, that drew
On Albion's head the curse to tyrants due.
But thou appeas'd submit to Heaven's decree,
That bids this realm of freedom rival thee.
Now sheathe the sword that bade the brave atone
With guiltless blood for madness not their own.
Sent from th' enjoyment of their native shore,
Ill-fated—never to behold her more.
From every kingdom on Europa's coast
Throng'd various troops, their glory, strength, and boast
With heart-felt pity fair Hibernia saw
Columbia menac'd by the Tyrant's law:
On hostile fields fraternal arms engage,
And mutual deaths, all dealt with mutual rage:
The muse's ear hears mother earth deplore
Her ample surface smoke with kindred gore:
The hostile field destroys the social ties,
And everlasting slumber seals their eyes.
Columbia mourns, the haughty foes deride,
Her treasures plunder'd and her towns destroy'd:
Witness how Charlestown's curling smokes arise,
In sable columns to the clouded skies.
The ample dome, high-wrought with curious toil,
In one sad hour the savage troops despoil.
Descending peace the power of war confounds;
From every tongue celestial peace resounds:
As from the east th' illustrious king of day,
With rising radiance drives the shades away,
So freedom comes array'd with charms divine,
And in her train commerce and plenty shine.
Britannia owns her independent reign,
Hibernia, Scotia, and the realms of Spain;
And great Germania's ample coast admires
The generous spirit that Columbia fires.
Auspicious Heaven shall fill with fav'ring gales,
Where'er Columbia spreads her swelling sails:
To every realm shall peace her charms display,
And heavenly freedom spread her golden ray.

By Phylis Wheatley

Carter G. Woodson

1875 - 1950

Historian

Carter G. Woodson was born in New Carrton, Virginia and educated at Berea College, the University of Chicago, Harvard University and the Sorbonne in Paris. Carter Woodson was the founder and director of the Association for the Study of Negro Life and History. Woodson taught both at the elementary and high school levels before becoming the Dean of Liberal Arts at Howard University in Washington, D.C. He traveled widely in Egypt, Asia and Europe. Woodson wrote many history books including "The Education of the Negro Prior to 1861" (1915); "A Century of Negro Migration" (1918); "The Negro in Our History" (1922). The cultural association he founded still has offices in Washington, D.C.

Name: Carter G. Woodson

Skill: Reading/Research skills

Procedure: Find in the word game the universities and colleges Dr. Woodson attended.

Variation: Take your class to the library to find some books by Carter G. Woodson. Use the card catalogue and any other source available to prepare a bibliography of his works. Use the proper format.

Carter G. Woodson
1875 - 1950
Historian

Carter G. Woodson was born in New Canton, Virginia and educated at Berea College, the University of Chicago, Harvard University and the Sorbonne in Paris. Carter Woodson was the founder and director of the Association for the Study of Negro Life and History. Woodson taught both at the elementary and high school levels before becoming the Dean of Liberal Arts at Howard University in Washington, D.C. He traveled widely in Egypt, Asia and Europe. Woodson wrote many history books including "The Education of the Negro Prior to 1861" (1915); "A Century of Negro Migration" (1918); "The Negro in Our History" (1922). The cultural association he founded still has offices in Washington, D.C.

THERE ARE 4 WORDS HERE - CAN YOU FIND THEM?

HERE ARE THE WORDS TO LOOK FOR:

BEREA COLLEGE   HARVARD
SARBONNE   UNIV OF CHICAGO

WOODSON

```
K W J D U N I V   O F   C H I C A G O H
V D V O X L A D Z D Z S Z U H S T C W T
B G V X T G N L E D A P T Q N C F E F R
N P T L F T J K J G D Q Y M D M T R E U
E Q J V C N U M X R X Q X R I O X F U F
L H J Z Q M G Y V G S N A F R U K H V C
X F X N Q K A L I A P V G O F M F S E B
W R K Z B R T X U L R J G E M Q U Y P O
I P B K S E N P W A J U I B G M M F V V
D X C Y U Y R K H O G K G D U M G X E M
M J S I H U T E E B E F O E A J S L X K
Q U T O P Y F N A T L J H H T M C F U Y
H R I C N B N E I   F H A P A C S T Z G
X R P I P O U L F P C P Q Z Z S A K T K
G I G F B U I T H W I O H T A Q I M S Y
P Q C R E R K B S R W T L U U O L D R C
U I A H E Z I I A Y V M D L U Q P V C T
D S F Q Z R G I K Q Q B M D E Y I U S O
Z T W W S J Y Q Z H W M Q B O G Y V R A
W C C Y T N K T I T E J T Y F V E U F Y
```

THERE ARE 4 WORDS HERE – CAN
YOU FIND THEM?

HERE ARE THE WORDS TO LOOK FOR:

BEREA COLLEGE   HARVARD
SARBONNE   UNIV OF CHICAGO

WOODSON

```
. . . . . U N I V   O F   C H I C A G O .
. . . . . . . . . . . . . . . . . . . . .
. . . . . . . . . . . . . . . . . . . . .
. . . . . . . . . . . . . . . . . D . . .
. . . . . . . . . . . . . . . R . . . . .
. . . . . . . . . . . . . . A . . . . . .
. . . . . . . . . . . . V . . . . . . . .
. . . . . B . . . . R . . . . . . . . . .
. . . . . . E . . . A . . . . . . . . . .
. . . . . . . R . H . . . . . . . . . . .
. . . . . . . . E E . . . . . . . . . . .
. . . . . . . . N A . . . . . . . . . . .
. . . . . . . N . . . . . . . . . . . . .
. . . . . . O . . . . C . . . . . . . . .
. . . . B . . . . . . O . . . . . . . . .
. . . R . . . . . . . . L . . . . . . . .
. . A . . . . . . . . . L . . . . . . . .
. S . . . . . . . . . . . E . . . . . . .
. . . . . . . . . . . . . . G . . . .
. . . . . . . . . . . . . . . E . . .
```

29

Richard Wright

1908 - 1960

Novelist

Richard Wright was born in Natchez, Mississippi. He used his childhood experiences in his books to dramatize the problem of racial injustice to a national audience. While a member of the Work Program Administration (WPA) of the Writers' Project, Wright published "Uncle Tom's Children" in 1938. This was a collection of four novels based on his Mississippi boyhood. The book won Wright several awards, among them the Guggenheim Fellowship. In 1940 he published his most famous work, "Native Son," which quickly became the Book-of-the-Month-Club choice. It was later made into a Broadway play produced by Orson Welles and then turned into a film with Wright himself playing the role of Bigger Thomas. His second best seller was "Black Boy," which was largely autobiographical. Wright moved to Paris and there wrote such outstanding books as "The Outsider," "Black Power," "The Color Curtain," and "The Long Dream."

Name: Richard Wright

Skill: Reading and comprehension.

Procedure: 1. Find the names of Richard Wright's books in the word game.

Variation: Check out one of Wright's books from the library. Read a chapter to your class. Ask questions about the racial injustice Wright describes.

WRIGHT'S BOOKS

```
C L Q P H C K M T B L A C K   P O W E R
C B H V Q O D J U J O T F E C T Q J I X
X D O Z T P E O I Y P V T G X Z I K I Q
L H W Y H J K M U S G W R E T I T W A R
U A E I E I C C B A B K U J K W H C V N
U S C C   O A U Y Y Q W P H L O K G S K
I O Y C O O K B I L J X V Y H K C Z Q N
F V M I U D E Y G F K R E W A B N V W K
W I Q P T B L A C K   B O Y V V A D G A
Q D G E S H J H E R Q L A G A Q T S V O
A M R O I A X U B B G B D X L J I P S O
M G S C D O R Z C P O P P T H X V H D S
Q E B H E S V I C V R M I E U K E A T F
G R E U R P I S R J C C R D E V   A R W
T W B G V V G A W G J Q Y S N U S J O Z
Q K W G O Y T T Y J A E X W K M O Q R N
A D T H E   L O N G   D R E A M N B R R
V B K F J V H X F V E C E C R P B L Y A
X T X Z L V A Z U G S H H X S G Z G E G
T K Y C O L O R   C U R T A I N W X U H
```

THERE ARE 6 WORDS HERE - CAN
YOU FIND THEM?

HERE ARE THE WORDS TO LOOK FOR:

BLACK BOY   BLACK POWER
COLOR CURTAIN   NATIVE SON
THE LONG DREAM   THE OUTSIDER

WRIGHT'S BOOKS

```
. . . . . . . . . B L A C K   P O W E R
. . . . . . . . . . . . . . . . . . . .
. . . . T . . . . . . . . . . . . . . .
. . . . H . . . . . . . . . . . . . . .
. . . . E . . . . . . . . . . . . . . .
. . . . . . . . . . . . . . . . . . . .
. . . . O . . . . . . . . . . . . . . .
. . . . U . . . . . . . . . . . N . . .
. . . . T B L A C K   B O Y . . A . . .
. . . . S . . . . . . . . . . . T . . .
. . . . I . . . . . . . . . . . I . . .
. . . . D . . . . . . . . . . . V . . .
. . . . E . . . . . . . . . . . E . . .
. . . . R . . . . . . . . . . . . . . .
. . . . . . . . . . . . . . . . S . . .
. . . . . . . . . . . . . . . . O . . .
. . T H E   L O N G   D R E A M N . . .
. . . . . . . . . . . . . . . . . . . .
. . . . C O L O R   C U R T A I N . . . .
```

32

IN EDUCATION

Mary McLeod Bethune

1875-1955

Educator

Mary McLeod Bethune was born in South Carolina and was educated to be a missionary. After being turned down for a missionary post in Africa by the Presbyterian Church, she turned to teaching. President Herbert Hoover asked her to attend a White House Conference on Child Health and Protection in 1930. A few years later President Franklin D. Roosevelt appointed her to serve on an advisory committee of the National Youth Administration (NYA). A year later she came to the President's attention again when he asked her to set up and head an Office of Minority Affairs in the NYA. This was the first post of this importance ever headed by an American Black woman. After 8 years, Mrs. Bethune's title was changed to Director of Negro Affairs. During the 1930s, Mary McLeod Bethune was a member of Roosevelt's unofficial "Black Cabinet" fighting for integration in the U.S. Government. She was the only woman in the group. Besides founding the "National Council of Negro Women," she also founded a school that is now known as Bethune-Cookman College in Daytona, Florida.

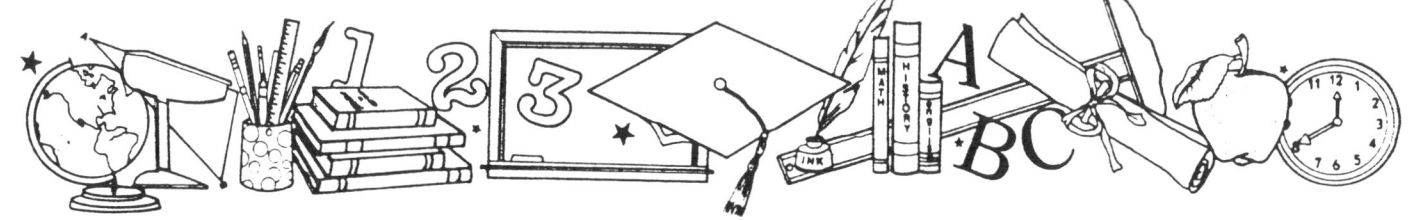

Name: Mary McLeod Bethune

Skill: Research skills/Social studies

Procedure: 1. Report on the unofficial "Black Cabinet." How would you locate? information in the library?

Variation: List some positions which Blacks now hold in government.

Benjamin Elizah Mays

1894 - 1984

Educator

Benjamin E. Mays, an educator, author and philosopher, was born in Epworth, South Carolina, on August 1, 1894. Benjamin's parents were barely literate farmers who had been slaves until the Civil War. His father was not in favor of Benjamin completing his elementary and secondary school education. He did finish, however, and left South Carolina for Bates College in Maine where he earned a degree in 1925. He continued his education at the University of Chicago where he earned a master's degree in 1929 and his Ph.D. in 1935. After completing his work in Chicago, he became Dean of the School of Religion at Howard University and later served as the President of Morehouse College in Atlanta, Georgia from 1940 until 1967. After Dr. Mays retired from Morehouse, he was elected to the Atlanta Board of Education where he served for twelve years. Dr. Mays wrote many inspirational books and 96 magazine articles. His philosophy is best demonstrated in his book *Quotable Quotes of Benjamin E. Mays*. He was an inspiration to all who knew him.

Name: Benjamin E. Mays

Skill: Research

Procedure:
1. Using resources from current events. Find out how decisions are made about running your local school system.
2. Draw a diagram of the "Chain of Command" of decision-making in your school system.

Variation:
1. Research the contributions to education of Alonzo Crim, the Superintendent of the Atlanta City School System and Dr. Manford Byrd, Jr., the Superintendent of the Chicago City Schools.
2. Choose one of Dr. Mays' quotes and explain its meaning in a paragraph.

Benjamin Elizah Mays
1894 - 1984
Educator

Benjamin E. Mays, an educator, author and philosopher, was born in Epworth, South Carolina, on August 1, 1894. Benjamin's parents were barely literate farmers who had been slaves until the Civil War. His father was not in favor of Benjamin completing his elementary and secondary school education. He did finish, however, and left South Carolina for Bates College in Maine where he earned a degree in 1925. He continued his education at the University of Chicago where he earned a master's degree in 1929 and his Ph.D. in 1935. After completing his work in Chicago, he became Dean of the School of Religion at Howard University and later served as the President of Morehouse College in Atlanta, Georgia from 1940 until 1967. After Dr. Mays retired from Morehouse, he was elected to the Atlanta Board of Education where he served for twelve years. Dr. Mays wrote many inspirational books and 96 magazine articles. His philosophy is best demonstrated in his book *Quotable Quotes of Benjamin E. Mays*. He was an inspiration to all who knew him.

QUOTES BY BENJAMIN E. MAYS

It is not your environment, it is you—
the quality of your minds, the integrity of
your souls, and the determination of
your wills—that decide your future and
shape your lives.

He who starts behind in the great race
of life must forever remain behind or
run faster than the man in front.

You are what you aspire to be, and not
what you now are; you are what you do
with your mind, and you are what
you do with your youth.

Whatever one touches, his aim should
always be to leave that which he touches
better than he found it.

BOOKS BY DR. MAYS

The Negro's Church
The Negro's God
A Gospel for the Social Awakening
Disturbed About Man
Born to Rebel
Lord, The People Have Driven Me On
Quotable Quotes of Benjamin E. Mays

QUOTES BY BENJAMIN E. MAYS

It is not your environment, it is you—
the quality of your minds, the integrity of
your souls, and the determination of
your wills—that decide your future and
shape your lives.

He who starts behind in the great race
of life must forever remain behind or
run faster than the man in front.

You are what you aspire to be, and not
what you now are; you are what you do
with your mind, and you are what
you do with your youth.

Whatever one touches, his aim should
always be to leave that which he touches
better than he found it.

BOOKS BY DR. MAYS

The Negro's Church

The Negro's God

A Gospel for the Social Awakening

Disturbed About Man

Born to Rebel

Lord, The People Have Driven Me On

Quotable Quotes of Benjamin E. Mays

contributed by Tom Garmon

Samuel Nabrit

1905 -

Member, Atomic Energy Commission

Samuel Nabrit was born in Macon, Georgia and educated in Augusta. He was the valedictorian of his high school class. After graduating from Morehouse College in Atlanta, he became a biology instructor at the college then a professor and dean at Atlanta University, both of which are United Negro College Fund Schools. In 1932 he became the first Black to receive his Ph.D. from Brown University. He taught at Columbia University and later did a year of research in Brussels, Belgium. President Dwight Eisenhower appointed him to the National Science Board. He was then named special ambassador to Niger in West Africa by President John Kennedy. In 1956 Dr. Nabrit was appointed President of Texas Southern University in Houston. Ten years later President Lyndon Johnson appointed him a member of the Atomic Energy Commission. For fourteen years he was also Executive Director of the Southern Fellowship Fund. Dr. Nabrit is now living in retirement in Atlanta.

Name: Samuel Nabrit

Skill: Reading

Procedure:
1. Find out more about the universities Dr. Samuel Nabrit was involved with.
2. Learn about the United Negro College Fund and discover which colleges belong to it.

Variation:
1. Use a map of the United States to locate the colleges that are institutional members of the United Negro College Fund.
2. Learn more about Dr. Douglas Patterson, the founder of the United Negro College Fund.

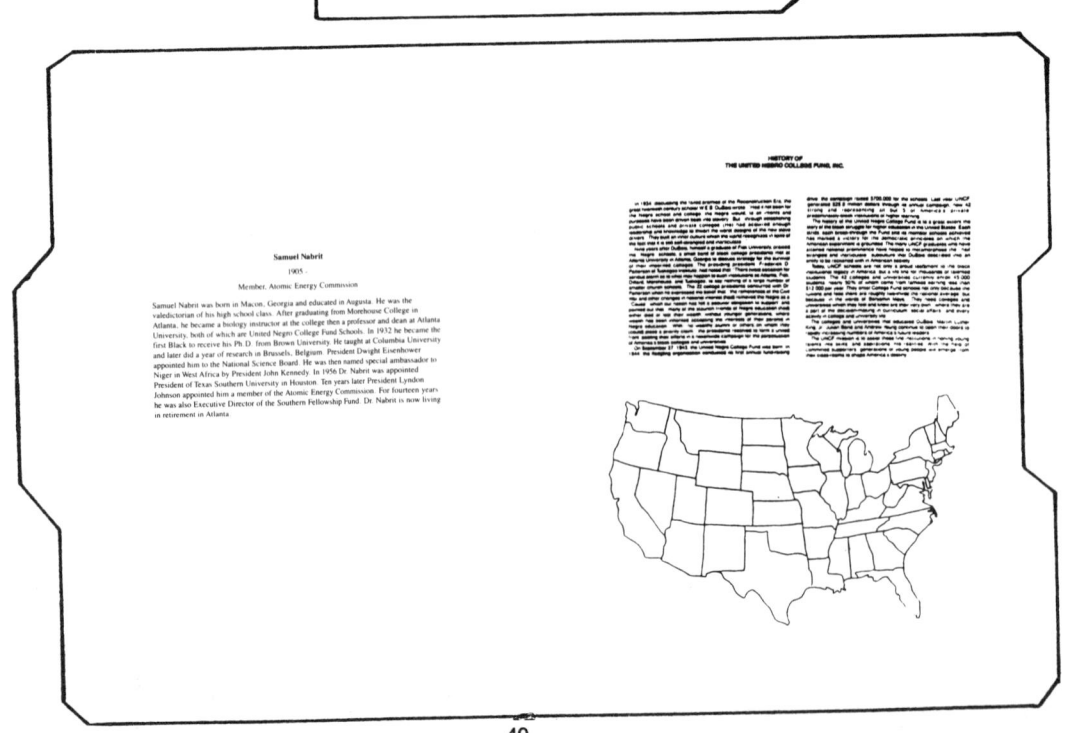

Samuel Nabrit
1905 -
Member, Atomic Energy Commission

Samuel Nabrit was born in Macon, Georgia and educated in Augusta. He was the valedictorian of his high school class. After graduating from Morehouse College in Atlanta, he became a biology instructor at the college then a professor and dean at Atlanta University, both of which are United Negro College Fund Schools. In 1932 he became the first Black to receive his Ph.D. from Brown University. He taught at Columbia University and later did a year of research in Brussels, Belgium. President Dwight Eisenhower appointed him to the National Science Board. He was then named special ambassador to Niger in West Africa by President John Kennedy. In 1956 Dr. Nabrit was appointed President of Texas Southern University in Houston. Ten years later President Lyndon Johnson appointed him a member of the Atomic Energy Commission. For fourteen years he was also Executive Director of the Southern Fellowship Fund. Dr. Nabrit is now living in retirement in Atlanta.

HISTORY OF
THE UNITED NEGRO COLLEGE FUND, INC.

HISTORY OF
THE UNITED NEGRO COLLEGE FUND, INC.

In 1934, discussing the failed promise of the Reconstruction Era, the great twentieth century scholar W.E.B. DuBois wrote: "Had it not been for the Negro school and college, the Negro would, to all intents and purposes have been driven back into slavery...But...through establishing public schools and private colleges..(He) had acquired enough leadership and knowledge to thwart the worst designs of the new slave drivers...They built an inner culture which the world recognizes in spite of the fact that it is still self-strangled and inarticulate..."

Nine years after DuBois, himself a graduate of Fisk University, praised the "Negro" schools, a small band of black college presidents met at Atlanta University in Atlanta, Georgia to discuss strategy for the survival of their imperiled colleges. The presiding president, Frederick D. Patterson of Tuskegee Institute, had noted that "There (was) occasion for serious alarm as to what may happen to such institutions as Atlanta, Fisk, Dillard, Morehouse, and Tuskegee, to say nothing of a large number of smaller church schools." The 22 college presidents concurred with Dr. Patterson when he expressed the belief that "the remoteness of the Civil War and other changes in national interest (had) removed the Negro as a "Cause" which our nation has felt a peculiar obligation to support' and pointed out that "many of the staunch friends of Negro education (had) either died or lost their wealth, without younger generations, where wealth has been inherited accepting the interests of their parents in Negro education." With "no wealthy alumni or others on whom they (could) place a priority claim," the presidents resolved to form a united front, pooling their efforts in a nationwide campaign for the perpetuation of America's black colleges and universities.

On September 27, 1943, the United Negro College Fund was born. In 1944, the fledgling organization conducted its first annual fund-raising drive; the campaign raised $700,000 for the schools. Last year UNCF generated $25.8 million dollars through its annual campaign, now 42 strong and representing all but 5 of America's private, predominately-black institutions of higher learning.

The history of the United Negro College Fund is to a great extent the story of the black struggle for higher education in the United States. Each stride, each break-through the Fund and its member schools achieved has marked a victory for the democratic principles on which the American experiment is grounded. The many UNCF graduates who have attained national prominence have helped to metamorphose the "half strangled and inarticulate" subculture that DuBois described into an entity to be reckoned with in American society.

Today, UNCF schools are not only a proud testament to the black institutional legacy in America, but a life line for thousands of talented students. The 42 colleges and universities currently enroll 45,000 students, nearly 50% of whom come from families earning less than $12,000 per year. They enter College Fund schools not only because the tuitions and fees there are roughly two-thirds the national average, but because, in the words of Benjamin Mays: "They need colleges and universities which they feel and know are their very own...where they are a part of the decision-making in curriculum, social affairs...and every activity in college and university life."

The colleges and universities that educated DuBois, Martin Luther King, Jr., Julian Bond and Andrew Young continue to open their doors to rapidly increasing numbers of America's future leaders.

The UNCF mission is to assist these fine institutions in honing young talents into skills, and aspirations into realities. With the help of committed supporters, generations of young people will emerge from their class-rooms to shape America's destiny.

UNITED NEGRO COLLEGE FUND, INC.
500 East 62nd Street
New York, New York 10021
(212) 644-9610

INSTITUTIONAL MEMBERS

ATLANTA UNIVERSITY
PRESIDENT LUTHER S. WILLIAMS
ATLANTA GA 30314

BARBER-SCOTIA COLLEGE
PRESIDENT MABLE P. MCLEAN
CONCORD NC 28025

BENEDICT COLLEGE
PRESIDENT MARSHALL C. GRIGSBY
COLUMBIA SC 29204

BENNETT COLLEGE
PRESIDENT ISAAC H. MILLER, JR.
GREENSBORO NC 27420

BETHUNE-COOKMAN COLLEGE
PRESIDENT OSWALD P. BRONSON, SR.
DAYTONA BEACH FL 32015

BISHOP COLLEGE
PRESIDENT WRIGHT L. LASSITER, JR.
DALLAS TX 75241

CLAFLIN COLLEGE
PRESIDENT OSCAR A. RODGERS, JR.
ORANGEBURG SC 29115

CLARK COLLEGE
PRESIDENT ELAIS BLAKE, JR.
ATLANTA GA 30314

DILLARD UNIVERSITY
PRESIDENT SAMUEL DUBOIS COOK
NEW ORLEANS LA 70122

EDWARDS WATERS COLLEGE
PRESIDENT CECIL W. CONE
JACKSONVILLE FL 32209

FISK UNIVERSITY
PRESIDENT HENRY PONDER
NASHVILLE TN 37203

FLORIDA MEMORIAL COLLEGE
PRESIDENT WILLIE C. ROBINSON
MIAMI FL 33054

HUSTON-TILLOTSON COLLEGE
PRESIDENT JOHN Q. TAYLOR KING
AUSTIN TX 78702

INTERDENOMINATIONAL THEOLOGICAL CENTER
PRESIDENT JAMES H. COSTEN
ATLANTA GA 30314

JARVIS CHRISTIAN COLLEGE
PRESIDENT CHARLES A. BERRY, JR.
HAWKINS TX 75765

JOHNSON C. SMITH UNIVERSITY
PRESIDENT ROBERT L. ALBRIGHT
CHARLOTTE NC 28216

KNOXVILLE COLLGE
ACTING PRESIDENT ROBERT SHEPHERD
KNOXVILLE TN 37921

LANE COLLEGE
PRESIDENT HERMAN STONE, JR.
JACKSON TN 38301

LEMOYNE-OWEN COLLEGE
PRESIDENT WALTER L. WALKER
MEMPHIS TN 38126

LIVINGSTONE COLLEGE
PRESIDENT WILLIAM H. GREENE
SALISBURY NC 28144

MILES COLLEGE
PRESIDENT W. CLYDE WILLIAMS
BIRMINGHAM AL 35208

MOREHOUSE COLLEGE
PRESIDENT HUGH M. GLOSTER
ATLANTA GA 30314

MORRIS COLLEGE
PRESIDENT LUNS C. RICHARDSON
SUMTER SC 29150

MORRIS BROWN COLLEGE
PRESIDENT CALVERT H. SMITH
ATLANTA GA 30314

OAKWOOD COLLEGE
PRESIDENT CALVIN B. ROCK
HUNTSVILLE AL 35896

PAINE COLLEGE
PRESIDENT WILLIAM H. HARRIS
AUGUSTA GA 30910

PAUL QUINN COLLEGE
PRESIDENT WARREN W. MORGAN
WACO TX 76704

PHILANDER SMITH COLLEGE
PRESIDENT HAZO W. CARTER
LITTLE ROCK AK 72203

RUST COLLEGE
PRESIDENT WILLIAM A. MCMILLAN
HOLLY SPRINGS MS 38635

SAINT AUGUSTINE'S COLLEGE
PRESIDENT PREZELL R. ROBINSON
RALEIGH NC 27611

SAINT PAUL'S COLLEGE
PRESIDENT S. DALLAS SIMMONS
LAWRENCEVILLE VA 23868

SHAW UNIVERSITY
PRESIDENT STANLEY H. SMITH
RALEIGH NC 27611

SPELMAN COLLEGE
PRESIDENT DONALD M. STEWART
ATLANTA GA 30314

STILLMAN COLLEGE
PRESIDENT CORDELL WYNN
TUSCALOOSA AL 35403

TALLADEGA COLLEGE
PRESIDENT PAUL B. MOHR, SR.
TALLADEGA AL 35160

TEXAS COLLEGE
PRESIDENT JIMMY ED CLARK
TYLER TX 75701

TOUGALOO COLLEGE
PRESIDENT J. HERMAN BLAKE
TOUGALOO MS 39174

TUSKEGEE UNIVERSITY
PRESIDENT BENJAMIN F. PAYTON
TUSKEGEE AL 36088

VIRGINIA UNION UNIVERSITY
PROVOST CAROLYN DAUGHTRY
RICHMOND VA 23220

VOORHEES COLLEGE
INTERIM PRESIDENT JOHN F. POTTS
DENMARK SC 29042

WILBERFORCE UNIVERSITY
PRESIDENT YVONNE WALKER-TAYLOR
WILBERFORCE OH 45384

WILEY COLLEGE
PRESIDENT ROBERT E. HAYES, SR.
MARSHALL TX 75670

XAVIER UNIVERSITY
PRESIDENT NORMAN C. FRANCIS
NEW ORLEANS LA 70125

Booker T. Washington

1856 - 1915

Educator

Booker Taliaferro Washington was born a slave in Hale's Ford, Virginia. He graduated from Hampton Institute in 1876 and taught school until he entered the seminary in Washington, D.C. He founded and became the first President of Tuskegee Institute in Alabama. He later established the National Negro Business League. Washington, a moderate leader, became the spokesman for the Blacks of his time. As the President of a major university, he believed that in order for Blacks to change their lives they had to develop more skills and be more self-reliant. Washington developed a large white as well as Black audience. After the election of President William McKinley, there was a movement to name him to the President's Cabinet. Washington publicly withdrew himself.

Name: Booker T. Washington

Skill: Reading/Writing

Procedure:
1. Locate more information on Booker T. Washington. Read the section on W.E.B. Dubois and find out more information about him.
2. In an essay, address the following: What were Washington's and Dubois' goals and their methods of achieving them? Were they really different?

Variation:
1. Study the progress made by Blacks in institutions such as the church and theology schools. Do research on Black leaders to see where and how they developed their leadership skills and styles.
2. Match the facts on the following page.

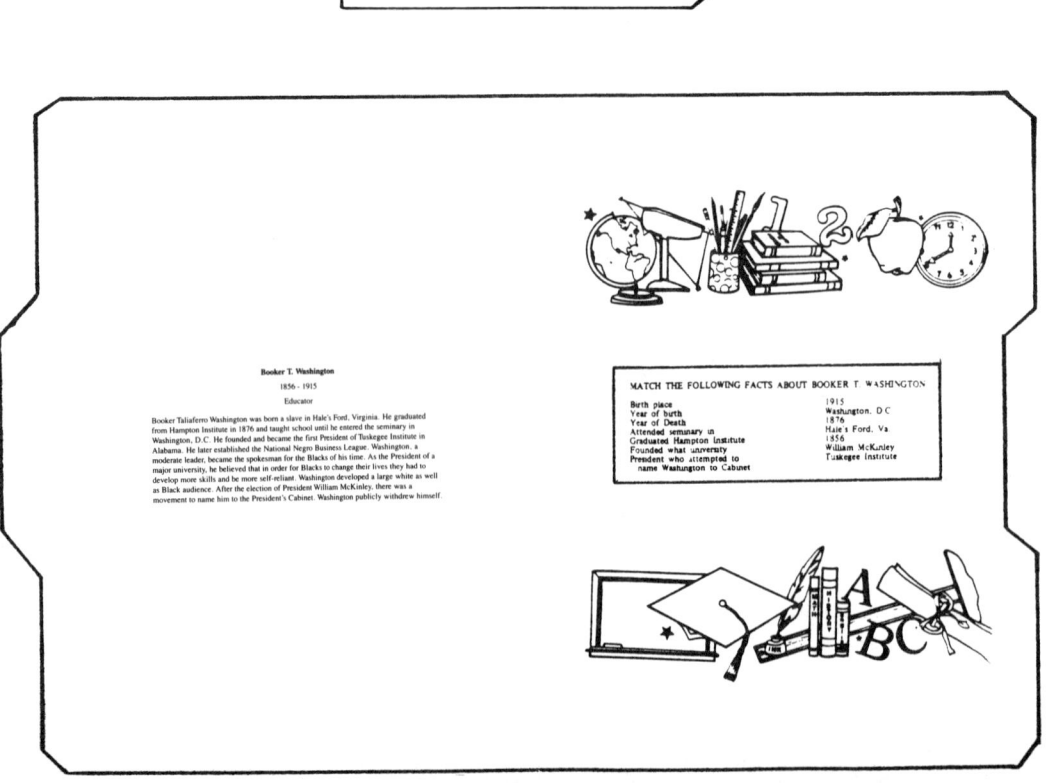

Booker T. Washington
1856 - 1915
Educator

Booker Taliaferro Washington was born a slave in Hale's Ford, Virginia. He graduated from Hampton Institute in 1876 and taught school until he entered the seminary in Washington, D.C. He founded and became the first President of Tuskegee Institute in Alabama. He later established the National Negro Business League. Washington, a moderate leader, became the spokesman for the Blacks of his time. As the President of a major university, he believed that in order for Blacks to change their lives they had to develop more skills and be more self-reliant. Washington developed a large white as well as Black audience. After the election of President William McKinley, there was a movement to name him to the President's Cabinet. Washington publicly withdrew himself.

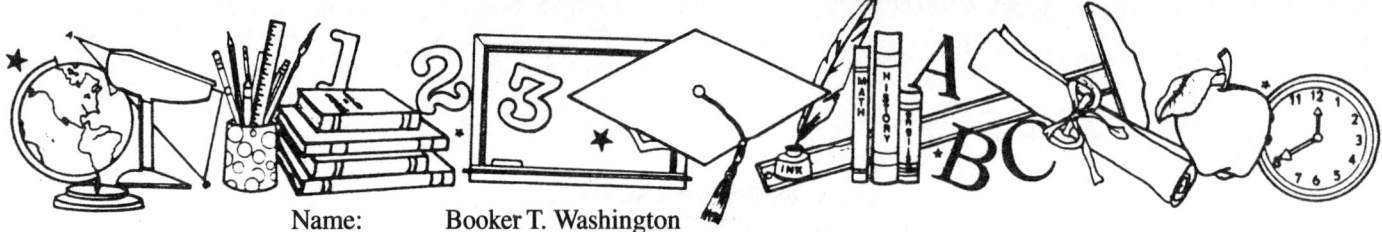

MATCH THE FOLLOWING FACTS ABOUT BOOKER T. WASHINGTON

Birth place — 1915
Year of birth — Washington, D.C.
Year of Death — 1876
Attended seminary in — Hale's Ford, Va
Graduated Hampton Institute — 1856
Founded what unversity — William McKinley
President who attempted to name Washington to Cabinet — Tuskegee Institute

44

MATCH THE FOLLOWING FACTS ABOUT BOOKER T WASHINGTON

Birth place	1915
Year of birth	Washington, D.C.
Year of death	1876
Attended seminary in	Hale's Ford, Va.
Graduated Hampton Institute	1856
Founded what university	William McKinley
President who attempted to name Washington to Cabinet	Tuskegee Institute

IN POLITICS

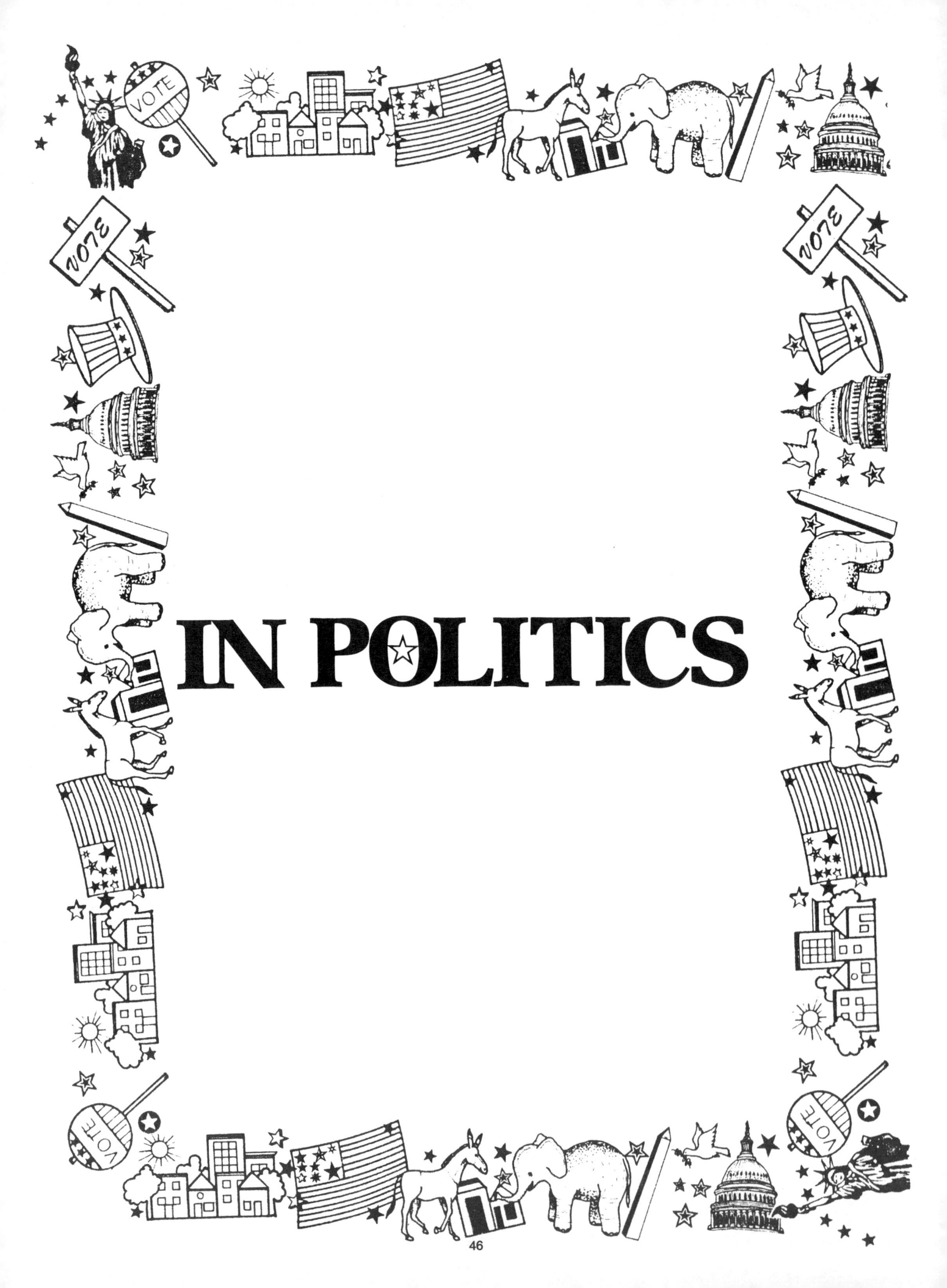

Edward Brooke

1919 -

U. S. Senator

Edward Brooke was born into a middle-class Washington, D.C. family. Brooke attended public schools and then Howard University. After World War II, he entered the Boston University Law School and set academic records for excellence. After several years of serving as an attorney in Boston, Brooke was nominated to run for the Attorney General of Massachusetts by the state's Republican Party. He was elected and served so well that he drew national attention to himself. In 1966 he was elected to the U.S. Senate from Massachusetts. Senator Edward Brooke became the first Black elected to the U.S. Senate since Reconstruction. During his years in the Senate (1966 to 1978), Edward Brooke worked on voting rights problems and was active in trying to get the United States to withdraw from Vietnam.

Name:	Edward Brooke
Skill:	Reading
Procedure:	Answer the questions on the following page referring to Senator Brooke and the political system.
Variation:	Find out more about Georgia State Senator Julian Bond whose name was placed in nomination at the Democratic National Convention in 1964. He was too young to run for President.

Edward Brooke
1919 -
U. S. Senator

Edward Brooke was born into a middle-class Washington, D.C. family. Brooke attended public schools and then Howard University. After World War II, he entered the Boston University Law School and set academic records for excellence. After several years of serving as an attorney in Boston, Brooke was nominated to run for the Attorney General of Massachusetts by the state's Republican Party. He was elected and served so well that he drew national attention to himself. In 1966 he was elected to the U.S. Senate from Massachusetts. Senator Edward Brooke became the first Black elected to the U.S. Senate since Reconstruction. During his years in the Senate (1966 to 1978), Edward Brooke worked on voting rights problems and was active in trying to get the United States to withdraw from Vietnam.

The U.S. Constitution describes the make-up of Congress. A decision made by the "Founding Fathers" determined that Congress would be bicameral (have two houses). This decision was called the Great Compromise. Congress is made up of the Senate and House of Representatives. There are two senators from each state. The number of representatives from a state is determined by that state's population. The number of people a state has is taken from the latest census. A census is an official count of the population that takes place every 10 years. All laws are made by Congress. Both houses must pass the same bill (proposed law) before it can become a law.

Answer the following

1. Why was Brooke's election in 1966 notable? What state was he representing?
2. List two of Brooke's accomplishments as a senator?
3. What does "Founding Fathers" and Great Compromise mean? (Look these up.)
4. How many representatives, U.S. Congressmen, does your state have?
5. Research how an idea evolves into a law.

The U.S. Constitution describes the make-up of Congress. A decision made by the "Founding Fathers" determined that Congress would be bicameral (have two houses). This decision was called the Great Compromise. Congress is made up of the Senate and House of Representatives. There are two senators from each state. The number of representatives from a state is determined by that state's population. The number of people a state has is taken from the latest census. A census is an official count of the population that takes place every 10 years. All laws are made by Congress. Both houses must pass the same bill (proposed law) before it can become a law.

Answer the following

1. Why was Brooke's election in 1966 notable? What state was he representing?

2. List two of Brooke's accomplishments as a senator.

3. What do "Founding Fathers" and 'Great Compromise' mean? (Look these up.)

4. How many representatives (U.S. Congressmen) does your state have?

5. Research how an idea evolves into a law.

contributed by Tom Gannon

Ralph J. Bunche

1904 - 1971

U. N. Diplomat

Ralph J. Bunche was born in Detroit, Michigan. He graduated from the University of California at Los Angeles in 1927. After receiving his master's degree in government at Harvard, he was named the head of the Department of Political Science at Howard University where he remained until 1932. He then obtained his doctorate from Harvard and later did further studies at Northwestern University, the London School of Economics, and Capetown University. Ralph Bunche became famous in 1948 when he was appointed Chief Assistant to the United Nations Mediator in the Palestine crisis. After the Mediator, Count Folke Bernadotte, was assassinated, Bunche took over the negotiations for the cease-fire talks between Egypt and Israel. After four weeks of intensive work, the "Four Armistice Agreements" led the two countries to stop their war. Upon his return to the United States he was given a hero's welcome. In 1950 Ralph Bunche was awarded the Nobel Peace Prize, the first Black American ever to receive the award. In 1955, Bunche was named U.N. Undersecretary for Special Political Affairs. This is the highest post ever held by a Black American in the world body.

Name: Ralph Bunche

Skill: Reading

Procedure: 1. Study the Egypt/Israel crisis and learn more about these countries.

Variation: Find out about the schools with which Dr. Bunche came into contact.
To get catalogs and other information, write to the admissions offices of the following schools: UCLA, Harvard University, Howard University, Northwestern University, the London School of Economics, and Capetown University.

Ralph J. Bunche
1904 - 1971
U. N. Diplomat

Ralph J. Bunche was born in Detroit, Michigan. He graduated from the University of California at Los Angeles in 1927. After receiving his master's degree in government at Harvard, he was named the head of the Department of Political Science at Howard University where he remained until 1932. He then obtained his doctorate from Harvard and took his further studies at Northwestern University, the London School of Economics, and Capetown University. Ralph Bunche became famous in 1946 when he was appointed Chief Assistant to the United Nations Mediator in the Palestine crisis. After the Mediator, Count Folke Bernadotte, was assassinated, Bunche took over the negotiations for the cease-fire talks between Egypt and Israel. After four weeks of intensive work, the "Four Armistice Agreements" led the two countries to stop their war. Upon his return to the United States he was given a hero's welcome. In 1950 Ralph Bunche was awarded the Nobel Peace Prize, the first Black American ever to receive the award. In 1955, Bunche was named U.N. Undersecretary for Special Political Affairs. This is the highest post ever held by a Black American in the world body.

EGYPT

Egypt is located on the northern coast of Africa with the Mediterranean Sea to its north and the Sahara desert to the south. Egypt, the land of the pharaohs, is one of the oldest civilized lands in the world—its history extending to 5000 years before the birth of Christ. It has a population of more than 45 million people. Most Egyptians live in the fertile Nile valley along the mighty Nile River. Finally, the desert constitutes 96% of the land area of Egypt and supports 4% of the population. The climate ranges from mild winters to summer temperatures in Upper Egypt which may go as high as 135°F. Egypt has gone four years without rain.

Egypt attracts many tourists. There are many historical sites to see including the Great Pyramid. These massive structures have endured as lasting monuments to ancient rulers and to the civilization which conceived and built them. The Great Pyramid, or Pyramid of Khufu (Cheops), was built by 600,000 men over a period of 20 years. The early Egyptians had a profound belief in immortality. By 3100 B.C. they were embalming the dead and building elaborate stone tombs shaped as pyramids for burial of the pharaoh. The Valley of the Kings lies on the west bank of the Nile across from Luxor. The rulers of the 18th, 19th and 20th Dynasties prepared tombs carved out of the underground rock. The smallest but most famous of the tombs in the Valley is that of King Tutankhamun, known as King Tut. The magnificent treasures of King Tut, housed in the Cairo Museum, were found by Howard Carter, a British archaeologist, in 1922, after 7 seasons of examining the area.

Egypt is one of the most modern, yet traditional Arab states. Many women still wear the long black garments with veils to cover their faces. They still carry burdens on their heads. In larger cities women dressed in western style clothing can be seen along with women who cling to the past. Much has been done to educate the children, create better housing for the poor and provide free medical services. Arabic is the official language of the country. It is written and read right to left. Books are read back to front. Hieroglyphics is a system of writing used in ancient Egypt in which pictures are used to indicate sound, words or ideas. The Hieroglyphic code was broken by the Rosetta Stone found in 1799 near Alexandria by a French officer of engineers. The cartouch, an oval shape around a name written in hieroglyphics, denotes royalty.

Cairo, the capital, is situated on the northern end of the Nile River. There are approximately 15 million people living in Cairo. As in other large cities there is a lot of noise from the cars and the usual hustle and bustle of city life. The small meal tents are scattered throughout Egypt and are much quieter. But even in the most modern towns one can always count on seeing a camel or two.

Education has become a major concern for Egyptians. Boys and girls between the ages of six and twelve are required to go to school. Many continue their education after high school and attend colleges and universities in Cairo and around the world. New schools are being opened in the desert to curb population density in Cairo. The curriculum of preparatory and secondary schools is becoming more diversified with foreign language and vocational studies becoming increasingly important. The children go to school six days a week. Friday, the Moslem sabbath, is like Sunday in the United States. All children study the usual courses: mathematics, geography, science, grammar, history, etc., but they also take religion classes so they can better understand their religion, Islam. Islam is the official religion of Egypt and is an important part of the Egyptian life. Since Moslems follow the Koran (the Moslem holy book, their "Bible") and use the laws of the Koran to govern their lives.

51

Egypt

Egypt is located on the northern coast of Africa with the Mediterranean Sea to its north and the Sahara desert to the south. Egypt, the land of the pharaohs, is one of the oldest civilized lands in the world---its history extending to 5000 years before the birth of Christ. It has a population of more than 45 million people. Most Egyptians live in the towns and villages along the Nile River Valley. The desert constitutes 96% of the land area of Egypt and supports only 4% of the population. The climate ranges from mild winters to summer temperatures in Upper Egypt which may go as high as 135°F. Egypt has gone for years without rain.

Egypt attracts many tourists. There are many historical sites to see including the Great Pyramids. These massive structures have endured as lasting monuments to ancient rulers and to the civilization which conceived and built them. The Great Pyramid, or Pyramid of Khufu (Cheops), was built by 100,000 men over a period of 20 years. The early Egyptians had a profound belief in immortality. By 2700 B.C. they were embalming the dead and building elaborate stone tombs shaped as pyramids for the burial of their pharaohs. The Valley of the Kings lies on the west bank of the Nile, across from Luxor. The rulers of the 18th, 19th and 20th Dynasties prepared tombs carved out of the underground rock. The smallest but most famous of the tombs in the Valley is that of King Tutankhamun, known as King Tut. The magnificient treasures of King Tut, housed in the Cairo Museum, were found by Howard Carter, a British archeologist, in 1922, after 7 years of examining the area.

Egypt is one of the most modern, yet traditional Arab states. Many women still wear the long black garments with veils to cover their faces. In larger cities women dressed in western-style clothing can be seen along with women who cling to the past. Much has been done to educate Egyptian children, create better housing for the poor and provide free medical services. Arabic is the official language of the country. It is written and read right to left. Books are read back to front. Hieroglyphics is a system of writing used in ancient Egypt in which pictures are used to represent sound, words or ideas. The Hieroglyphic code was broken by a French officer of engineers using the Rosetta Stone found in 1799 near Alexandria. The cartouche, an oval shape around a name written in hieroglyphics, denotes royalty.

Cairo, the capital, is situated near the northern end of the Nile River. There are approximately 15 million people living in Cairo. As in other large cities there is a lot of noise from the cars and the usual hustle and bustle of city life. Small, rural towns are scattered throughout Egypt and are much quieter. But even in the most modern towns one can always count on seeing a camel or two.

Education has become a major concern for Egyptians. Boys and girls between the ages of six and twelve are required to go to school. Many continue their education after high school and attend colleges and universities in Cairo and around the world. New schools are being opened in the desert to curb the population density of Cairo. The curriculum of preparatory and secondary schools is becoming more diversified with foreign language and vocational studies becoming increasingly important. Egyptian children go to school six days a week. (Friday, the Moslem Sabbath, is like Sunday in the United States.) All children study the usual courses: mathematics, geography, science, grammar, history, etc., but they also take religion classes so they can better understand their religion, Islam. Islam is the official religion of Egypt and is an important part of Egyptian life since Moslems follow the Koran (the Moslem holy book, their "Bible") and use its laws to govern their lives.

Israel

Israel is a small country in the Middle East. It is about the size of New Jersey. Its neighbors are Lebanon, Syria, Jordan, Saudi Arabia and Egypt. The capital of Israel is Jerusalem. There are beautiful lush green valleys, deserts of sand (called the Negev), tall mountains and areas below sea level. Israel's Dead Sea is so salty that no plant or other living thing can grow in it---so salty in fact that it's impossible to sink in it when swimming because the salt holds you up!

Israel is a young country. It was established as a homeland for the Jewish people and was recognized as a nation by the United Nations on May 14, 1948. It is also a holy land for Christians and Moslems. Many of the events recorded in the Bible took place in what is now the country of Israel. The people of Israel were Jews who came from all over the world seeking religious freedom and escape from persecution and fear.

The people who came to Israel when it was a new country found the land a barren desert. The entire country virtually had to be built from scratch. These early Israelis were called *Chalutzim* or pioneers. Today, life in Israel is still very hard. Children born in Israel are call *Sabras,* named after the cactus which is hard on the outside and soft and sweet on the inside.

Since the people who come to live in Israel speak many different languages, they are required to learn one: Hebrew, the official language of Israel. Hebrew was the ancient language of the Jews who originally lived in this area nearly two thousand years ago. When the Jews were forced to leave Israel because of religious persecution, they had to disperse all over the world. Hebrew was no longer spoken. However, when Israel was established as the Jewish homeland in 1948, modern Israelis decided to revive their ancient language. The people learn Hebrew in special classes called *Ulpans*. All street signs in Israel are in Hebrew and Arabic. Hebrew is read from right to left and has a completely different alphabet from the English alphabet.

In Israel groups of people sometimes choose to live together in a collective settlement called a *kibbutz*. All the people living in a kibbutz share the work that must be done, and in return each member of the kibbutz receives food, clothing, medical care and education from the resources of the kibbutz. The first kibbutz in Israel, called Degania, was founded in 1909.

Israel is a land of much variety. It has modern cities, such as Tel Aviv, as well as ancient encampments where Bedouin Arabs live in tents and ride camels. Travelers to Israel can visit ancient Roman ruins, the sites of events recorded in the Bible as well as modern colleges and universities. They can see the national dance of Israel, the *Hora,* performed. Or they can attend a soccer game. Soccer is one of the most popular sports in Israel.

A typical Israeli breakfast includes tomatoes, cucumbers, cheese, eggs and bread. Israelis usually eat their main meal at noon. It usually consists of chicken or fish since there is very little beef in Israel. *Felafel* is a delicious national dish of Israel. It can be bought at felafel stands on street corners.

Most Israeli children start nursery school at age three since both parents usually work outside the home. Children in Israel belong to scouts and other youth groups as they are growing up. They continue their education through high school. The government pays for this schooling. At age 18, every Jewish boy and girl must go into the army. The boys serve for three years and girls serve for twenty months. Upon completing their military service, many young people in Israel go to college.

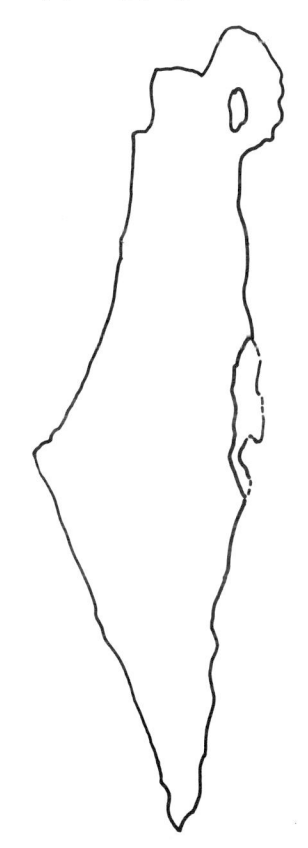

Shirley Chisholm

1926 -

U. S. Congresswoman

Shirley St. Hill Chisholm was born in New York to a mother from Barbados and a father from British Guiana. She was sent to Barbados at age three to live with family until the age of eleven when she returned to Brooklyn, New York. She attended grade school, then high school and earned a scholarship to pursue higher education. She graduated from both Brooklyn College and Columbia University and has a master's degree in elementary education. Before becoming a state representative in Albany, Shirley Chisholm was a nursery school teacher, the director of a daycare center and a consultant for the New York Department of Social Services. After her election to the U.S. Congress in 1969, Chisholm became one of the first members of Congress to fight the committee system and demand committees dealing with education, labor management, city conditions, and social services. She soon became an outspoken defender of the basic decency of Black people and in 1971 mounted a campaign to get the Democratic nomination for the Presidency. She polled well in several states. She retired from Congress in 1982 and now lives in New York City.

Name: Shirley Chisholm

Skill: Reading

Procedure: Read the biography and answer the questions about the life of Shirley Chisholm.

Variation:
1. While observing children in a day care center or while babysitting, conduct a case study to see how much you can learn about a child. Ms. Chisholm conscientiously observed children as a teacher and as a day care director so she could better know and meet their needs when she was a politician.
2. Compare the contributions toward children's rights of Chisholm and Marion Wright Edelman.

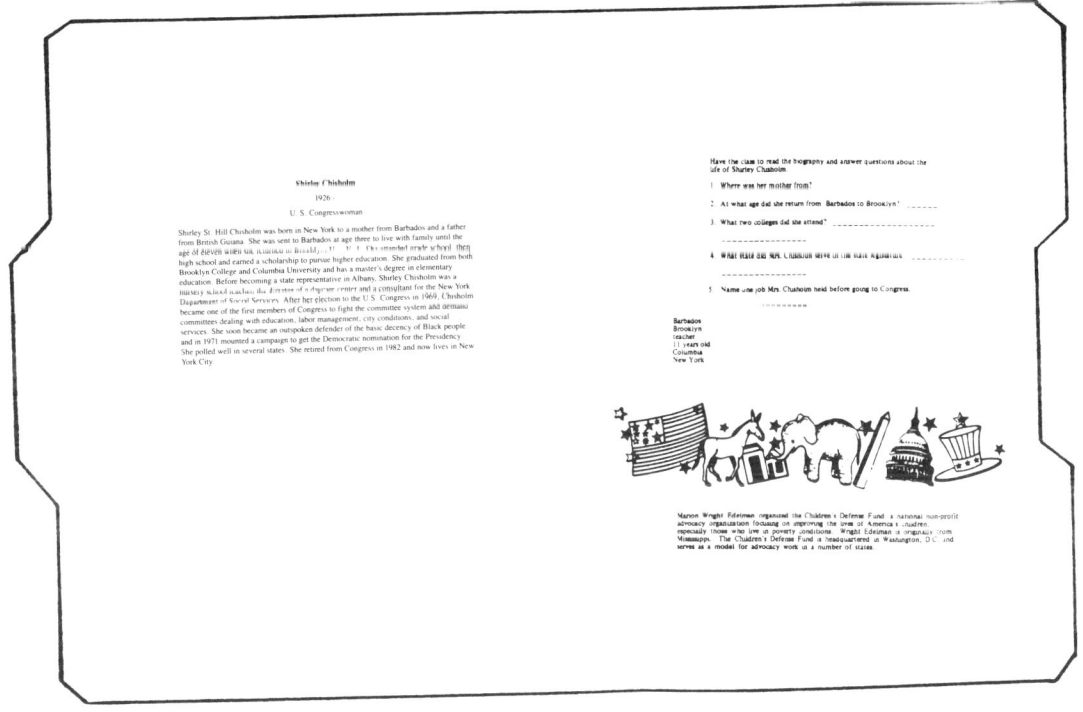

Shirley Chisholm
1926 –
U. S. Congresswoman

Shirley St. Hill Chisholm was born in New York to a mother from Barbados and a father from British Guiana. She was sent to Barbados at age three to live with family until the age of eleven when she returned to Brooklyn, N. Y. She attended grade school, then high school and earned a scholarship to pursue higher education. She graduated from both Brooklyn College and Columbia University and has a master's degree in elementary education. Before becoming a state representative in Albany, Shirley Chisholm was a nursery school teacher, the director of a daycare center and a consultant for the New York Department of Social Services. After her election to the U.S. Congress in 1969, Chisholm became one of the first members of Congress to fight the committee system and demand committees dealing with education, labor management, city conditions, and social services. She soon became an outspoken defender of the basic decency of Black people and in 1971 mounted a campaign to get the Democratic nomination for the Presidency. She polled well in several states. She retired from Congress in 1982 and now lives in New York City.

Have the class to read the biography and answer questions about the life of Shirley Chisholm.

1. Where was her mother from? _____
2. At what age did she return from Barbados to Brooklyn? _____
3. What two colleges did she attend? _____
4. What state did Mrs. Chisholm serve in the state legislature? _____
5. Name one job Mrs. Chisholm held before going to Congress. _____

Barbados
Brooklyn
teacher
11 years old
Columbia
New York

Marion Wright Edelman organized the Children's Defense Fund, a national non-profit advocacy organization focusing on improving the lives of America's children, especially those who live in poverty conditions. Wright Edelman is originally from Mississippi. The Children's Defense Fund is headquartered in Washington, D.C. and serves as a model for advocacy work in a number of states.

Have the class read Shirley Chisholm's biography and answer questions about her life.

1. Where was her mother from? _____

2. At what age did she return to Brooklyn from Barbados? _____

3. What two colleges did she attend? _____
   _____

4. For what state did Mrs. Chisholm serve in the state legislature?
   _____

5. Name one job Mrs. Chisholm held before going to Congress.
   _____

Barbados
Brooklyn College
teacher
11 years old
Columbia University
New York

Marion Wright Edelman organized the Children's Defense Fund, a national non-profit advocacy group trying to improve the lives of America's children, especially those who live in poverty conditions. Wright Edelman is originally from Mississippi. The Children's Defense Fund is headquartered in Washington, D.C. and serves as a model for advocacy programs in a number of other states.

OUTLINE FOR CASE STUDY

Mrs. Chisholm used similar case structures as she observed children.

I. BASIC INFORMATION
A. Age
B. Sex
C. Grade Level
D. Family Members
E. Unusual Facts

II. PHYSICAL STATUS
A. Height and Weight
B. General Appearance
C. General Health Conditions
D. Defects
E. Motor Characteristics

III. SOCIAL DEVELOPMENT
A. Living Conditions
B. Experience Opportunity
C. Activities Available
D. Family Status
E. Acceptance of Individual
F. Hobbies Indulged in
G. Vocational Ambitions/Plans
H. Values Displayed

IV. SELF CONCEPT
A. Personal Appraisal
B. Strength Recognized in Self
C. Weakness Recognized in Self
D. Forms of Compensation
E. Stated Fears
F. Personality Traits
G. Attitudes Toward Others
H. Values Recognized

V. EMOTIONAL DEVELOPMENT
A. Attitudes Developed
B. Emotions Displayed
C. Nervous Disorders

VI. MENTAL DEVELOPMENT
A. Intelligence Category
B. Special Aptitudes
C. Thinking Patterns
D. Maturity of Thought

VII. COMMUNICATION PATTERNS
A. Vocabulary
B. Sentence Structure
C. Content
D. Listening Habits
E. Oral and Written Patterns

PROCEDURE IN MAKING A CASE STUDY:

1. Begin with an average or normal case, if possible.
2. Study all available records.
3. Observe for an extended period of time, taking documented anecdotes.
4. Talk informally with the individual as often as is natural.
5. Talk with peers on an informal basis at first.
6. Talk with adults who are responsible for the individual.
7. Take careful notes after each experience, recording what you learned.
8. Observe specifically the reactions of others to the individual.
9. Up to this point you have made no judgments or formalized study.
10. Conduct a series of conferences alone with the person.
11. Analyze any specific work or achievements of the child: writing, drawing, construction, play, habits, or show of interests.
12. Visit the child's home, if possible.
13. Record the facts in detail.
14. Interpret the data, noting related conditions.
15. Recommend action.

Richard Hatcher

1923 -

Mayor of Gary, Indiana

Richard Hatcher was born in rural Georgia, the 12th of 13 children. With the help of his older brothers and sisters and an athletic scholarship, he was able to go to college. He then attended Valparaiso University Law School while working full-time at a mental hospital. He moved to Gary, Indiana, in 1959 to practice law, became interested in politics and was elected President of the City Council in 1963. In 1967 Hatcher realized that his time had come. He announced his candidacy for mayor. With little support from the county Democratic Party and even though the city was divided strictly on racial lines, Hatcher was still able to defeat two white candidates, one of whom was the incumbent mayor. In the general election, Hatcher defeated the Republican candidate by only 1400 votes. Mayor Hatcher's next problem was to govern a city that had a long history of graft and vice. Police officers were accused of overlooking crime. Organized crime had a base of operation there for the entire state. Mayor Hatcher's car was bombed and he was under constant death threats, but he cracked down on crime, lifted the morale of the Police Department and gained the support of Gary's white citizens and the ethnic community. Hatcher has served as the Mayor of Gary, Indiana, for twenty years.

Name: Richard Hatcher

Skill: Reading

Procedure:
1. Play the word search game.
2. Find out about the Mayor of New Orleans, Ernest "Dutch" Morial, the President of the U.S. Conference of Mayors during the 1980s.

Variation:
1. Write to your state's department of tourism for brochures and other materials describing your state.
2. Find out who your mayor is, when he/she was elected, his/her political party, etc.
3. Find the words in the wordgame of Mayor Hatcher's life in the biographical data.

Richard Hatcher

1923 -

Mayor of Gary, Indiana

Richard Hatcher was born in rural Georgia, the 12th of 13 children. With the help of his older brothers and sisters and an athletic scholarship, he was able to go to college. He then attended Valparaiso University Law School while working full-time at a mental hospital. He moved to Gary, Indiana, in 1959 to practice law, became interested in politics and was elected President of the City Council in 1963. In 1967 Hatcher realized that his time had come. He announced his candidacy for mayor. With little support from the county Democratic Party and even though the city was divided racially, campaign funds Hatcher was still able to defeat two white candidates, one of whom was the incumbent mayor. In the general election, Hatcher defeated the Republican candidate by only 1400 votes. Mayor Hatcher's next problem was to govern a city that had a long history of graft and vice. Police officers were accused of overlooking crime. Organized crime had a base of operation there for the entire state. Mayor Hatcher's car was bombed and he was under constant death threats, but he cracked down on crime, lifted the morale of the Police department and gained the support of Gary's white citizens and the ethnic community. Hatcher has served as the Mayor of Gary, Indiana, for twenty years.

MAYOR HATCHER

THERE ARE 10 WORDS HERE - CAN YOU FIND THEM?

HERE ARE THE WORDS TO LOOK FOR:

ATHLETIC
DEMOCRATIC
EUROPEAN
ORGANIZED
PROFESSIONAL

CROOKED
ETHNIC
HOSPITAL
POLICE
REPUBLICAN

59

MAYOR HATCHER

```
P D Z S Z U H S T C W T B G V X T G N L
R E D A P T Q N C F E F R N P T L O C F
O T J A T H L E T I C P O L I C E R R K
F J G D Q Y M M T R E U E Q J V C G A N
E U M X R X Q X I O X F U F L H J A C Z
S Q M G Y V G S N F R U K H V C X N K F
S X N Q K A L I A P G O D F M F R I E S
I E B W R K Z R T X U L E J G E E Z D M
O H O S P I T A L Q U Y M P O I P E P B
N K S N P W J U I B G M O M F V U D V D
A X C Y U Y K O G K G E C D U M B G X E
L M M J S I H U T B E U R F O E L A J S
L X K Q U T O P Y F T R A L J H I H T M
C F U Y H R I C E N B O T E I F C H A P
A C S T Z G X R T P I P I P U L A F P P
Q Z Z S A K T K H G I E C G F U N I T H
W I H T A Q I M N S Y A P Q C E R K B S
R W T U U O L D I R C N U I H E Z I I A
Y V M D U Q P V C C T D F Q Z R G I K Q
Q B M D Y I U S O Z T W W S J Y Q Z H W
```

THERE ARE 10 WORDS HERE - CAN
YOU FIND THEM?

HERE ARE THE WORDS TO LOOK FOR:

ATHLETIC	CRACKED
DEMOCRATIC	ETHNIC
EUROPEAN	HOSPITAL
ORGANIZED	POLICE
PROFESSIONAL	REPUBLICAN

MAYOR HATCHER

```
P . . . . . . . . . . . . . . . . . . .
R . . . . . . . . . . . . . . . . . . .
O . . A T H L E T I C P O L I C E R R .
F . . . . . . . . . . . . . . . . G A .
E . . . . . . . . . . . . . . . . . . .
S . . . . . . . . . . . . . . . . N K .
S . . . . . . . . . . . D . . . R I E .
I . . . . . . . . . . . E . . . E Z D .
O H O S P I T A L . . . M . . . P E . .
N . . . . . . . . . . . O . . . U D . .
A . . . . . . . . . . . E C . . . B . . .
L . . . . . . . . . . . U R . . . L . . .
. . . . . . . . . . . . R A . . . I . . .
. . . . . . . . . . E . . O T . . . C . . .
. . . . . . . . . . T . . P I . . . A . . .
. . . . . . . . . . H . . E C . . . N . . .
. . . . . . . . . . N . . . A . . . . . . .
. . . . . . . . . . I . . N . . . . . . . .
. . . . . . . . . . C . . . . . . . . . . .
```

Adam Clayton Powell, Jr.

1908 - 1972

U.S. Congressman

Adam Clayton Powell, Jr. was born in New York City. He attended Colgate University, in Hamilton, New York. At an early age, Powell became involved in several large demonstrations that made a name for him in Harlem. He also organized the integration of the medical staff at Harlem Hospital and helped many Blacks to find employment along Harlem's main street, 125th Street. When his father, Adam Clayton Powell, Sr. retired from the Abyssinian Baptist Church in 1937, young Adam Jr. was named as his successor. In 1939 when the World's Fair was to open in New York, Powell served as the Chairman of the Coordinating Committee on Employment. He forced the state to employ hundreds of Blacks in jobs at the fair. In 1941 Powell won a seat on the New York City Council and served until 1945 when he was elected to the U.S. Congress. He represented more than 300,000 people, 89% of whom were Black. He was quickly called "Mr. Civil Rights" for his work on behalf of Blacks. At the time Powell was elected to the Congress of the United States, he could not rent a room in Washington's downtown hotels, nor could he attend a movie in which his wife Hazel Scott had been starring. He couldn't eat in the congressional dining room or use the showers or the barber shop available to the white congressmen. As a freshman legislator, Powell used all of these facilities and insisted that his staff follow his lead. He engaged in public debate with segregationists and fought to abolish discrimination in the U.S. Military. He introduced what came to be known as the Powell Amendments which denied federal funds to any project where discrimination existed. He was the first Black Congressman to have legislation passed by both houses. While he was Chairman of the House Committee on Education and Labor, his committee was credited with processing more legislation than any other committee in the House of Representatives. President Kennedy called him the most productive in Congress legislator. When he was accused of misconduct in 1967, the House of Representatives voted to exclude him from his seat. Two years later the Supreme Court ruled that the House had violated Powell's Constitutional rights and reseated him. In the Democratic Primary of 1970 the voters of New York did not renominate him for the congressional seat he had held for twenty-five years.

Name: Adam Clayton Powell, Jr.

Skill: Reading/Spelling

Procedure:
1. Find the words on the following page that were important in Powell's life.
2. Play the word search game.

Variation: Answer the questions.

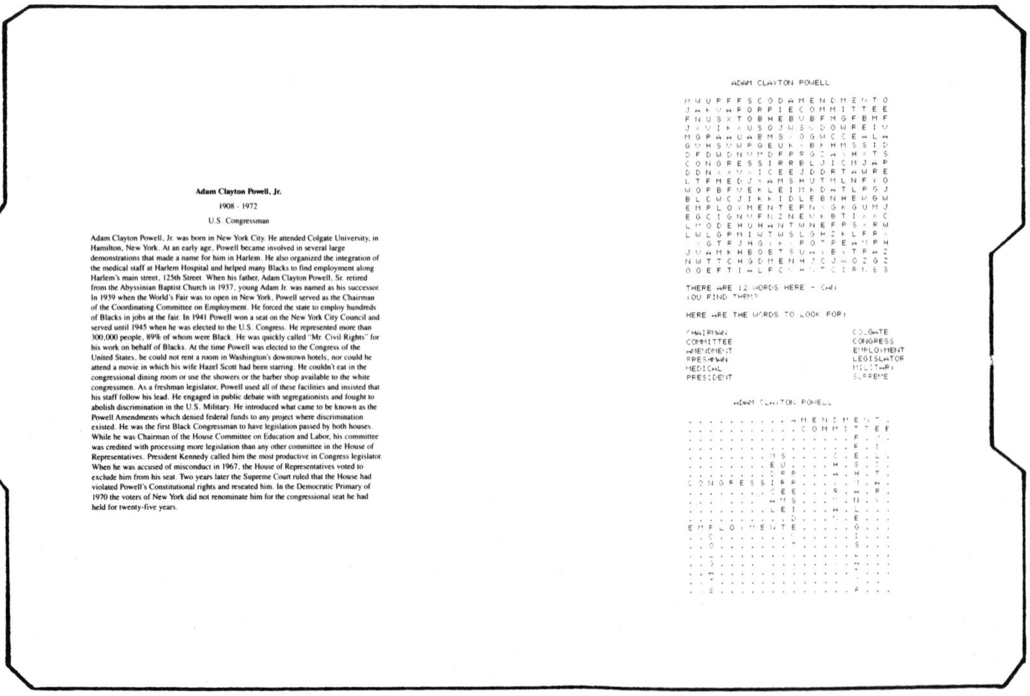

ADAM CLAYTON POWELL

```
M W U P F F S C O D A M E N D M E N T O
J A K V A R Q R P I E C O M M I T T E E
F N U S X T Q B H E B V B F M G F B M F
J X V I K X U S Q J W S V D O W R E I V
M G P A A U A B M S X Q G W C C E A L A
G V H S V W P G E U K X B K H M S S I D
D F D W D N V M D P P R G Z A X H X T S
C O N G R E S S I R R B L J I C M J A P
D D N X X V X I C E E J D D R T A W R E
L T F M E D J X A M S H U T M L N F Y O
W O F B F V E K L E I M K D A T L P G J
B L C W C J I K K I D L E B N H E W G W
E M P L O Y M E N T E P N X G K G U M J
E G C I G N V F N Z N E W K B T I X X C
L M O D E H U H A N T W N E F P S X R W
L W L G P M I W T W S L G H Z K L P R X
Y X G T R J H G Y K X P O T R E A M P H
J V A M K H B Q B T S U A Y B Y T P A Z
N W T T C H G D M E N H J C J W O Z G Z
O Q E F T I A L F C V H N T C I R N B S
```

THERE ARE 12 WORDS HERE - CAN
YOU FIND THEM?

HERE ARE THE WORDS TO LOOK FOR:

CHAIRMAN   COLGATE
COMMITTEE   CONGRESS
AMENDMENT   EMPLOYMENT
FRESHMAN   LEGISLATOR
MEDICAL   MILITARY
PRESIDENT   SUPREME

ADAM CLAYTON POWELL

```
. . . . . . . . . . . A M E N D M E N T .
. . . . . . . . . . . . C O M M I T T E E
. . . . . . . . . . . . . . . . . F . M .
. . . . . . . . . . . . . . . . . R . I .
. . . . . . . . . M S . . . . C . E . L .
. . . . . . . . . E U . . . . H . S . I .
. . . . . . . . . D P P . . . A . H . T .
C O N G R E S S I R R . . . I . M . A .
. . . . . . . . . C E E . . . R . A . R .
. . . . . . . . . A M S . . . M . N . Y .
. . . . . . . . . L E I . . . A . L . . .
. . . . . . . . . . . D . . . N . E . . .
E M P L O Y M E N T E . . . . . G . . .
. . C . . . . . . . N . . . . . I . . .
. . O . . . . . . . T . . . . . S . . .
. . L . . . . . . . . . . . . . L . . .
. . G . . . . . . . . . . . . . A . . .
. . A . . . . . . . . . . . . . T . . .
. . T . . . . . . . . . . . . . O . . .
. . E . . . . . . . . . . . . . R . . .
```

63

Answer these questions.

1. Adam Clayton Powell, Jr. represented what community in Congress? _____
2. What is the main street in Harlem? _____
3. What was Powell called when he was in Congress? _____
4. What did Powell amendments deny to projects that discriminated against Blacks? _____
5. Congressman Powell was the first Black to pass legislation through both what? _____

House of Congress
Harlem
Civil Rights
Federal funds
125th Street

Hiram Rhoades Revels

1822- 1901

U.S. Senator

Hiram Rhoades Revels was born in Fayetteville County, North Carolina, and was educated in Indiana and Illinois. After his ordination, Revels was a minister for churches in Kentucky, Missouri, and Maryland. He also worked as a school principal and organized a Black regiment in the Civil War. At the end of the war he moved to Natchez, Mississippi. He organized several churches in Jackson, the state capital, and other Mississippi cities. The Union military governor of the state appointed Revels as an Alderman of Jackson. Revels thought that he would not be accepted by the people, but in time his constituents respected his alert grasp of important state and local issues. He supported legislation which would have given voting and office-holding rights back to white Southerners. In 1870 the governor appointed Hiram Revels to the U.S. Senate and he served for one year until the regular elections. Revels retired from politics and became the president of Alcorn University in Lorman, Mississippi. He spent the rest of his life developing Alcorn into a first-rate university for Black students.

Name: Hiram Rhoades Revels

Skill: Geography

Procedure: Find the states where Revels lived on the map. Trace his route from North Carolina to Mississippi.

Variation: Have students read Revels' biography to complete a more detailed map and list the dates Revels lived in each state. Library skills will need to be used.

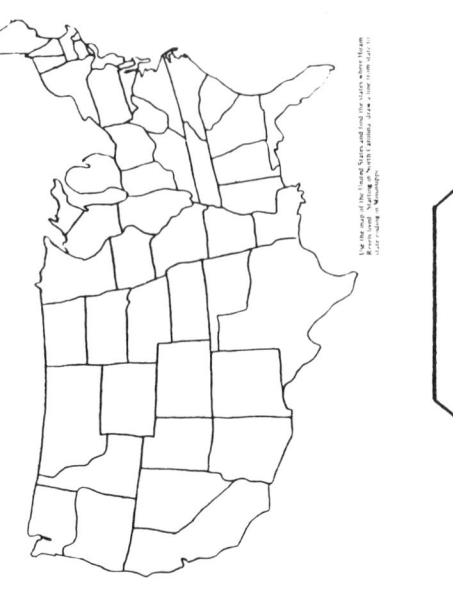

Hiram Rhoades Revels
1822–1901
U.S. Senator

Hiram Rhoades Revels was born in Fayetteville County, North Carolina, and was educated in Indiana and Illinois. After his ordination, Revels was a minister for churches in Kentucky, Missouri, and Maryland. He also worked as a school principal and organized a Black regiment in the Civil War. At the end of the war he moved to Natchez, Mississippi. He organized several churches in Jackson, the state capital, and other Mississippi cities. The Union military governor of the state appointed Revels as an Alderman of Jackson. Revels thought that he would not be accepted by the people, but in time his constituents respected his alert grasp of important state and local issues. He supported legislation which would have given voting and office-holding rights back to white Southerners. In 1870 the governor appointed Hiram Revels to the U.S. Senate and he served for one year until the regular elections. Revels retired from politics and became the president of Alcorn University in Lorman, Mississippi. He spent the rest of his life developing Alcorn into a first-rate university for Black students.

Use the map of the United States and find the states where Hiram Revels lived. Starting in North Carolina, draw a line from state to state ending in Mississippi.

Robert C. Weaver

1907-

Presidential Cabinet Member

Robert C. Weaver was born in Washington, D.C. and attended school there. He received his Ph.D. in economics from Harvard University. Weaver's grandfather was the first Black to receive a doctor's degree in dentistry from Harvard. In 1933, Weaver was hired as an aid to the Secretary of the Interior under President Franklin Roosevelt. Dr. Weaver became a member of what came to be known as Roosevelt's "Black Cabinet." In 1934, Robert Weaver was named a consultant in the Public Works Admininstration. By 1938, Weaver was a special assistant to the Administrator of the U.S. Housing Authority. During the 1940s, Dr. Weaver was a professor of economics at North Carolina A&T in Greensboro. From 1949 to 1955, he was the Director of the Opportunity Fellowships Program of the Whitney Foundation and a Consultant to the Ford Foundation. Weaver was the first Black to serve on the Cabinet of the governor of New York before he was appointed by President Kennedy as head of the Housing and Home Finance Agency. In 1966, when the Housing and Urban Development Department was formed, President Lyndon B. Johnson named him as its Secretary which made him the first Black to serve officially on a Presidential Cabinet.

Name: Dr. Robert Weaver

Skill: Vocabulary/Spelling

Procedure: 1. Match the phrases relating to Dr. Weaver's life on the following page.
2. Play the word search game.

Variation: Spell the words in the Weaver biography.

Robert C. Weaver

1907-

Presidential Cabinet Member

Robert C. Weaver was born in Washington, D.C. and attended school there. He received his Ph.D. in economics from Harvard University. Weaver's grandfather was the first Black [illegible] Hat [illegible]. In 1933, Weaver was hired as an aid to the Secretary of the Interior under President Franklin Roosevelt. Dr. Weaver became a member of what came to be known as Roosevelt's "Black Cabinet." In 1934, Robert Weaver was named a consultant in the Public Works Administration. By 1938, Weaver was a special assistant to the Administrator of the U.S. Housing Authority. During the 1940s, Dr. Weaver was a professor of [illegible] at North Carolina A&T in Greensboro. From 1949 to 1955, he was the Director of the Opportunity Fellowships Program of the Whitney Foundation and a Consultant to the Ford Foundation. Weaver was the first Black to serve on the Cabinet of the governor of New York before he was appointed by President Kennedy as head of the Housing and Home Finance Agency. In 1966, when the Housing and Urban Development Department was formed, President Lyndon B. Johnson named him as its Secretary which made him the first Black to serve officially on a Presidential Cabinet.

Draw lines to associate the following phrases which are related to Dr. Weaver's life.

Housing and Urban Development
Professor of Economics
President Franklin Roosevelt
First Black on Governor's Cabinet
President John Kennedy

North Carolina A & T
New York State
Housing and Home Finance Agency
President Lyndon B. Johnson
Black Cabinet

Have the class to spell words in the Weaver biography.

Franklin
Roosevelt
Cabinet
Kennedy
Carolina
Development
Finance
Dentistry
Harvard
President

DR. WEAVER

THERE ARE 10 WORDS HERE - CAN YOU FIND THEM?

HERE ARE THE WORDS TO LOOK FOR:

CABINET   CAROLINA
DENTISTRY   DEVELOPMENT
FINANCE   FRANKLIN
HARVARD   KENNEDY
PRESIDENT   ROOSEVELT

69

Draw lines to match the following phrases relating to Dr. Weaver's life.

Housing and Urban Development	North Carolina A&T
Professor of Economics	New York State
President Franklin Roosevelt	Housing and Home Finance Agency
First Black on Governor's Cabinet	President Lyndon B. Johnson
President John Kennedy	Black Cabinet

Have the class spell words in the Weaver biography.

Franklin
Roosevelt
Cabinet
Kennedy
Carolina
Development
Finance
Denistry
Harvard
President

DR. WEAVER

```
V V K A J O R Z B S A A A A E B A L D B
R G I Y S P K A H V S T O H I G M V E Z
F H H A R V A R D U Z W Z T P S H M N U
V B G S R A R S P N A E F X L I T Q T B
S L M Z X S K X R T C G Q V A S I Y I Y
D Q S A N W O D E H A U K K M G X Y S S
C O L L R N M Q S D Z N Z S C M P Z T B
M L V L O X D O I L H S R Y I Z B Q R A
T Y V M O T R O D F I N A N C E A E Y N
D T Q L S Y S D E B W T X W U G E I W M
Q L B J E J Y M N M G F J F A V P B W U
Z A S I V C A W T E B C A R O L I N A U
N Y M F E A V J S Q N V L A S T P W Y I
O L H L L B N I X U N H H N Z J N S M A
P M M G T I P K K T Y R H K P C V T F V
J M O S U N J W T J M S M L K F L B P E
L O W V S E I J W X T U D I M P H O J V
Z E X U Q T K E N N E D Y N N H M A Q D
X U E E X E D R V P G D X S Q Z C T Y X
R L Z D E V E L O P M E N T H H L E X O
```

THERE ARE 10 WORDS HERE - CAN
YOU FIND THEM?

HERE ARE THE WORDS TO LOOK FOR:

CABINET	CAROLINA
DENTISTRY	DEVELOPMENT
FINANCE	FRANKLIN
HARVARD	KENNEDY
PRESIDENT	ROOSEVELT

DR. WEAVER

```
. . . . . . . . . . . . . . . . . . . D .
. . . . . . . . . . . . . . . . . . . E .
. . H A R V A R D . . . . . . . . . . N .
. . . . . . . . P . . . . . . . . . . T .
. . . . . . . . R . . . . . . . . . . I .
. . . . . . . . E . . . . . . . . . . S .
. . . . . R . . S . . . . . . . . . . T .
. . . . O . . . I . . . . . . . . . . R .
. . . . O . . . D F I N A N C E . . . Y .
. . . . . S . . E . . . . . . . . . . . .
. . . . . . E . . N . . . . F . . . . . .
. . . . . . V C . . T . . C A R O L I N A .
. . . . . . . E A . . . . . A . . . . . .
. . . . . . . L B . . . . . N . . . . . .
. . . . . . . T I . . . . . K . . . . . .
. . . . . . . . N . . . . . L . . . . . .
. . . . . . . E . . . . . . I . . . . . .
. . . . . T K E N N E D Y N . . . . . . .
. . . . . . . . . . . . . . . . . . . . .
. . . D E V E L O P M E N T . . . . . . .
```

Andrew Young

1932 -

Mayor of Atlanta, Georgia

Andrew Young was born in New Orleans, Louisiana, in March of 1932. His father was a prominent dentist and his mother an educator. He attended elementary and secondary schools in New Orleans, received a bachelor's degree from Howard University and then graduated from the Hartford Theological Seminary. He moved to Atlanta, Georgia, where in the late 50s he became involved with the civil rights movement through Dr. Martin Luther King, later becoming one of his chief aides. After Dr. King's death in 1968, Young worked with many civil rights organizations including the Southern Christian Leadership Conference which he had helped to form with Dr. King. In 1972, Andrew Young was elected to the United States Congress from the Fifth District of Georgia. He was the first Black to win a congressional seat in Georgia in more than 100 years. Young served in Congress with such distinction that when the former Governor of Georgia, Jimmy Carter, was elected President in 1976, he asked Andrew Young to be the American Ambassador to the United Nations. As the U.N. Ambassador he also served as a member of the President's Cabinet and the National Security Council. During his time as U.N. Ambassador, Young traveled to nearly every country in the world and became an expert on international affairs. In late 1981, Young was elected the Mayor of Atlanta, Georgia, succeeding Maynard Jackson. Jackson had been the first Black mayor of Atlanta. A follower of Dr. Martin Luther King's teachings, Young is committed to nonviolent change in the world. Andrew Young has been presented with the nation's highest civilian award, the Presidential Medal of Freedom.

Name: Andrew Young

Skill: Reading comprehension

Procedure:
1. Answer the questions about Andrew Young's life.
2. Study the American political system which is explained on the next page.

Variation:
1. Learn about the political contributions of other Black mayors in the United States: Sidney Bartholomy of New Orleans, Louisiana; Marion Barry of Washington, D.C.; and Tom Bradley of Los Angeles, California.

Andrew Young
1932
Mayor of Atlanta, Georgia

Andrew Young was born in New Orleans, Louisiana, in March of 1932. His father was a prominent dentist and his mother an educator. He attended elementary and secondary schools in New Orleans, received a bachelor's degree from Howard University and then graduated from the Hartford Theological Seminary. He settled in Atlanta, Georgia, where in the late 50s, he became involved with the civil rights movement through Dr. Martin Luther King, later becoming one of his chief aides. After Dr. King's death in 1968, Young worked with many civil rights organizations including the Southern Christian Leadership Conference which he then helped to form with Dr. King. In 1972, Andrew Young was elected to the United States Congress from the Fifth District of Georgia. He was the first Black to win a congressional seat in Georgia in more than 100 years. Young served in Congress with such distinction that when the former Governor of Georgia, Jimmy Carter, was elected President in 1976, he asked Andrew Young to be the American Ambassador to the United Nations. As the U.N. Ambassador he also served as a member of the President's Cabinet and the National Security Council. During his time as U.N. Ambassador, Young traveled to nearly every country in the world and became an expert on international affairs. In late 1981, Young was elected the Mayor of Atlanta, Georgia, succeeding Maynard Jackson who had been the first Black mayor of Atlanta. A follower of Dr. Martin Luther King's teachings, Young is committed to nonviolent change in the world. Andrew Young has been presented with the nation's highest civilian award, the Presidential Medal of Freedom.

QUESTIONS ABOUT THE LIFE OF ANDREW YOUNG

1. Andrew Young has spent most of his life in what two cities?
   _____ _____

2. What are the public offices which Andrew Young has been elected to?
   _____ _____

3. Name two of the jobs Andrew Young held in President Jimmy Carter's administration?
   _____ _____

4. What university did Andrew Young attend? _____

5. The highest award presented to Andrew Young in the United States was the
   _____.

Answers
Congress
Cabinet member
Howard University
Atlanta, Ga.
Mayor
National Security Council
Presidential Medal of Freedom
U.N. Ambassador
New Orleans, La.

Political System

The United States Constitution gives our plan of government

The government of the United States has three equal branches, executive, legislative, and judicial. The President is sometimes called the chief executive because he heads the executive branch. This branch is responsible for carrying out the laws passed by Congress, the legislative branch. The Congress is bicameral, consisting of two houses: the Senate and the House of Representatives. Each state sends two senators who are elected in statewide elections to represent them in Congress. The number of representatives a state sends to Congress depends on its population as recorded in the last census. The last census, the official count of our nation's population, takes place every ten years. The last one occurred in 1980. States with a large population have more representatives in Congress than states with a small population. There are 435 Representatives in the House. When a state's population changes, the number of its representatives changes also. This is called reapportionment. When one state gains a representative another state must lose one.

A proposed law is called a bill. It is not a law until it has been passed by a majority in both houses of Congress, and the president has signed it. All laws must be in accord with the Constitution since it is the ultimate law of the land. When there is a question about a law being allowed by the Constitution, the Supreme Court rules on it. If the law violates the Constitution, the court strikes it down.

Each branch of our government has enough power to prevent the others from getting too much authority. This is called the system of checks and balances. It has served us well for almost 2 centuries. Like a footstool with 3 legs, our 3 branches of government have proved to be stable, helping us pursue the American ideals of life, liberty, and the pursuit of happiness.

contributed by Tom Garmon

QUESTIONS ABOUT THE LIFE OF ANDREW YOUNG

1. Andrew Young has spent most of his life in what two cities?
   _____   _____

2. What public offices has Andrew Young been elected to?
   _____   _____

3. Name two of the jobs Andrew Young held in President Jimmy Carter's administration.
   _____   _____

4. What university did Andrew Young attend? _____

5. The highest civilian award in the United States was presented to Andrew Young. It was the _____

Answers

Congress
Cabinet member
Howard University
Atlanta, Ga.
Mayor
National Security Council
Presidential Medal of Freedom
U.N. Ambassador
New Orleans, La.

Study Hard & Keep Faith —

Peace & Blessings

Andrew Young

IN SCIENCE & MATH

Benjamin Banneker

1731 - 1806

Inventor, Mathematician

Benjamin Banneker was born in Ellicott, Maryland, of a free mother and a slave father. Banneker was always considered free. He received the equivalent of an eighth-grade education. His knowledge of astronomy and mathematics enabled him to predict the solar eclipse of 1789. His almanac, published for more than 10 years, was the first book written by an American Black on a scientific subject. It contained tide tables and predictions of future eclipses as well as directions for using medical products. Banneker was best known because he was the surveyor on a six-man team that laid out the blueprint for the city of Washington, D.C. When Major Pierre L'Enfant, the engineer who designed the plans for the federal city, resigned and went back to France with the plans, Banneker reproduced all of the plans of Washington, D.C. from memory. Banneker is also credited with building the first all wooden clock.

Name: Benjamin Banneker

Skill: Map reading

Procedure:
1. Study the map of Washington, D.C. on the next page and find the buildings noted.
2. Design a city map.

Variation: Get a copy of an almanac and explain its usefulness to your class.

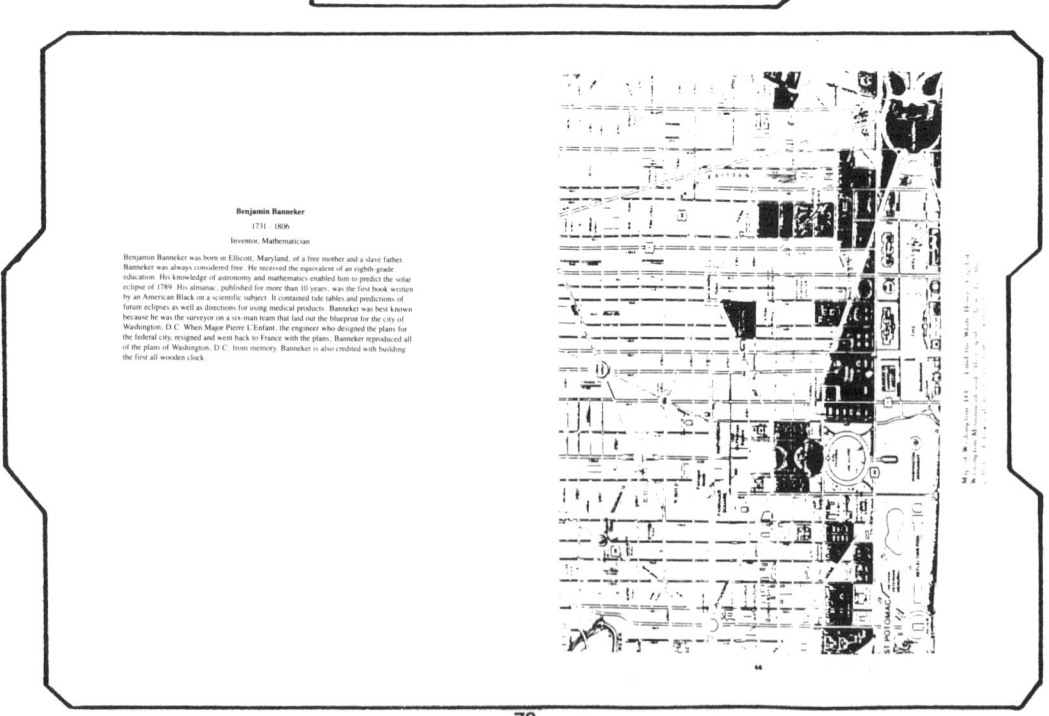

Benjamin Banneker
1731 - 1806
Inventor, Mathematician

Benjamin Banneker was born in Ellicott, Maryland, of a free mother and a slave father. Banneker was always considered free. He received the equivalent of an eighth-grade education. His knowledge of astronomy and mathematics enabled him to predict the solar eclipse of 1789. His almanac, published for more than 10 years, was the first book written by an American Black on a scientific subject. It contained tide tables and predictions of future eclipses as well as directions for using medical products. Banneker was best known because he was the surveyor on a six-man team that laid out the blueprint for the city of Washington, D.C. When Major Pierre L'Enfant, the engineer who designed the plans for the federal city, resigned and went back to France with the plans, Banneker reproduced all of the plans of Washington, D.C. from memory. Banneker is also credited with building the first all wooden clock.

78

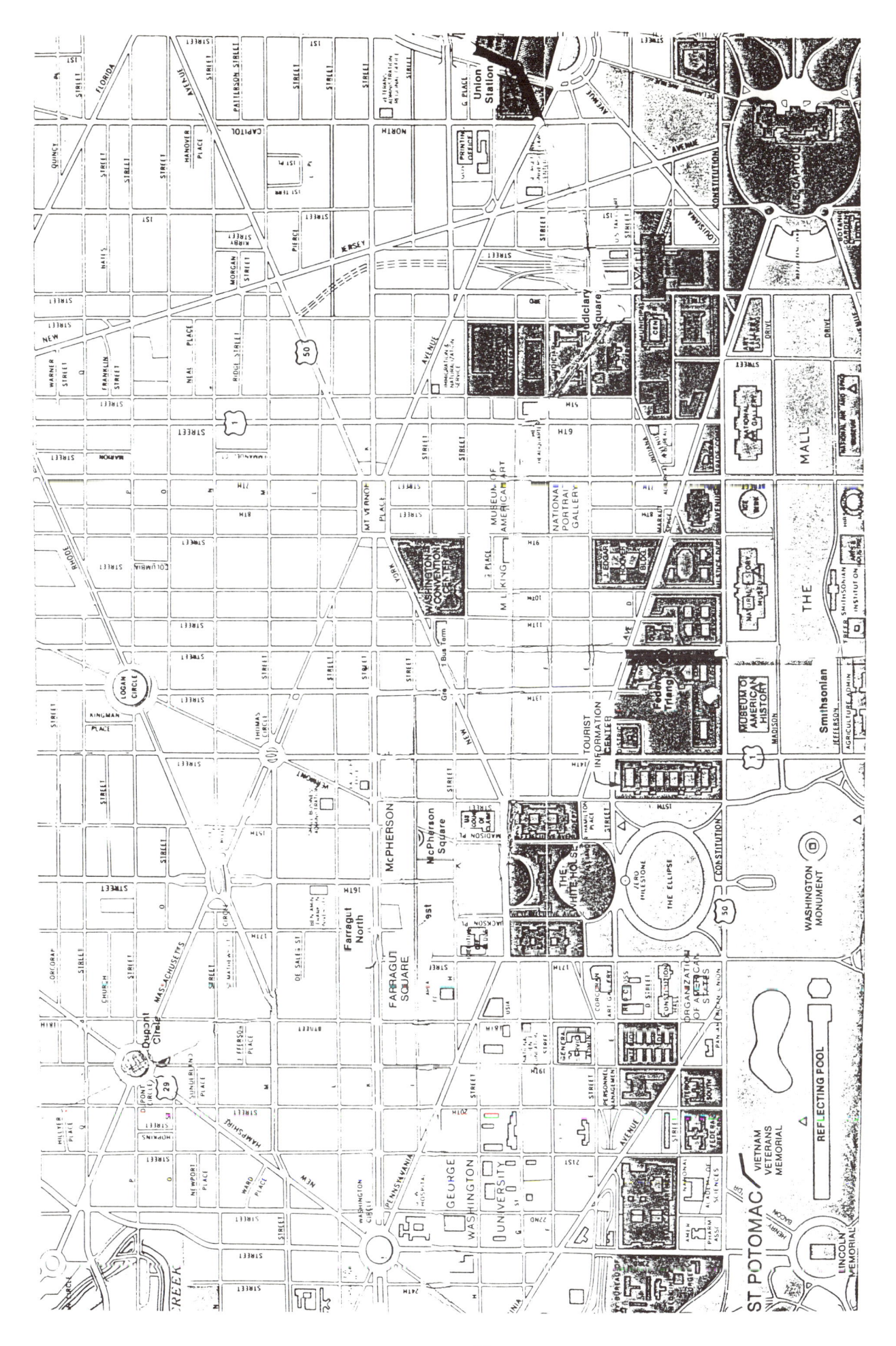

Map of Washington, D.C.: Find the White House, Capitol, Washington Monument and other landmarks. Show your class the pattern of diagonal streets that Banneker laid out to allow troops to get across the city quickly.

DESIGN A CITY MAP

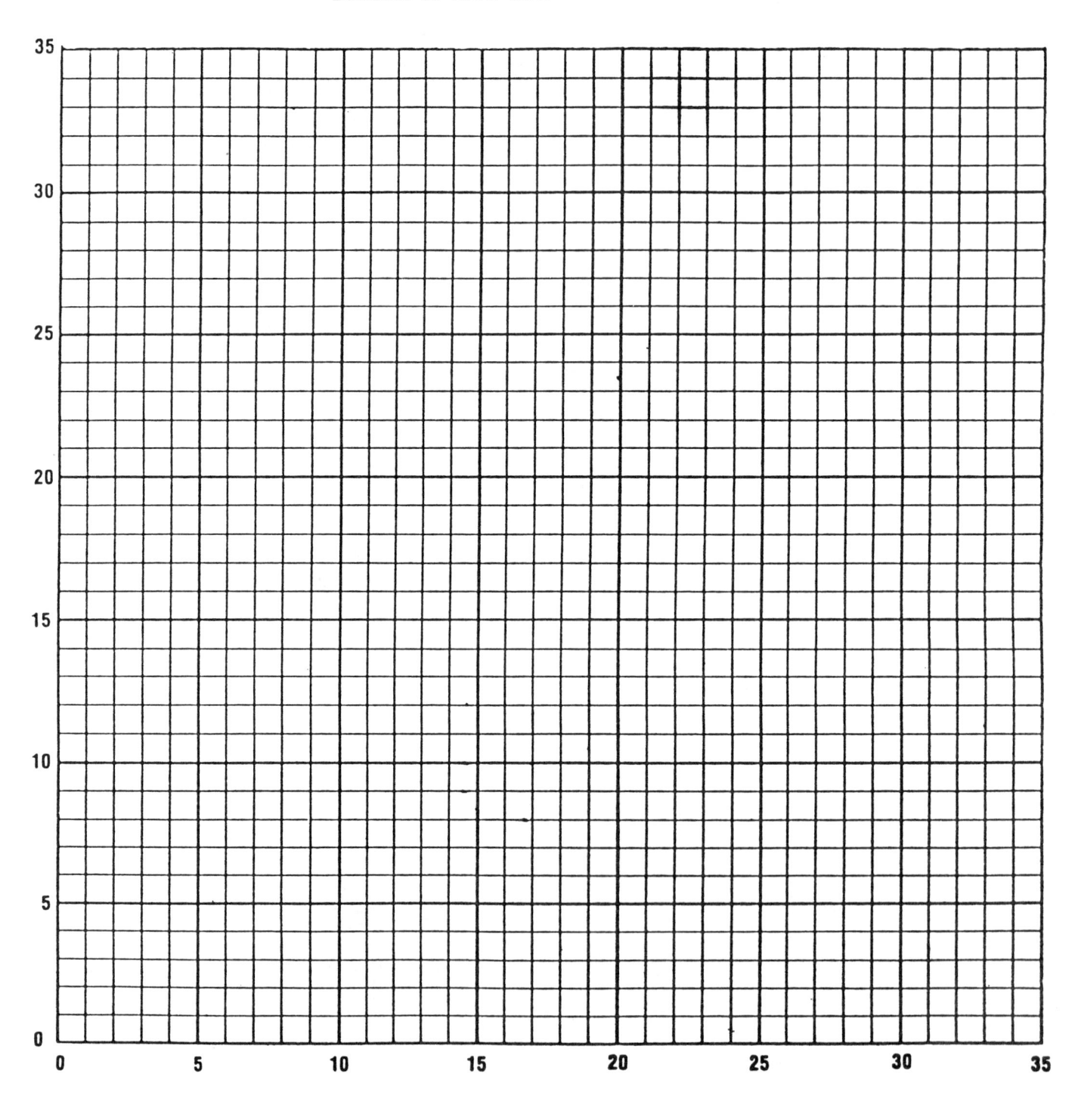

Name_____

Guion S. Bluford, Jr.

1941 -

Astronaut

Guion Bluford, Jr. was born in Philadelphia, Pennsylvania, and attended the public schools there. He received his Bachelor of Science degree from Pennsylvania State University in Aerospace Engineering and both his master's and doctorate in Aerospace Engineering from the Air Force Institute of Technology. After his graduation from college in 1964, he entered the Air Force, and was trained as a pilot. He went on to do combat training in F4C planes in both Arizona and Florida. After flying combat missions in Vietnam he became a T38 trainer pilot at Sheppard Air Force Base in Texas. During the time he worked on his master's and doctorate degrees he was a Staff Development Engineer at Wright Patterson Air Force Base in Ohio. Before joining NASA as an astronaut candidate in 1978, he wrote and presented many scientific papers on computational fluid dynamics. At NASA he became a Mission Specialist Astronaut (scientific astronaut) and on the eighth shuttle flight in August of 1983, became the first Black American to go into space. He took a second ride into space on the first German/American scientific space mission in November of 1985. He now lives in Houston, Texas, where he continues his work as a Mission Specialist Astronaut for NASA.

Name: Guion S. Bluford, Jr.

Skill: Reading, geography

Procedure:
1. Make the space shuttle model.
2. Identify on the map all the states where Colonel Bluford lived, worked, and received training. Trace the route from Philadelphia to Houston.

Variation: Write to NASA or visit the library to find out about Dr. Ronald McNair (the second Black American in space) who was killed in the Challenger accident (Mission 51-L) in January, 1986. Like Col. Bluford, he was a scientist and a Mission Specialist Astronaut.

Guion S. Bluford, Jr.

1941 -

Astronaut

Guion Bluford, Jr. was born in Philadelphia, Pennsylvania, and attended the public schools there. He received his Bachelor of Science degree from Pennsylvania State University in Aerospace Engineering and both his master's and doctorate in Aerospace Engineering from the Air Force Institute of Technology. After his graduation from college in 1964, he entered the Air Force, and was trained as a pilot. He went on to do combat training in F4C planes in both Arizona and Florida. After flying combat missions in Vietnam he became a T38 trainer pilot at Sheppard Air Force Base in Texas. During the time he worked on his master's and doctorate degrees he was a Staff Development Engineer at Wright Patterson Air Force Base in Ohio. Before joining NASA as an astronaut candidate in 1978, he wrote and presented many scientific papers on computational fluid dynamics. At NASA he became a Mission Specialist Astronaut (scientific astronaut) and on the eighth shuttle flight in August of 1983, became the first Black American to go into space. He took a second ride into space on the first German-American scientific space mission in November of 1985. He now lives in Houston, Texas, where he continues his work as a Mission Specialist Astronaut for NASA.

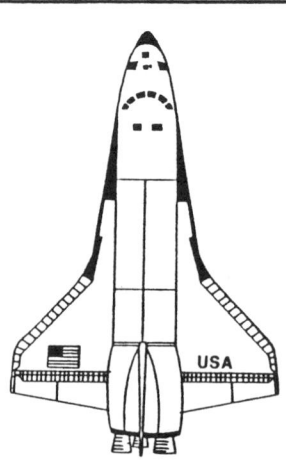

1. Ask the class how many degrees Dr. Bluford has.
   B.S., M.S., Ph.D.
2. How many airplanes was he trained to fly? 2
   Name them. F4C and T38
3. When was he selected as an astronaut? 1978
4. In what year was his historic flight in the space shuttle?
   1983

82

SPACE SHUTTLE MODEL

ASSEMBLY INSTRUCTIONS

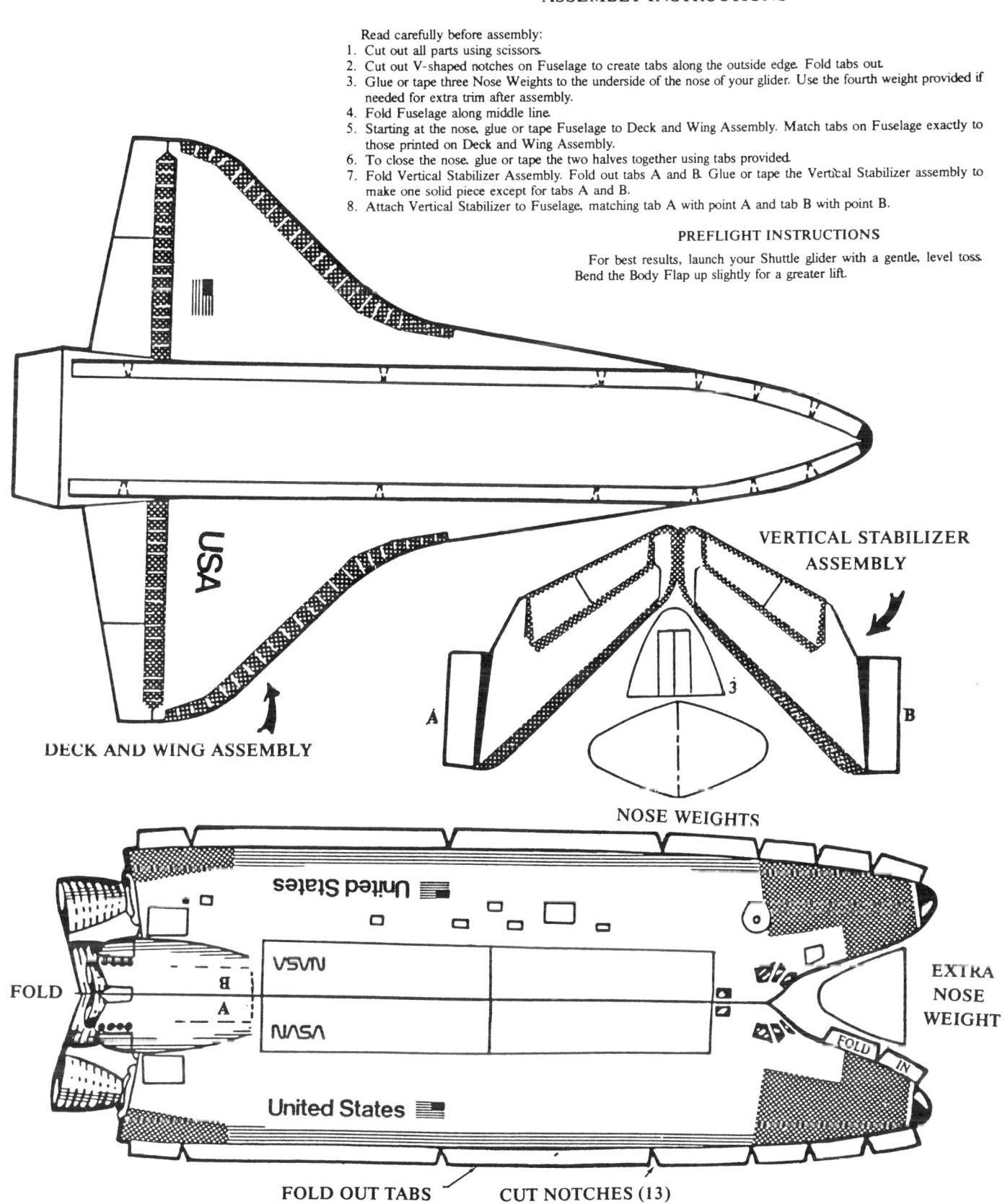

Read carefully before assembly:
1. Cut out all parts using scissors.
2. Cut out V-shaped notches on Fuselage to create tabs along the outside edge. Fold tabs out.
3. Glue or tape three Nose Weights to the underside of the nose of your glider. Use the fourth weight provided if needed for extra trim after assembly.
4. Fold Fuselage along middle line.
5. Starting at the nose, glue or tape Fuselage to Deck and Wing Assembly. Match tabs on Fuselage exactly to those printed on Deck and Wing Assembly.
6. To close the nose, glue or tape the two halves together using tabs provided.
7. Fold Vertical Stabilizer Assembly. Fold out tabs A and B. Glue or tape the Vertical Stabilizer assembly to make one solid piece except for tabs A and B.
8. Attach Vertical Stabilizer to Fuselage, matching tab A with point A and tab B with point B.

PREFLIGHT INSTRUCTIONS

For best results, launch your Shuttle glider with a gentle, level toss. Bend the Body Flap up slightly for a greater lift.

DECK AND WING ASSEMBLY

VERTICAL STABILIZER ASSEMBLY

NOSE WEIGHTS

FOLD

EXTRA NOSE WEIGHT

FOLD OUT TABS   CUT NOTCHES (13)

1. Ask the class how many degrees Dr. Bluford has. B.S., M.S., Ph.D.
2. How many airplanes was he trained to fly? 2 Name them. F4C and T38.
3. When was he selected as an astronaut? 1978
4. In what year was his historic flight in the space shuttle? 1983

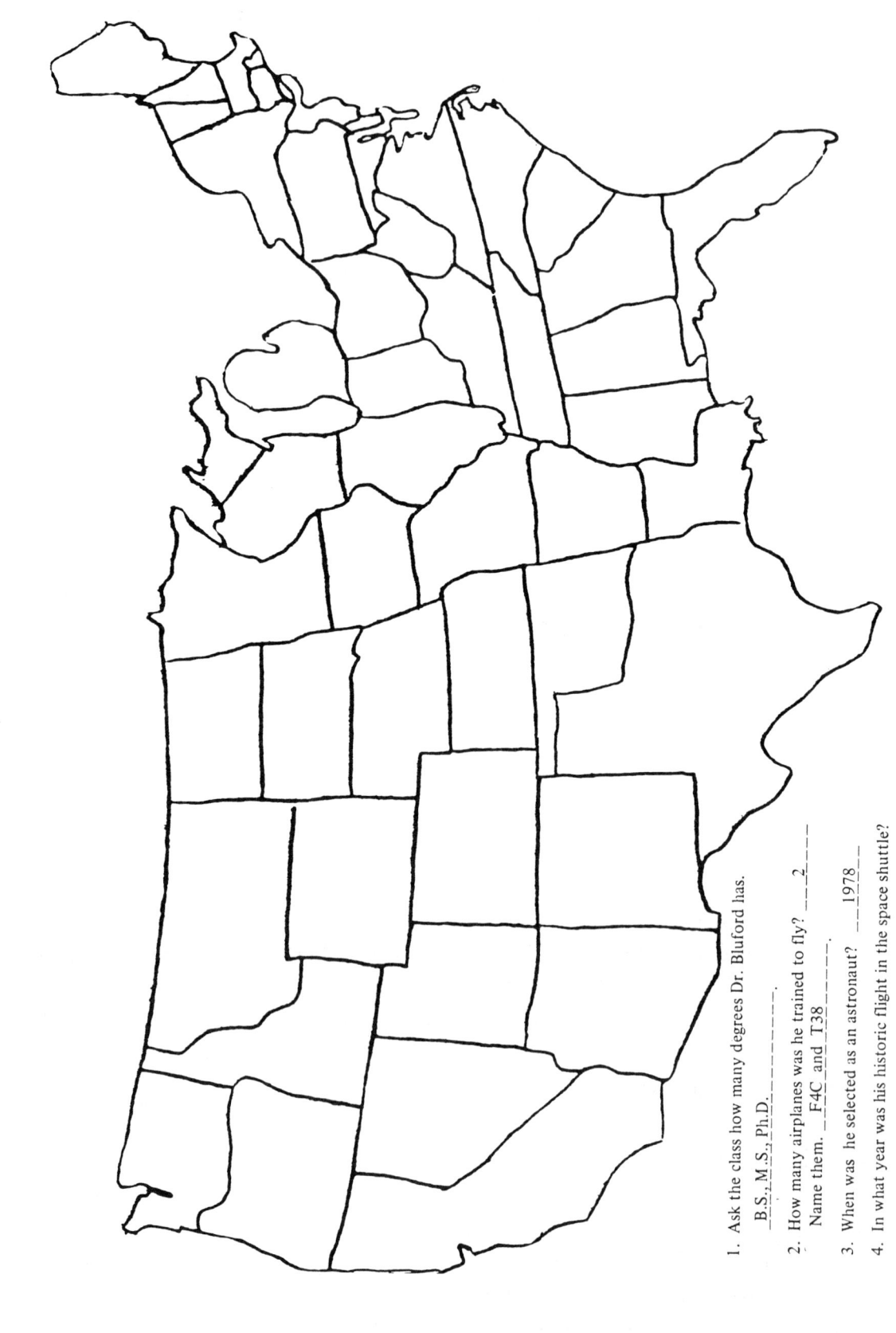

George Washington Carver

1864 - 1943

Agricultural Scientist

George Washington Carver was born a slave in Diamond Grave, Missouri, where he and his mother were taken from his owner's plantation by a group of slave raiders. The master was not able to get the mother before she was sold at a slave auction but he was able to ransom little George, in exchange for a race horse. Carver managed to obtain a high school education but was turned down by many colleges before Simpson College in Indianola, Iowa, agreed to take him as their first Black student. He earned money for his degree in agricultural science by working nights as the school's janitor. He later received his master's and became the college's first Black faculty member. Booker T. Washington, then the President of Tuskegee Institute, heard about him and brought him to the Alabama campus. Dr. Carver never obtained a patent for any of his agricultural discoveries. With his life savings of $30,000 he established the George Washington Carver Foundation in order for his work to be carried on after his death. When Carver died in 1943 he was buried alongside Booker T. Washington on the campus of Tuskegee Institute. His epitaph reads: "He could have added fortune to fame, but caring for neither, he found happiness and honor in being helpful to the world."

Name: George Washington Carver

Skill: Health and nutrition awareness/Library skills

Procedure:
1. Read about peanuts, then prepare the recipies as described.
2. Complete the peanut family tree.
3. Locate peanut producing states on the U.S. map.
4. List by-products made from peanuts and peanut shells.

Variation: Obtain raw peanuts from a health food or seed store. Remove peanuts from shell. Plant them in a container filled with sandy soil. Plant the peanut so that the pointed end is up and the nub, the germ or round end, is down. Place container in warm sunny location and keep soil moist. The peanuts will start to sprout in 5-7 days.

George Washington Carver
1864 - 1943
Agricultural Scientist

George Washington Carver was born a slave in Diamond Grove, Missouri, where he and his mother were taken from his owner's plantation by a group of slave raiders. The master was not able to get the mother before she was sold at a slave auction but he was able to ransom little George, in exchange for a race horse. Carver managed to obtain a high school education but was turned down by many colleges before Simpson College in Indianola, Iowa, agreed to take him as their first Black student. He earned money for his degree in agricultural science by working nights as the school's janitor. He later received his master's and became the college's first Black faculty member. Booker T. Washington, then the President of Tuskegee Institute, heard about him and brought him to the Alabama campus. Dr. Carver never obtained a patent for any of his agricultural discoveries. With his life savings of $30,000 he established the George Washington Carver Foundation in order for his work to be carried on after his death. When Carver died in 1943 he was buried alongside Booker T. Washington on the campus of Tuskegee Institute. His epitaph reads. "He could have added fortune to fame, but caring for neither, he found happiness and honor in being helpful to the world."

Peanuts are one of the world's oldest foods. The Spanish explorers found peanuts in the 16th century when they explored the land now known as Peru. Peanuts are presently grown on over 42,000,000 acres in the world and is one of the six basic United States farm crops valued at over 400 million dollars. The Spanish and Portuguese traders used peanuts in exchange for spices and elephant tusks in the African nations. The Africans liked these "goobers" and they were put on ships along with the slaves bound for America. Although this food for the poor was not accepted by Americans at first, Union soldiers fed on peanuts during the War and took them back North after the War. After the War the cotton crop began to fail due to the boll weevil. Dr. George Washington Carver showed the southern farmers how to replenish their income by growing peanuts. Now peanuts are grown by over 84,000 farmers in numerous states: Georgia, Texas, Alabama, North Carolina, Oklahoma, Virginia, Florida, New Mexico and Mississippi. Carver rose to fame as the world-renowned botanist and received numerous honors in scientific research. He was director of the Department of Agriculture at Tuskegee Institute from 1896 to 1943. He performed numerous experiments in soil-building, cotton growing and developed hundreds of peanut by-products.

RECIPES

Peanut Butter

1 cup freshly roasted or salted peanuts
1½ tablespoons of peanut oil

Blend mixture in a blender until smooth. Gradually add another tablespoon of oil until the peanut butter is the proper consistency.

Chocolate Crunchies

1 6 ounce package semi-sweet chocolate pieces
1 tablespoon peanut oil
½ cup smooth peanut butter
2 tablespoons confectioners' sugar
75 - 80 miniature shredded whole wheat biscuits
whole peanuts

In a small saucepan over hot water, heat chocolate and oil until melted. Stir in peanut butter and sugar until smooth. Dip each miniature biscuit in peanut mixture to coat and place on waxed paper. Top each with a peanut half. Chill.

Peanut Butter Balls

1/3 cup honey
½ cup crunchy peanut butter
½ cup non-fat dry milk

Mix honey and peanut butter in bowl. Stir in non-fat dry milk until blended. Shape into balls.

Peanuts are one of the world's oldest foods. The Spanish explorers discovered peanuts in the 16th century when they explored the land now known as Peru. Peanuts are presently grown on over 42,000,000 acres in the world. Peanut farming is among the six basic United States farm crops valued at over 400 million dollars. The Spanish and Portuguese traders used peanuts in exchange for spices and elephant tusks when bartering with African nations. Because the Africans liked these "goobers," peanuts were put on slave ships bound for America. Although white Americans did not accept this food at first because they considered it fit only for slaves, Union soldiers ate peanuts during the Civil War and took them back North after the war. After the war, when the cotton crop began to fail because of the boll weevil, Dr. George Washington Carver showed Southern farmers how to replenish their income by growing peanuts. Now peanuts are grown by over 84,000 farmers in numerous states: Georgia, Texas, Alabama, North Carolina, Oklahoma, Virginia, Florida, New Mexico and Mississippi. Carver rose to fame as a world-renowned botanist, receiving numerous honors in scientific research. He was the director of the Department of Agriculture at Tuskegee Institute from 1896 to 1943. He performed numerous experiments in soil-building and cotton growing, and also developed hundreds of peanut by-products.

RECIPES

Peanut Butter

1 cup freshly roasted or salted peanuts
1 ½ tablespoons of peanut oil

Blend mixture in a blender until smooth. Gradually add another tablespoon of oil until the peanut butter is the proper consistency.

Chocolate Crunchies

1 6-ounce package semi-sweet chocolate pieces
1 tablespoon peanut oil
½ cup smooth peanut butter
2 tablespoons confectioners' sugar
75-80 miniature shredded whole wheat biscuits
whole peanuts

In a small saucepan over hot water, heat chocolate and oil until melted. Stir in peanut butter and sugar until smooth. Dip each miniature biscuit in peanut mixture to coat it and then place on waxed paper. Top each with a peanut half. Chill.

Peanut Butter Balls

⅓ cup honey
½ cup crunchy peanut butter
½ cup non-fat dry milk

Mix honey and peanut butter in bowl. Stir in non-fat dry milk until blended. Shape into balls.

Complete the peanut tree. Extend the limbs as much as you can.

contributed by Tom Garmon

Charles R. Drew

1904 - 1950

Blood Plasma Researcher

Charles R. Drew was born in Washington, D.C., and graduated from Amherst College in Massachusetts where he received a trophy for having brought the most honor to the school during his four years. He was also captain of the track team and the star halfback on the college's football team. He received his medical degree from McGill University in 1933, and returned to Washington, D.C. to teach pathology at Howard University. He wrote his Columbia University dissertation in 1940 on "banked blood." He became an expert in the field and British government called upon him to set up the first blood bank in England. During World War II, Dr. Drew was appointed the director of the Red Cross Blood Donor Project. He also served as a surgeon at Howard University's Freedman's Hospital. Dr. Drew was killed in an auto accident in Alabama. His nephew Frederick Drew Gregory became the first Black space shuttle pilot.

Name: Charles R. Drew

Skill: Health

Procedure:
1. Discuss with the class the importance of preserving and storing blood to save lives.
2. Write to Morehouse College, a member of the United Negro College Fund, about their new medical school.

Variation: Introduce the idea of how AIDS may be transmitted if blood is collected from a donor infected with the virus; hence, the careful procedures a blood bank must use to collect and preserve blood.

Charles R. Drew
1904 - 1950
Blood Plasma Researcher

Charles R. Drew was born in Washington, D.C., and graduated from Amherst College in Massachusetts where he received a trophy for having brought the most honor to the school during his four years. He was also captain of the track team and the star halfback on the college's football team. He received his medical degree from McGill University in 1933, and received his Ph.D. from Columbia University. He wrote his Columbia University dissertation in 1940 on "banked blood." He became an expert in the field and British government called upon him to set up the first blood bank in England. During World War II, Dr. Drew was appointed the director of the Red Cross Blood Donor Project. He also served as a surgeon at Howard University's Freedman's Hospital. Dr. Drew was killed in an auto accident in Alabama. His nephew Frederick Drew Gregory became the first Black space shuttle pilot.

Garrett A. Morgan

1877 - 1963

Inventor

Garrett A. Morgan was born in Paris, Kentucky and raised in Cleveland, Ohio. He sold his first invention, an improvement on the sewing machine, for $150.00. The invention which gained him fame was a gas inhalator that firemen used to avoid smoke asphyxiation. Orders for the Morgan inhalator came into Cleveland from fire companies all over the nation until it became known that Morgan was Black. At the beginning of World War I, Morgan's inhalator was transformed into a gas mask for the use of combat troops. By 1923 Morgan's inventions were so well known that the General Electric Company agreed to pay him $40,000 for his automatic stop sign, the traffic light.

Name: Garrett A. Morgan

Skill: Spelling/Reading comprehension

Procedure:
1. Play the word search game.
2. Use the words on the following page for a class spelling bee after the students have read the biography.

Variation: Ask the class to tell how each of the words fits into Garrett Morgan's life story.

Garrett A. Morgan
1877 - 1963
Inventor

Garrett A. Morgan was born in Paris, Kentucky and raised in Cleveland, Ohio. He sold his first invention, an improvement on the sewing machine, for $150.00. The invention which gained him fame was a gas inhalator that firemen used to avoid smoke asphyxiation. Orders for the Morgan inhalator came into Cleveland from fire companies all over the nation until it became known that Morgan was Black. At the beginning of World War I, Morgan's inhalator was transformed into a gas mask for the use of combat troops. By 1923 Morgan's inventions were so well known that the General Electric Company agreed to pay him $40,000 for his automatic stop sign, the traffic light.

THERE ARE 12 WORDS HERE — CAN YOU FIND THEM?

HERE ARE THE WORDS TO LOOK FOR:

ASPHYXIATION
CLEVELAND
GARRETT
INVENTOR
OHIO
1923

AUTOMATIC
ELECTRIC
INHALATOR
KENTUCKY
MORGAN
PARIS

91

```
A M M R J J K C S L A N N E P N A Z F L
G O A R U B E H A U T O M A T I C I J Q
L N V W I A P E F V U J P Y M I M P J F
K B B K H S A R T D O I G M Y O K N O S
E N D S Y P R A P E M B R Q E W L P Z O
N O K R N H I W Z E E P V B Y N J I E P
T X W D V Y S Q A O L P L R Y V L C Y B
U G M G H S I L W K E C L E V E L A N D
C A A M T I N V B H C O H I O D I Y D K
K R S O Z A H I I X T C L A X G N J X H
Y R K R Q T A G A K R Z T E V G V O O H
N E U G E I L F T D I K Q V Q L E B K Y
Y T G A M O A V F I C A U J L I N Y F R
W T D N W N T X Z L S N L A H Z T Y D A
T O S T G D O V V N P S X Y S T O B I G
N Z W T S N R I P E V K L S H N R I T Y
W O O N V P R K V L A W Q J C K B A E W
I L O J X M O W C E N O B N X A Z X J J
O J X P H W C S W D J L Y N D K Y I J U
D Q Y P B P D P Y D V X Z Y J S E P S L
```

THERE ARE 12 WORDS HERE - CAN
YOU FIND THEM?

HERE ARE THE WORDS TO LOOK FOR:

ASPHYSIATION   **AUTOMATIC**
CLEVELAND   **ELECTRIC**
GARRETT   **INHALATOR**
INVENTOR   **KENTUCKY**
MASK   **MORGAN**
OHIO   **PARIS**

```
. . . . . . . . . . . . . . . . . . . .
. . . . . . . . A U T O M A T I C . . .
. . . . . A P . . . . . . . . . . . . .
K . . . . S A . . . . . . . . . . . . .
E . . . . P R . . . . . . . . . . . . .
N . . . . H I . . . E . . . . . . . . .
T . . . . Y S . . . L . . . . . . . . .
U G M . . S I . . . E C L E V E L A N D
C A A M . I N . . . C O H I O . I . . .
K R S O . A H . . . T . . . . . N . . .
Y R K R . T A . . . R . . . . . V . . .
. E . G . I L . . . I . . . . . E . . .
. T . A . O A . . . C . . . . . N . . .
. T . N . N T . . . . . . . . . T . . .
. . . . . . O . . . . . . . . . O . . .
. . . . . . R . . . . . . . . . R . . .
. . . . . . . . . . . . . . . . . . . .
. . . . . . . . . . . . . . . . . . . .
. . . . . . . . . . . . . . . . . . . .
. . . . . . . . . . . . . . . . . . . .
```

92

Daniel Hale Williams

1856 - 1931

Surgeon

Daniel Hale Williams was born in Holidaysburg, Pennsylvania. His father died when he was only 11 years old and his mother deserted him soon after that. He worked as a cobbler, a roustabout on a lake steamer, and a barber before he finished Chicago Medical College in 1883. At that time Chicago hospitals would not allow Black doctors to use their facilities so Dr. Williams performed operations on kitchen tables and other makeshift places in southside homes until he founded the Provident Hospital, which he opened to all people. Dr. Williams performed an operation which gained him national fame. On the 10th of July a patient who had a knife wound in an artery just a fraction of an inch from the heart was admitted to Provident Hospital. Aided by 6 surgeons, Dr. Williams made an incision in the patient's chest and successfully operated on the artery. After a second operation, considered minor surgery, and after recuperating for several weeks the patient recovered completely. This was the first open heart surgery in the history of the world Skeptics doubted that a Black doctor had performed such a delicate and astonishing operation. Williams moved to Washington, D.C. and practiced medicine and surgery at Howard University's Freedmen's Hospital. He devoted his life to the construction of hospitals and training schools for Black doctors and nurses.

Name: Daniel Hale Williams

Skill: Reading/Writing/Health

Procedure:
1. Discuss how much heart surgery has advanced since 1893.
2. Define the following tersm: cobbler, roustabout, facility, incision, recuperate, skeptic, national fame.

Variation:
1. Make a list of health practices that are believed to strengthen the heart (i.e. exercise, no smoking, avoiding high cholesterol, etc.) Discuss some innovations related to heart surgery (i.e. bypass surgery, mechanical hearts).
2. The first woman neurosurgeon is from Laurel, Mississippi. See if you can find out who she is and what her specialty, angioplasty, is.
3. Take your pulse rate before and after exercise.

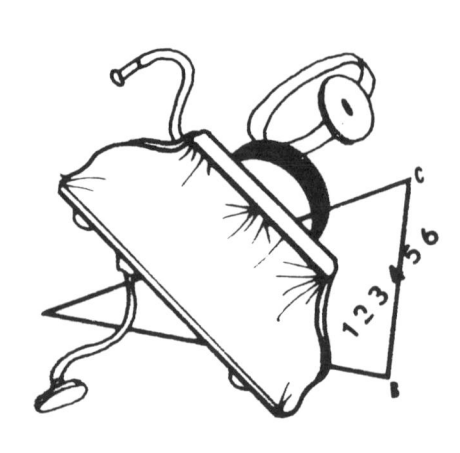

Daniel Hale Williams
1856 - 1931
Surgeon

Daniel Hale Williams was born in Holidaysburg, Pennsylvania. His father died when he was only 11 years old and his mother deserted him soon after that. He worked as a cobbler, a roustabout on a lake steamer, and a barber before he finished Chicago Medical College in 1883. At that time Chicago hospitals would not allow Black doctors to use their facilities so Dr. Williams performed operations on kitchen tables and other makeshift places in southside homes until he founded the Provident Hospital, which he opened to all people. Dr. Williams performed an operation which gained him national fame. On the 10th of July a patient who had a knife wound in an artery just a fraction of an inch from the heart was admitted to Provident Hospital. Aided by 6 surgeons, Dr. Williams made an incision in the patient's chest and successfully operated on the artery. After a second operation, considered minor surgery, and after recuperating for several weeks the patient recovered completely. This was the first open heart surgery in the history of the world. Skeptics doubted that a Black doctor had performed such a delicate and astonishing operation. Williams moved to Washington, D.C. and practiced medicine and surgery at Howard University's Freedmen's Hospital. He devoted his life to the construction of hospitals and training schools for Black doctors and nurses.

94

Civil Rights LEADERS

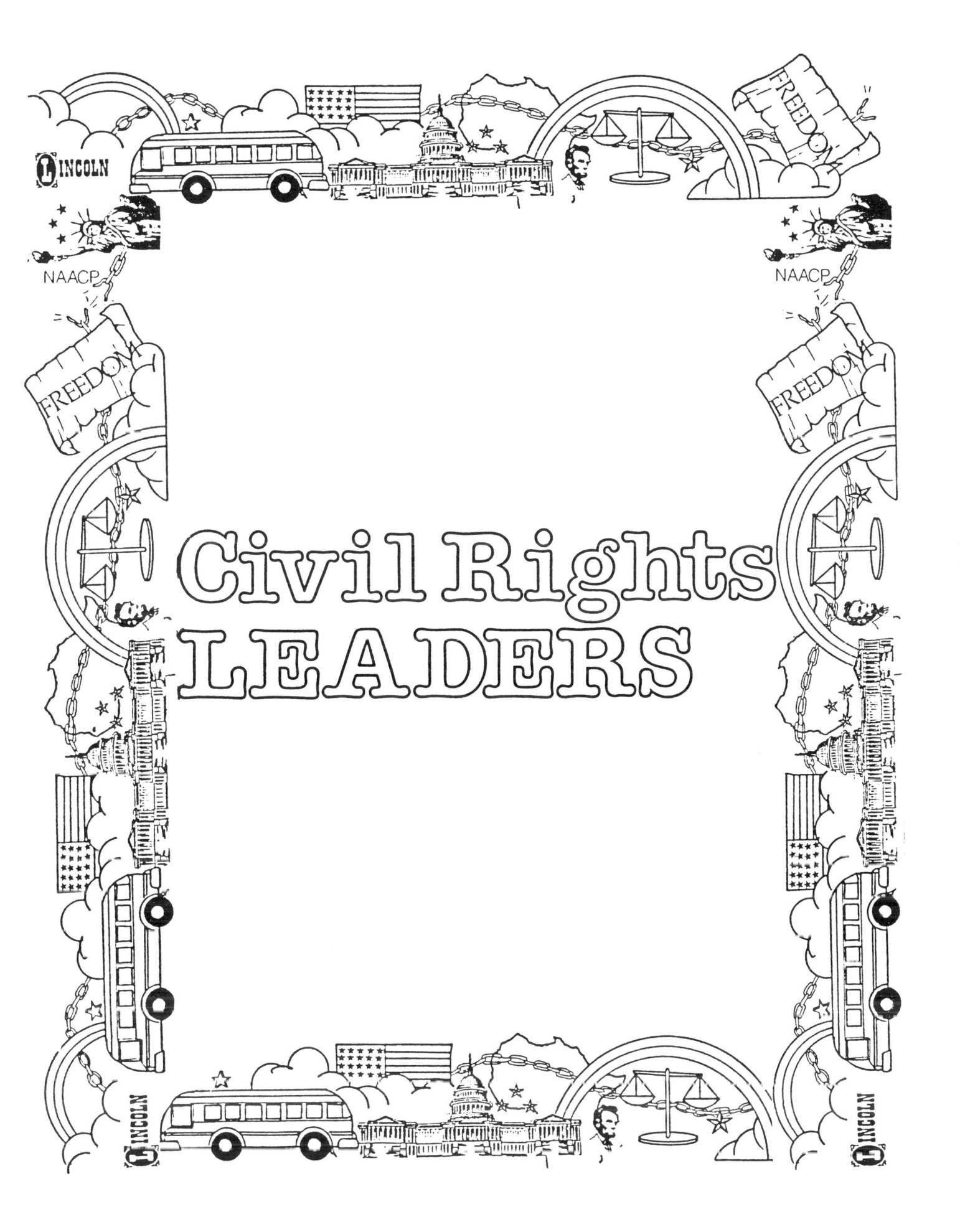

Frederick Douglass

1812 - 1895

Abolitionist

Frederick Douglass was born in Talbot Country, Maryland. At the age of eight he was sent to Baltimore to be a house servant. There his mistress taught him how to read and write. After one unsuccessful attempt, Douglass managed to escape from his slavery to New York. In New York, Frederick Douglass found his calling as a leader in the anti-slavery crusade. As time went on, Douglass became an increasingly important figure in the abolitionists' movement. In the 1840s, Douglass went to England, where he raised enough money by lecturing on slavery and women's rights to buy his freedom. Back in the United States, Douglass founded a newspaper, "The North Star," in Washington, D.C. When the Civil War started, Douglass met with President Abraham Lincoln and assisted in recruiting the 54th and 55th Massachusetts Negro regiments. After the war in 1871, Douglass was appointed to the territorial legislature of the district of columbia. He later became the police commissioner and then U.S. Marshal of the District of Columbia. In 1889 by the new president to be the Consul General of the Republic of Haiti and later was named chargé d' affaires to Santo Domingo. Douglass resigned in 1891 and died in his Washington, D.C., home four years later.

Name: Frederick Douglass

Skill: Communication (Language Arts)

Procedure:
1. Discuss how the print and broadcast media affect our thoughts. Name some newspapers, television stations, radio stations in your area. Discuss the use of media in getting messages across to viewers (e.g., No Smoking campaigns; Mothers Against Drunk Drivers, editorials against apartheid, nuclear energy, etc.)
2. Learn about the various jobs Douglass held.

Variation:
1. Research the concepts of freedom and liberty that originated during the Enlightenment.
2. In an essay, discuss Frederick Douglass' beliefs and the concepts of the Enlightenment.

97

EXPLAIN THE MANY JOBS FREDERICK DOUGLASS HELD DURING HIS LIFE TIME.

1. A house servant is a person who does jobs around the house.
2. A crusader is a person who works for a cause.
3. An abolitionist is a person who works for the freedom of slaves.
4. A lecturer is a person who speaks publicly about a subject.
5. A newspaper publisher is a person who owns and prints a newspaper.
6. A recruiter is a person who encourages people to join the military.
7. A member of the territorial legislature is a person who serves in a governing role of a territory.
8. A police commissioner is a person who has control of a police department.
9. A U.S. Marshal is a law enforcement officer for the Federal Courts System.
10. A counsul general assists an ambassador in a foreign country.
11. A chargé d'affaires (in charge of affairs) works in place of an ambassador in a foreign country.

W. E. B. DuBois

1868 - 1963

Author, Historian

W.E.B. DuBois was born in Great Barrington, Massachusetts. He received a bachelor's degree from Fisk University, then a second bachelor's degree and a Ph.D. from Harvard University. He was a professor of Latin, Greek, economics and history at Wilberforce University, the University of Pennsylvania and Atlanta University. A critic, editor, educator, scholar, author and civil rights leader, Dr. DuBois was one of the founders of the NAACP in 1909. He was the editor of the organization's magazine "Crisis" until 1934. After emigrating to Africa in 1961, he became the editor-in-chief of the "Encyclopedia Africana." Some of his works include "Black Folk: Then and Now" (1939); "Dusk of Dawn" (1940); "The World and Africa" (1947); "In Battle for Peace" (1952). He died at age 95 in Ghana, West Africa.

Name: W.E.B. Dubois

Skill: Reading/Research

Procedure: Read about the NAACP. Watch the news to see what the organization does to help minorities.

Variation: Locate one of Dubois' books. Read it and report on how it applies today.

W. E. B. DuBois
1868 - 1963
Author, Historian

W.E.B. DuBois was born in Great Barrington, Massachusetts. He received a bachelor's degree from Fisk University, then a second bachelor's degree and a Ph.D. from Harvard University. He was a professor of Latin, Greek, economics and history at Wilberforce University, the University of Pennsylvania and Atlanta University. A critic, editor, educator, scholar, author and civil rights leader, Dr. DuBois was one of the founders of the NAACP in 1909. He was the editor of the organization's magazine "Crisis" until 1934. After emigrating to Africa in 1961, he became the editor-in-chief of the "Encyclopedia Africana." Some of his works include: "Black Folk: Then and Now" (1939); "Dusk of Dawn" (1940); "The World and Africa" (1947); "In Battle for Peace" (1952). He died at age 95 in Ghana, West Africa.

NAACP

The National Association for the Advancement of Colored People (NAACP) has traditionally been a leading advocate of civil rights for minorities. The NAACP, a United States based organization, assumed leadership of the civil rights movement early in this century. The organization grew from the 1905 Niagara Movement led by W.E.B. DuBois. Prominent white liberals were attracted to the Niagara Movement following the violent race riot in Springfield, Illinois, in 1908. This led to the founding of the NAACP which was incorporated in 1910. DuBois served as editor of the NAACP's journal Crisis.

The Association has always sought to advance the ideals of democracy by focusing on social, political, and economic equality for all Americans. The main instruments employed to achieve these aims has been litigation, agitation, and education. This function was first the responsibility of the Association's Legal Redress Committee. In 1939 this was split from the NAACP to become the Legal Defense and Educational Fund. Its first success was in 1915 when the United States Supreme Court ruled to protect black voting rights. Other important cases were the 1917 case that ended municipal housing segregation ordinances, and the 1954 Brown verses Board of Education, Topeka, Kansas that ended school segregation.

The NAACP has experienced recent difficulties resulting from internal dissension and loss of interest in the movement. Disputes with their traditional allies, labor unions and liberals over busing and affirmative action have resulted in the diminished support for the Association.

Over the years the organization has provided for a climate more favorable to the emergence of more activist organizations.

100

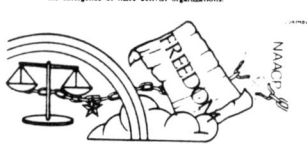

NAACP

The National Association for the Advancement of Colored People (NAACP) has traditionally been a leading advocate of civil rights for minorities. The NAACP, a United States-based organization, assumed leadership of the civil rights movement early in this century. The organization grew from the 1905 Niagara Movement led by W.E.B. DuBois. Prominent white liberals were attracted to the Niagara Movement following the violent race riot that occurred in Springfield, Illinois, in 1908. This led to the founding of the NAACP which was incorporated in 1910. DuBois served as editor of the NAACP's journal, "Crisis." The Association has always sought to advance the ideals of democracy by focusing on social, political, and economic equality for all Americans. The main instruments employed to achieve these aims have been litigation, legislation, and education. This function was first the responsibility of the Association's Legal Redress Committee. In 1939 this aim split from the NAACP to become the Legal Defense and Educational Fund. The separate group's first success was in 1915 when the United States Supreme Court ruled to protect Black voting rights. Other important cases were the 1917 case that ended municipal housing segregation ordinances, and the 1954 ruling in Brown versus Board of Education, Topeka, Kansas, that ended school segregation.

Recently, the NAACP has experienced difficulties resulting from internal dissension and a loss of public interest in the movement. Disputes with their traditional allies, labor unions and white liberals, over busing and affirmative action have resulted in diminished support for the Association.

Over the years the organization has provided for a climate more favorable to the emergence of more activist organizations.

contributed by Tom Garmon

Marcus Garvey

1887 - 1940

Freedom Fighter

Marcus Garvey was born in Jamaica, West Indies, the youngest of eleven children. At the age of fourteen he became an apprentice to a printer. After a hurricane destroyed the land on his mother's estate in 1903, he moved to Kingston, the capital of Jamaica. He took a job as a foreman in a print shop and after a few years was working in the Jamaican's Government Printing Office. In 1911 he founded the Universal Negro Improvement Association (UNIA) in Jamaica. Garvey left Jamaica for England in 1912, seeking funds to support his movement. In 1916, Marcus Garvey came to the United States and settled in New York to establish his popular movement in America. His "Back to Africa" program involved the resettlement of American Blacks in Africa. He was one of the first to tour the country preaching Black Nationalism to large audiences. In a very short time he had established thirty chapters of his organization. With one and a half million members in UNIA, Garvey founded a Black steam ship company. "The Black Star Line" operated three vessels traveling from New York to Central America and the West Indies. In 1920, Garvey convened a thirty-one day conclave in Madison Square Garden in New York on the "Back to Africa" movement. He wanted American Blacks to resettle in Liberia, West Africa. Garvey incurred many financial problems and was finally charged in the mid-1920s with defrauding investors by use of the U.S. mails. He was imprisoned in the Atlanta Federal Penitentiary and in 1927, after serving his sentence, he was deported to Jamaica by order of President Calvin Coolidge. A year after returning to Jamaica, Marcus Garvey organized a second international convention to look at the deplorable conditions of Blacks the world over. In 1935 Garvey left for England and died five years later in near obscurity. He has been called everything from a crank to a genius. More than forty years after his death we can say that he was a visionary with enormous ideas who was driven by the concept that there should be a separate empire in Africa for Black Americans.

Name: Marcus Garvey

Skill: Social studies/Geography

Procedure: Read about Liberia and Jamaica. Learn the countries' flags and locate them on a world map or globe.

Variation: Ask someone who has visited one or both of the countries to talk to your class.

LIBERIA

Liberia is the oldest republic in Africa and until 1957 was the only independent Black-ruled state on the continent.

The creation of the modern state of Liberia is tied to the abolitionist movement in the United States in the early 19th century. With the assistance of the United States government, Francis Scott Key, and President James Monroe, the American Colonization Society initiated an experiment to repatriate free slaves to their ancestral home, Africa. In 1821 the first ship landed at Providence Island with a group of former slaves from the United States. This port of entry for freed slaves was later named Monrovia after James Monroe. Today it is Liberia's capital.

In 1847 Liberia declared its independence from the United States. The tiny republic was forced to defend itself against European colonialists with only minor diplomatic assistance from the United States. The hostility of the tribes who originally inhabited the area against the American Blacks continued into the 20th century.

The descendants of former slaves from the United States make up about 5% of the population. They are known as Americo-Liberians and until the 1980 coup were the social and political leaders of the country.

The official language in Liberia is English and its economy is tied to that of the United States. Liberia has one of the world's largest merchant marines because of its lenient terms for ship registry. Many refer to the Liberian registry as a "flag of convenience." The country became a member of the United Nations in 1945 and in 1960 was the first African nation to serve on the Security Council. Liberia has traditionally been a leader in African unification, economic and cultural cooperation, human rights, and economic development. The country was a founding member of the Organization of African Unity in 1963. In the coup of April 12, 1980, the president was killed and replaced with a 17-member junta. The constitution has been suspended. Liberia's future is uncertain.

Color the Liberian flag with alternate red and white stripes then color the white star on a blue background.

contributed by Tom Garmon

Color the Liberian flag alternate red and white stripes with a white star on a blue background.

JAMAICA

The island of Jamaica is an independent country located in the Caribbean Sea, approximately ninety miles south of Cuba. It is strategically important since its location controls the entrance to the Caribbean Sea. A United States naval and air base is located near Kingston. The island was discovered by Columbus in 1494 and ruled by Spain for over one hundred and fifty years. Under Spanish rule, approximately 100,000 Arawak Indians died in slavery; only a few hundred survived the Spaniards' harsh rule.

When Jamaica was seized by Britain in 1655, Indians and Africans--former Spanish slaves--fled into the mountain areas. They were subsequently referred to as "Maroons" because of the unique culture they evolved due to their ability to avoid British authority until the early 1700's. During Spanish rule, a few Africans were imported to Jamaica to be sold into slavery. However, during the 18th century, under British rule, many Africans were imported and at one point, as many as 300,000 African slaves were at work on the plantations that made Jamaica the leading sugar producer in the world. Slavery was abolished in Jamaica in 1838.

The political system of Jamaica reflects the influence of the British parliamentary form of government. In 1962, the country became an independent member of the British Commonwealth of Nations. In Jamaica there are two major political parties: The People's National Party and the Jamaica Labor Party. In 1980, The People's National Party, a socialist party in favor of government ownership of businesses, was defeated in the election. The Jamaica Labor Party, a pro-business socialist party more in favor of free enterprise, was elected to power.

Tourism is an important industry in Jamaica. Ocho Rios, a port town sixty miles east of Montego Bay, is a popular area. Beautiful hotels line the tranquil north coast. Dunn's River Falls, a 690-foot fall, opens into the sea. The natural stairway leading up to the Falls can be climbed with the aid of a guide. Working plantations are also located near Ocho Rios. The Rio Grande River is a popular place for rafting. Rafts can often be observed going down the river. Local women wash their clothes in the river and lay them on the rocks to dry. Jamaica is known for its straw goods, wooden statues and beautiful batiks. These popular items are sold in the straw markets.

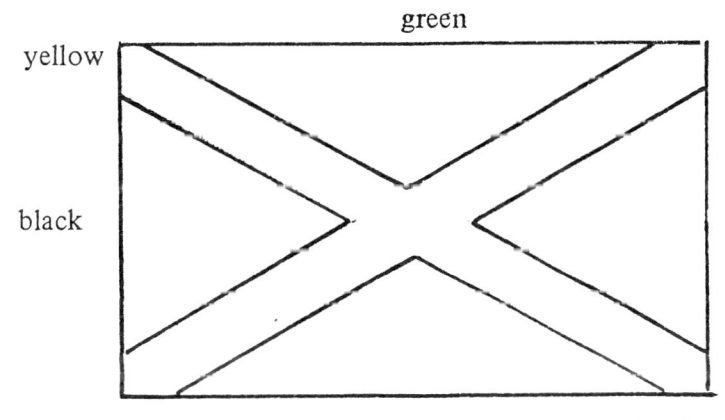

Color the Jamacian flag green, yellow and black.

Reprinted with permission from Children Around the World, Humanics Limited.

Jesse Jackson

1942 -

Civil Rights Leader

Jesse Jackson was born in Greenville, South Carolina and was educated at North Carolina A & T University in Greensboro. In the summer of 1963, Jackson became active in sit-ins to protest discrimination against Blacks. His jailing during the Greensboro civil rights movement made him make a life-time commitment to working in this field. He studied for the ministry at Chicago Theological Seminary. In 1965 Jesse Jackson met Martin Luther King, Jr. during the famous march in Selma, Alabama. By 1968 Jackson was one of King's chief lieutenants running the Chicago-based Operation Breadbasket, a part of the Southern Christian Leadership Conference. Operation Breadbasket worked on the economic needs of the Black community. In 1984 Jesse Jackson ran for the Democratic nomination for the presidency of the United States. He carried several States and his call for racial and economic unity in America became the moral voice of the campaign. Jesse Jackson lives in Chicago, Illinois with his wife and family.

Name: Jesse Jackson

Skill: Spelling

Procedure: Have the class first spell the words on the following page and then find them in the word search.

Variation: Discuss what Jackson means by "Rainbow Coalition."

Jesse Jackson

1942 -

Civil Rights Leader

Jesse Jackson was born in Greenville, South Carolina and was educated at North Carolina A & T University in Greensboro. In the summer of 1963, Jackson became active in sit-ins to protest discrimination against Blacks. His jailing during the Greensboro civil rights movement made him make a life-time commitment to working in this area. He studied for the ministry at Chicago Theological Seminary. In 1965 Jesse Jackson met Martin Luther King, Jr. during the famous march in Selma, Alabama. By 1968 Jackson was one of King's chief lieutenants running the Chicago-based Operation Breadbasket, a part of the Southern Christian Leadership Conference. Operation Breadbasket worked on the economic needs of the Black community. In 1984 Jesse Jackson ran for the Democratic nomination for the presidency of the United States. He carried several States and his call for racial and economic unity in America became the moral voice of the campaign. Jesse Jackson lives in Chicago, Illinois with his wife and family.

THERE ARE 13 WORDS HERE — CAN YOU FIND THEM?

HERE ARE THE WORDS TO LOOK FOR:

ALABAMA
CAROLINA
COMMITMENT
CONFERENCE
GREENVILLE
SELMA
BREADBASKET
CHICAGO
COMMUNITY
GREENSBORO
MINISTRY
SEMINARY

107

JESSE JACKSON

```
J G J L X M L A P W W G B H K G S Y D L
K B S U R M S I L G P I Y H O U E O F O
W V I D K Y S D Z Z H F W N J F M M I X
P D U A S T A R C O T I K X A Y I T Y Y
F R P L J B R E A D B A S K E T N I T Y
C Q Z A O I T L G N X R A J O D A I P X
A V G B G T J L J O W N L W H B R V G X
R T R A R K D P F C C A H Y V V Y U Y J
O H E M E K H H W O M I N I S T R Y S A
L D E A E C T X I M N B F H X D H X H V
I K N C N O E B W M L C Z J I S H O I O
N R V U S S B W P U M J J F O E Z I P N
A M I V B E U D C N C O N F E R E N C E
I K L Q O Y F O U I L O R C B X J D M Z
Y Z L M R I X U E T E E H H I S M Z T W
V J E U O H B M N Y T C L P W P Z E J M
W J J H W Q S O S C F G W Y S M O D K G
R G U Y W O J X F V F E W A V M B N K M
S E L M A E F C O M M I T M E N T M L X
M S K I W P C H I C A G O P K K O A I O
```

THERE ARE 12 WORDS HERE - CAN
YOU FIND THEM?

HERE ARE THE WORDS TO LOOK FOR:

ALABAMA	BREADBASKET
CAROLINA	CHICAGO
COMMITMENT	COMMUNITY
CONFERENCE	GREENSBORO
GREENVILLE	MINISTRY
SELMA	SEMINARY

JESSE JACKSON

```
. . . . . . . . . . . . . . . . . . S . . .
. . . . . . . . . . . . . . . . . . E . . .
. . . . . . . . . . . . . . . . . . M . . .
. . . A . . . . . . . . . . . . . . I . . .
. . . L . B R E A D B A S K E T N . . .
C . . A . . . . . . . . . . . . A . . .
A . G B G . . . . . . . . . . . R . . .
R . R A R . . . . C . . . . . . Y . . .
O . E M E . . . . O M I N I S T R Y . . .
L . E A E . . . . M . . . . . . . . .
I . N . N . . . . M . . . . . . . . .
N . V . S . . . . U . . . . . . . . .
A . I . B . . . . N C O N F E R E N C E
. . L . O . . . . I . . . . . . . . .
. . L . R . . . . T . . . . . . . . .
. . E . O . . . . Y . . . . . . . . .
. . . . . . . . . . . . . . . . . . . . .
S E L M A . . C O M M I T M E N T . . .
. . . . . . C H I C A G O . . . . . . .
```

108

Martin Luther King, Jr.

1929-1968

Martin Luther King, Jr., was born in Atlanta, Georgia to Martin Luther King, Sr., and Alberta Williams King. Martin attended public school in Atlanta. In 1948 King graduated from Morehouse College in Atlanta and decided to enter the ministry. In 1955, after completing his dissertation at Crozer Theological Seminary in Chester, King was awarded his doctorate degree. After his marriage to Coretta Scott, he went south to become the pastor of the Dexter Avenue Baptist Church in Montgomery, Alabama. When Rosa Parks refused to stand on the bus, it was King who organized the 382-day boycott of the city's bus lines. Dr. King was arrested and had his house bombed before the U.S. Supreme Court declared the Alabama laws on bus segregation unconstitutional. He became a national hero, and in 1957 organized the Southern Christian Leadership Conference. In 1960, Dr. King moved to Atlanta to join his father as co-pastor of the Ebenezer Baptist Church. In Birmingham three years later Dr. King was arrested again and there wrote his classic "Letter from a Birmingham Jail." In 1963, Martin Luther King, Jr., delivered the most passionate speech of his career during the "March on Washington": the speech called "I Have a Dream." He was TIME Magazine's "Man of the Year" in 1963 and a year later was named the recipient of the Nobel Peace Prize. King then decided to start a new coalition that would include the peace movement. Speaking at the United Nations, he said, "Let us save our national honor--stop the bombing. Let us save American lives and Vietnamese lives." Throughout his life, Dr. King spoke out for non-violence. It was within that context that he went to Memphis, Tennessee in support of the sanitation workers' strike. The striking workers wanted raises in their salaries and union representation. By that time in his life he had conquered the fear of death. In the speech Dr. King made on the night before he was killed, he said, "I don't know what will happen now…but it really doesn't matter." On April 4, 1968, while standing with Jesse Jackson, Andy Young, and Ralph Abernathy on a balcony of the Lorraine Motel, Martin Luther King, Jr., was shot with a rifle bullet in the neck and within a short time died. His birthdate has become a national holiday celebrated on the third Monday of January.

Name: Martin Luther King, Jr.

Skill: Social studies

Procedure:
1. Review the time line on the next page and discuss the events of Dr. King's life.
2. Discuss the Jim Crow laws.
3. Study the speech "I Have a Dream" and the song "We Shall Overcome."

Variation: Think about your dreams and write essays about them.

Martin Luther King, Jr. Time Line

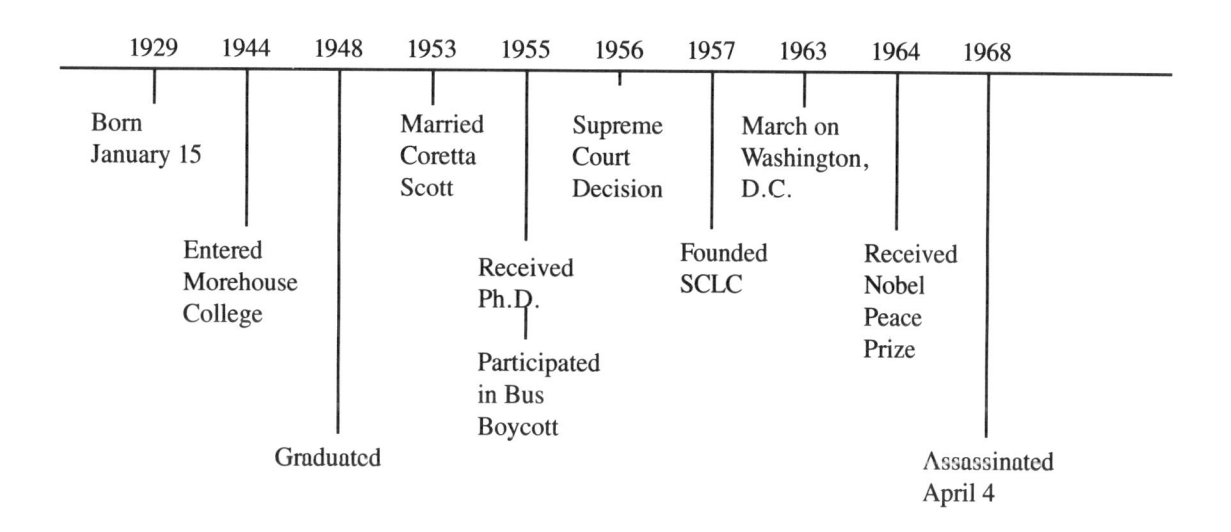

1929	1944	1948	1953	1955	1956	1957	1963	1964	1968
Born January 15			Married Coretta Scott		Supreme Court Decision		March on Washington, D.C.		
	Entered Morehouse College			Received Ph.D.		Founded SCLC		Received Nobel Peace Prize	
				Participated in Bus Boycott					
		Graduated							Assassinated April 4

Review the time line of Martin Luther King, Jr. Discuss the events that had significance in his life. Discuss the life of Martin Luther King, Jr. and his contributions to the civil rights movement.

Discuss the Jim Crow laws. (Segregation laws were commonly known as Jim Crow laws.) Ask questions such as:
What do you think of the Jim Crow laws?
How do you think these laws made Whites feel?
How do you think these laws made Blacks feel?
Discuss the segregation policies of South Africa. Compare them to the laws in the United States prior to 1954.

Get a copy of the speech "I Have a Dream." Read the speech focusing on the following topics:
What was King's dream?
Do you feel his dream has come true? Why? Why not?

Get a copy of the song "We Shall Overcome." Discuss the words of the song and how it was used as a protest song of the 1960s.

Think about King's dream. Then think about a dream that you have. Fill in the following.
I have a dream for myself......
        for my family......
        for my community......
        for the world......

Thurgood Marshall

1908 -

Justice, U.S. Supreme Court

Thurgood Marshall was born in Baltimore, Maryland, and received his Bachelor of Arts degree from Lincoln University as a pre-dental student. Deciding to become a lawyer, he attended Howard University Law School, graduating at the top of his class in 1933. After five years of private practice, Marshall joined the NAACP as special counsel handling all cases involving constitutional rights. With a string of successes he was named the director-counsel of the NAACP's Legal Defense and Educational Fund in 1950. In 1954, Thurgood Marshall led a team of lawyers that won the historic Supreme Court decision permitting school desegregation. Justice Marshall also was the lead attorney in the Smith versus Allwright case that gave Blacks the right to vote in the Texas Democratic primaries. In 1967, when Thurgood Marshall was fifty-nine years old, he became the ninety-sixth man and the first Black to sit as justice of the U.S. Supreme Court. Marshall, whose grandfather was a slave and whose father was a sleeping-car porter, has served under several presidents and rendered many historic decisions that will affect the nation for years to come.

Name: Thurgood Marshall

Skill: Library skills/Use of chronology

Procedure:
1. Do research (interview older citizens) to find out about how different life was when "separate but equal" was the law of the land. Describe a typical" day during that time. (e.g. where did one eat: go to school? go to church? go to a movie?
2. What was the 1954 Supreme Court decision? Why is it called a "landmark decision?"
3. Enact court room cases on Civil Rights.

Variation: Use the biography as the basis for constructing a time line listing events in Marshall's life. Further research in the library will help add more details and dates.

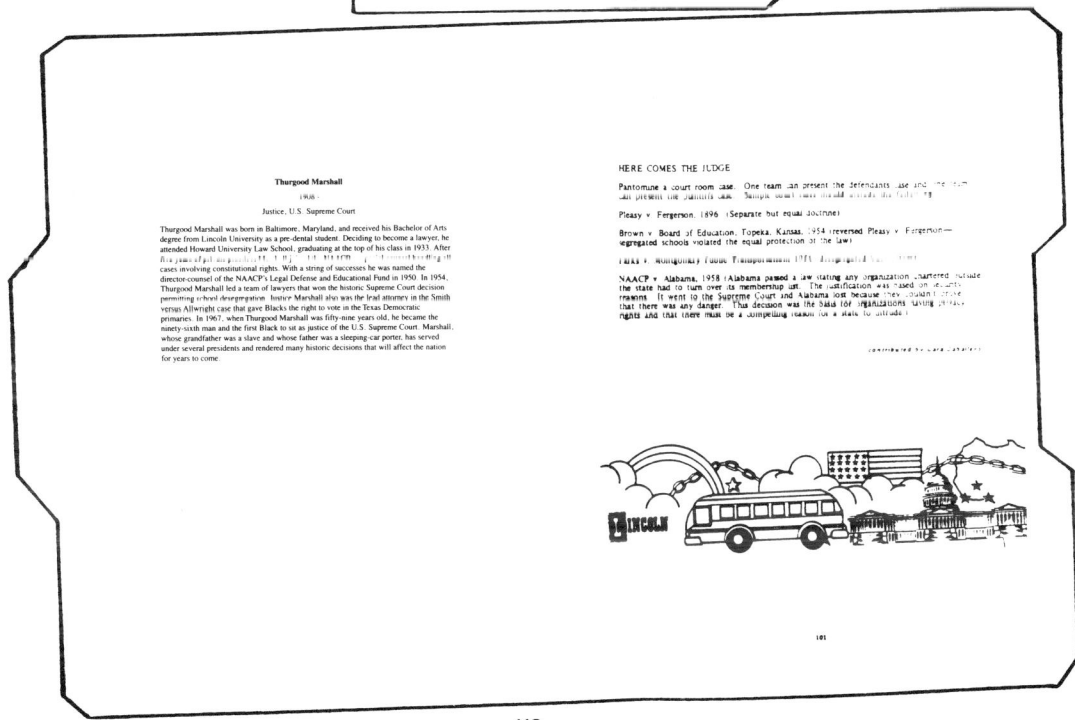

Thurgood Marshall

1908 –

Justice, U.S. Supreme Court

Thurgood Marshall was born in Baltimore, Maryland, and received his Bachelor of Arts degree from Lincoln University as a pre-dental student. Deciding to become a lawyer, he attended Howard University Law School, graduating at the top of his class in 1933. After five years of private practice, he began handling cases involving constitutional rights. With a string of successes he was named the director-counsel of the NAACP's Legal Defense and Educational Fund in 1950. In 1954, Thurgood Marshall led a team of lawyers that won the historic Supreme Court decision permitting school desegregation. Justice Marshall also was the lead attorney in the Smith versus Allwright case that gave Blacks the right to vote in the Texas Democratic primaries. In 1967, when Thurgood Marshall was fifty-nine years old, he became the ninety-sixth man and the first Black to sit as justice of the U.S. Supreme Court. Marshall, whose grandfather was a slave and whose father was a sleeping-car porter, has served under several presidents and rendered many historic decisions that will affect the nation for years to come.

HERE COMES THE JUDGE

Pantomime a court room case. One team can present the defendants case and the other can present the plaintiffs case. Sample court cases should include the following:

Plessy v. Ferguson, 1896. (Separate but equal doctrine)

Brown v. Board of Education, Topeka, Kansas, 1954 (reversed Plessy v. Ferguson—segregated schools violated the equal protection of the law)

Gayle v. Montgomery Public Transportation 1956 (desegregated buses)

NAACP v. Alabama, 1958 (Alabama passed a law stating any organization chartered outside the state had to turn over its membership list. The justification was based on security reasons. It went to the Supreme Court and Alabama lost because they couldn't prove that there was any danger. This decision was the basis for organizations suing for civil rights and that there must be a competing reason for a state to intrude.)

Here Comes The Judge

Enact a court room case. One team can present the defendant's case, the other the plaintiff's. Sample court cases should include the following:

Pleasy v. Fergerson, 1896 (Separate but equal doctrine)

Brown v. Board of Education, Topeka, Kansas, 1954 (This reversed Pleasy v. Fergerson - segregated schools violated equal protection of the law)

Parks v. Montgomery Public Transportation, 1956 (desegregated bus system)

NAACP v. Alabama, 1958 (Alabama passed a law stating any organization chartered outside the state had to turn over its membership list. The state's legal justification for this law was based on security reasons. The case went to the Supreme Court and Alabama lost because the state couldn't prove that there was any danger. This decision was the basis for organizations getting privacy rights. Now there must be a compelling reason for a state to intrude in an organization's activities.)

contributed by Lara Caballero

Rosa Parks

1913 -

Civil Rights Activist

Rosa Parks was born in Montgomery, Alabama, where she worked as a dressmaker. Rosa Parks started the Montgomery bus boycott which caused the world to take notice of Martin Luther King, Jr. Returning from work one day in 1955, she sat down in the white section of the bus and then refused to move when asked by the bus driver to let a white man sit down. Bercause of Mrs. Park's arrest, jailing and trial, the Black community refused to ride the buses in Montgomery, Alabama. This single act started a movement that caused the U.S. Congress to pass laws that allow Blacks and whites to use the same hotels, buses, stores and other places of public accommodations in this country.

Name: Rosa Parks

Skill: Spelling

Procedure: Have the class spell the words on the following page. Then define each word and write sentences using each word.

Variation: Why did Rosa Parks refuse to move from her seat? Discuss in a paper.

CLASSROOM LANGUAGE ARTS ACTIVITIES

Have the class spell the following words:

Alabama
movement
driver
arrest
community
boycott
dressmaker
section
Luther
Congress
refused

Define each of the above words.

Write a sentence using each word.

Write an essay discussing why Rosa Parks refused to move from her seat on the Montgomery bus.

Rosa Parks
1913 -
Civil Rights Activist

Rosa Parks was born in Montgomery, Alabama, where she worked as a dressmaker. Rosa Parks started the Montgomery bus boycott which caused the world to take notice of Martin Luther King, Jr. Returning from work one day in 1955, she sat down in the white section of the bus and then refused to move when asked by the bus driver to let a white man sit down. Because of Mrs. Park's arrest, jailing and trial, the Black community refused to ride the buses in Montgomery, Alabama. This single act started a movement that caused the U.S. Congress to pass laws that allow Blacks and whites to use the same hotels, buses, stores and other places of public accommodations in this country.

Classroom Language Arts Activities

Have the class spell the following words.

Alabama
movement
driver
arrest
community
boycott
dressmaker
section
Congress
refused

Define each of the above words.

Write a sentence using each word.

Write an essay discussing why Rosa Parks refused to move from her seat on the Montgomery bus.

Sojourner Truth

1797 - 1883

Abolitionist

    Sojourner Truth was born Isbella Baumfree in Ulster County, New York. Sojourner Truth, as she is known, was freed from slavery by a law passed in New York in 1827. She took the name Sojourner Truth and became a traveling preacher, drawing large crowds everywhere she spoke. During the Civil War she raised money by lecturing and singing to buy gifts for the soldiers, which she distributed in the camps herself. She became known as a person who would help runaway slaves from the South find work and places to live in the North. Even after the war Sojourner Truth continued to travel around the country on behalf of better education for the newly freed slaves. In 1875, she published a narrative that recounted her war experiences as well as her meeting with Abraham Lincoln.

Name: Sojourner Truth

Skill: Reading

Procedure: Learn the Gettysburg Address. What do you think Lincoln meant by the phrases: liberty, unfinished work; all men are created equal; honored dead; new birth of freedom; government of the people, by the people, for the people.

Variation:
1. Report on the "Underground Railroad."
2. Discuss the Civil War and Lincoln's efforts to provide freedom for the slaves.

Sojourner Truth
1797 - 1883
Abolitionist

Sojourner Truth was born Isabella Baumfree in Ulster County, New York. Sojourner Truth, as she is known, was freed from slavery by a law passed in New York in 1827. She took the name Sojourner Truth and became a traveling preacher, drawing large crowds everywhere she spoke. During the Civil War she raised money by lecturing and singing to buy gifts for the soldiers, which she distributed in the camps herself. She became known as a person who would help runaway slaves from the South find work and places to live in the North. Even after the war Sojourner Truth continued to travel around the country on behalf of better education for the newly freed slaves. In 1875, she published a narrative that recounted her war experiences as well as her meeting with Abraham Lincoln.

LINCOLN'S GETTYSBURG ADDRESS

Four score and seven years ago our fathers brought forth on this continent a new nation conceived in liberty and dedicated to the proposition that all men are created equal.

Now we are engaged in a great civil war testing whether that nation or any nation so conceived and so dedicated can long endure. We are met on a great battlefield of that war. We have come to dedicate a portion of that field as a final resting place for those who here gave their lives that that nation might live. It is altogether fitting and proper that we should do this. But in a larger sense we can not dedicate—we can not consecrate—we can not hallow—this ground. The brave men living and dead who struggled here have consecrated it far above our poor power to add or detract. The world will little note nor long remember what we say here but it can never forget what they did here. It is for us the living rather to be dedicated here to the unfinished work which they who fought here have thus far so nobly advanced. It is rather for us to be here dedicated to the great task remaining before us—that from these honored dead we take increased devotion to that cause for which they gave the last full measure of devotion—that we here highly resolve that these dead shall not have died in vain—that this nation under God shall have a new birth of freedom—and that government of the people by the people for the people shall not perish from the earth.

LINCOLN'S GETTYSBURG ADDRESS

Four score and seven years ago our fathers brought forth on this continent a new nation, conceived in Liberty, and dedicated to the proposition that all men are created equal.

Now we are engaged in a great civil war, testing whether that nation, or any nation so conceived and so dedicated, can long endure. We are met on a great battlefield of that war. We have come to dedicate a portion of that field as a final resting-place for those who here gave their lives that that nation might live. It is altogether fitting and proper that we should do this. But in a larger sense we cannot dedicate--we cannot consecrate--we cannot hallow--this ground. The brave men, living and dead, who struggled here have consecrated it far above our poor power to add or detract. The world will little note, nor long remember, what we say here, but it can never forget what they did here. It is for us the living, rather, to be dedicated here to the unfinished work which they who fought here have thus far so nobly advanced. It is rather for us to be here dedicated to the great task remaining before us--that from these honored dead we take increased devotion to that cause for which they gave the last full measure of devotion; that we here highly resolve that these dead shall not have died in vain; that this nation, under God, shall have a new birth of freedom; and that government of the people, by the people, for the people, shall not perish from the earth.

IN THE MILITARY

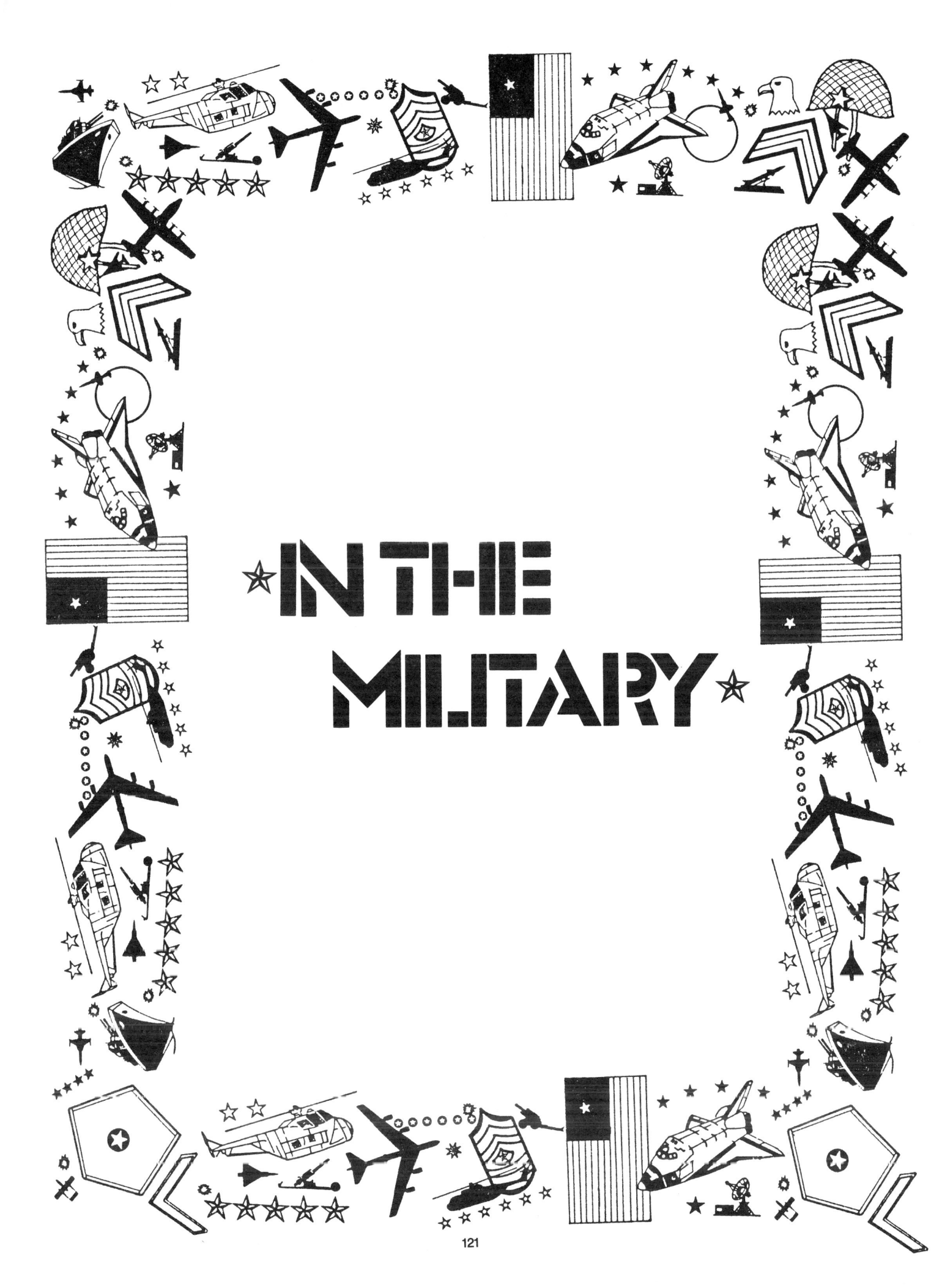

General Benjamin O. Davis, Jr.

1912-

Air Force General

Benjamin O. Davis, Jr. was born in Washington, D.C. and educated in Alabama where his father taught military science at Tuskegee Institute. His father was the first Black general in the history of the United States Army. Davis, Jr. attended both Western Reserve University and the University of Chicago before entering the U.S. Military Academy in 1932. His fellow cadets gave him the silent treatment but he persevered, graduating 35th in a class of 276 students. After serving in the infantry for five years, he transferred to the Army Air Corps in 1941. He became one of six Blacks to become an air cadet and graduated in 1942 from flying school. As commander of the all-Black 99th Fighter Squadron and the 332nd Fighter Group, Davis flew sixty missions in 224 combat hours in World War II. Lieutenant General Benjamin Davis, Jr.'s last command was as head of the U.S. Strike Command at McDill Air Force Base in Tampa, Florida.

Name: General Benjamin O. Davis, Jr.

Skill: Comprehensive/Career awareness

Procedure: Learn the Army/Air Force rank order.
Make a time line of Davis' military career rise.
Answer the questions about General Davis' life:

a. General Davis, Sr. was a general in what branch of the military?
_____

b. General Davis, Jr. was born in what year? _____

c. In _____ (year), Davis, Jr. was accepted by the U.S. Military Academy.

d. Name the U.S. Air Force Base General Davis, Jr. commanded.
_____

e. Name one of the universities Davis, Jr. attended _____

Learn the Military Ranks

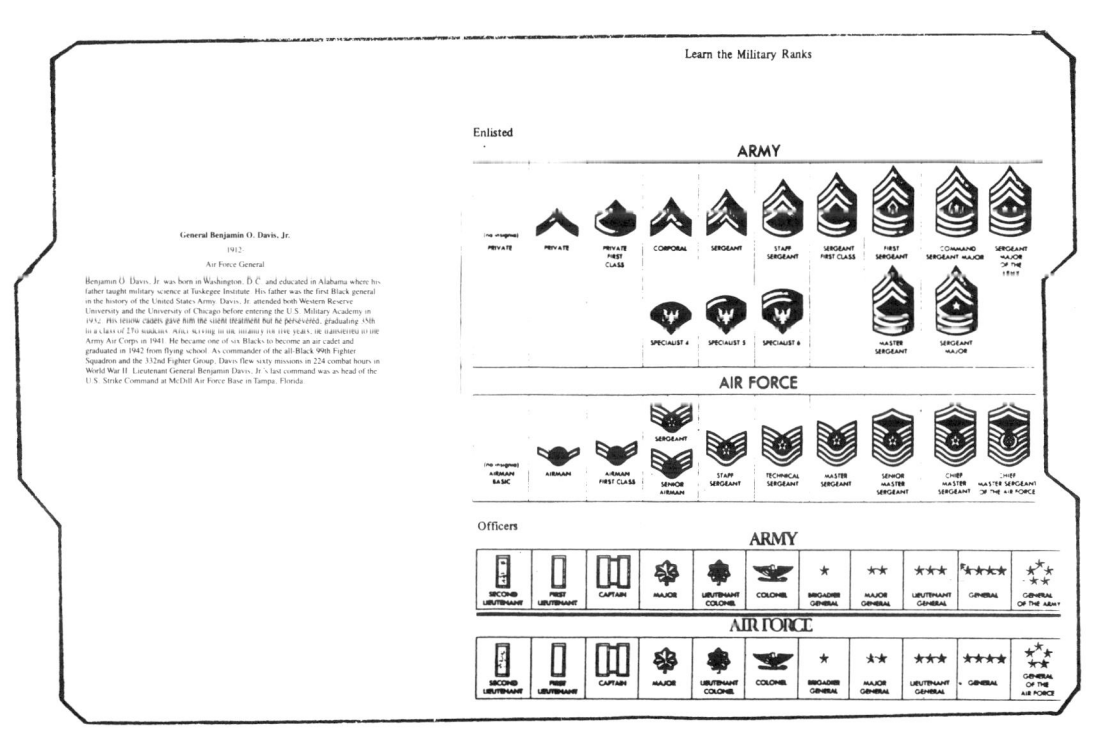

General Benjamin O. Davis, Jr.
1912-
Air Force General

Benjamin O. Davis, Jr. was born in Washington, D.C. and educated in Alabama where his father taught military science at Tuskegee Institute. His father was the first Black general in the history of the United States Army. Davis, Jr. attended both Western Reserve University and the University of Chicago before entering the U.S. Military Academy in 1932. His fellow cadets gave him the silent treatment but he persevered, graduating 35th in a class of 276 students. After serving in the infantry for five years, he transferred to the Army Air Corps in 1941. He became one of six Blacks to become an air cadet and graduated in 1942 from flying school. As commander of the all-Black 99th Fighter Squadron and the 332nd Fighter Group, Davis flew sixty missions in 224 combat hours in World War II. Lieutenant General Benjamin Davis, Jr.'s last command was as head of the U.S. Strike Command at McDill Air Force Base in Tampa, Florida.

123

Learn the Military Ranks

Enlisted

ARMY

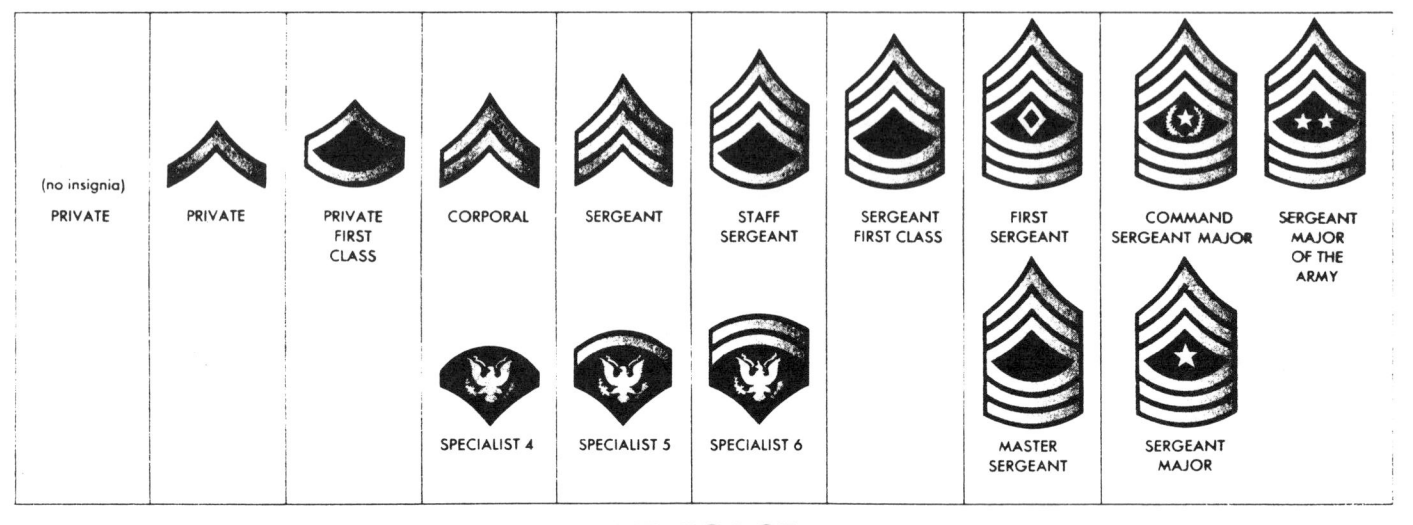

(no insignia) PRIVATE	PRIVATE	PRIVATE FIRST CLASS	CORPORAL	SERGEANT	STAFF SERGEANT	SERGEANT FIRST CLASS	FIRST SERGEANT	COMMAND SERGEANT MAJOR	SERGEANT MAJOR OF THE ARMY
			SPECIALIST 4	SPECIALIST 5	SPECIALIST 6		MASTER SERGEANT	SERGEANT MAJOR	

AIR FORCE

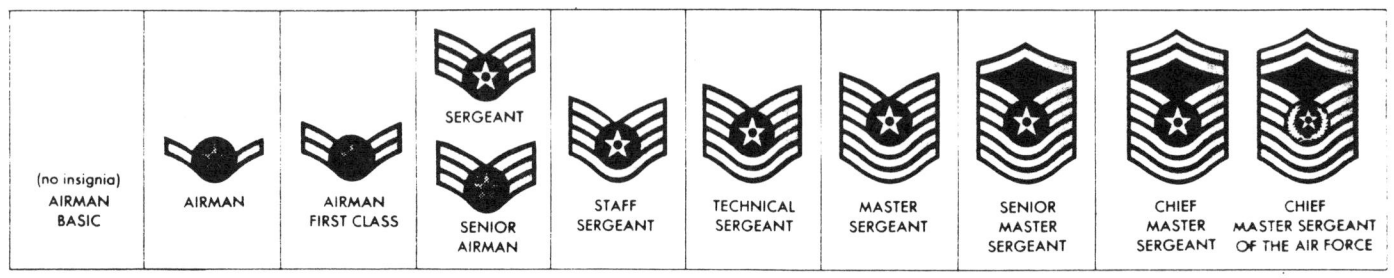

| (no insignia) AIRMAN BASIC | AIRMAN | AIRMAN FIRST CLASS | SERGEANT / SENIOR AIRMAN | STAFF SERGEANT | TECHNICAL SERGEANT | MASTER SERGEANT | SENIOR MASTER SERGEANT | CHIEF MASTER SERGEANT | CHIEF MASTER SERGEANT OF THE AIR FORCE |

Officers

ARMY

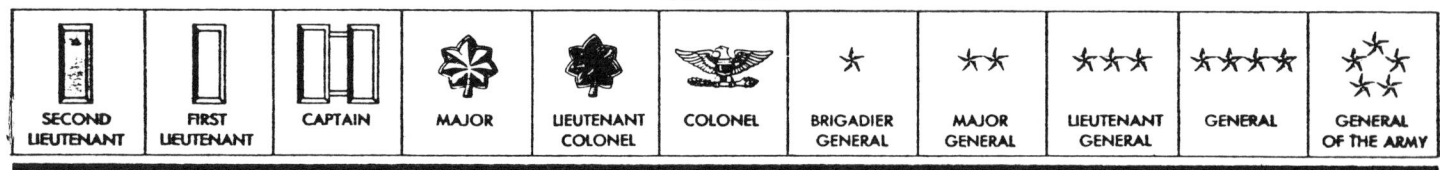

| SECOND LIEUTENANT | FIRST LIEUTENANT | CAPTAIN | MAJOR | LIEUTENANT COLONEL | COLONEL | BRIGADIER GENERAL | MAJOR GENERAL | LIEUTENANT GENERAL | GENERAL | GENERAL OF THE ARMY |

AIR FORCE

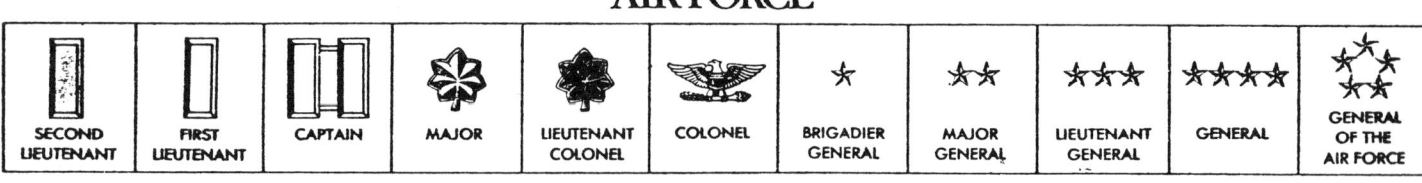

| SECOND LIEUTENANT | FIRST LIEUTENANT | CAPTAIN | MAJOR | LIEUTENANT COLONEL | COLONEL | BRIGADIER GENERAL | MAJOR GENERAL | LIEUTENANT GENERAL | GENERAL | GENERAL OF THE AIR FORCE |

Frederick Drew Gregory

1941 -

Pilot Astronaut

Born and reared in Washington D.C., Frederick Drew Gregory graduated from Anacostia High School in the city. After being nominated by Congressman Adam Clayton Powell, Jr., he attended and was the fourth Black to graduate from the United States Air Force Academy in Colorado Springs, Colorado. As a young Air Force officer, he flew helicopters on rescue operations in the Vietnam conflict. He later was trained in jet aircraft and was one of the first Blacks to graduate from the Naval Test Pilot School. In 1971, Gregory was assigned as a research engineering pilot at Wright Patterson Air Force Base in Ohio, and then a research engineering test pilot for four years at NASA Langley Research Center in Hampton, Virginia. In 1978 he was selected for Astronaut Training by NASA and moved to the Johnson Space Center in Houston, Texas. He has flown more than forty different types of experimental and operational aircraft, logging more than 5600 hours of flying time. On April 29, 1985, Gregory, at this time an Air Force Colonel, became the first Black ever to pilot a spacecraft and the third U.S. Black astronaut in space. His historic flight aboard "Challenger" 51-B was called Spacelab 3 and was a scientific mission. It landed one week after completing 110 earth orbits.

Name: Colonel Frederick Gregory

Skill: Matching facts and visual awareness

Procedure:
1. Match the facts on the following page about Colonel Gregory's life.
2. Identify the military planes.

Variation: Write NASA for Spacelab 3 (17M484) – information on Gregory's mission on the Shuttle and for the NASA photograph of Colonel Gregory: NASA, Code LE, Washington, D.C. 20546.

Find out more about Colonel Charles Bolden, the second Black space shuttle pilot.

Frederick Drew Gregory
1941 -
Pilot Astronaut

Born and reared in Washington D.C., Frederick Drew Gregory graduated from Anacostia High School in the city. After being nominated by Congressman Adam Clayton Powell, Jr., he attended and was the fourth Black to graduate from the United States Air Force Academy in Colorado Springs, Colorado. As a young Air Force officer, he flew helicopters on rescue operations in the Vietnam conflict. He later was trained in jet aircraft and was one of the first Blacks to graduate from the Naval Test Pilot School. In 1971, Gregory was assigned as a research engineering pilot at Wright Patterson Air Force Base in Ohio, and then a research engineering test pilot for four years at NASA Langley Research Center in Hampton, Virginia. In 1978 he was selected for Astronaut Training by NASA and moved to the Johnson Space Center in Houston, Texas. He has flown more than forty different types of experimental and operational aircraft, logging more than 5600 hours of flying time. On April 29, 1985, Gregory, at this time an Air Force Colonel, became the first Black ever to pilot a spacecraft and the third U.S. Black astronaut in space. His historic flight aboard "Challenger" 51-B was called Spacelab 3 and was a scientific mission. It landed one week after completing 110 earth orbits.

MATCH THE FOLLOWING FACTS ABOUT COLONEL GREGORY'S LIFE

Dr. Charles Drew	Vietnam
Adam Clayton Powell	Flight time
helicopter pilot	uncle
4500 hours	Air Force Academy sponsor
Washington D.C.	birth place
1978 to 1985	training for shuttle piloting

126

MATCH THE FOLLOWING FACTS ABOUT COLONEL GREGORY'S LIFE

Adam Clayton Powell	Vietnam
Helicopter pilot	Flight time
4500 hours	Air Force Academy sponsor
Washington D.C.	Birth place
1978 to 1985	Training for shuttle piloting
Research pilot	April 29, 1985
Selected as NASA astronaut	1978
Historic space flight	Wright Patterson AFB

NAME THE AIRPLANES ON THE FOLLOWING PAGE

Beginning Pilot Training
1 Cessna T-41

Basic Training
2 Cessna T-37

Advanced Training
3 Northrop T-38

Transport
4 Lockheed C-141

5 Lockheed C-5

Fighter
6 McDonnell Douglas F-4

7 General Dynamics F-111

8 McDonnell Douglas F-15

Bombers

9 Boeing B-52

10 North American Rockwell B-1

1

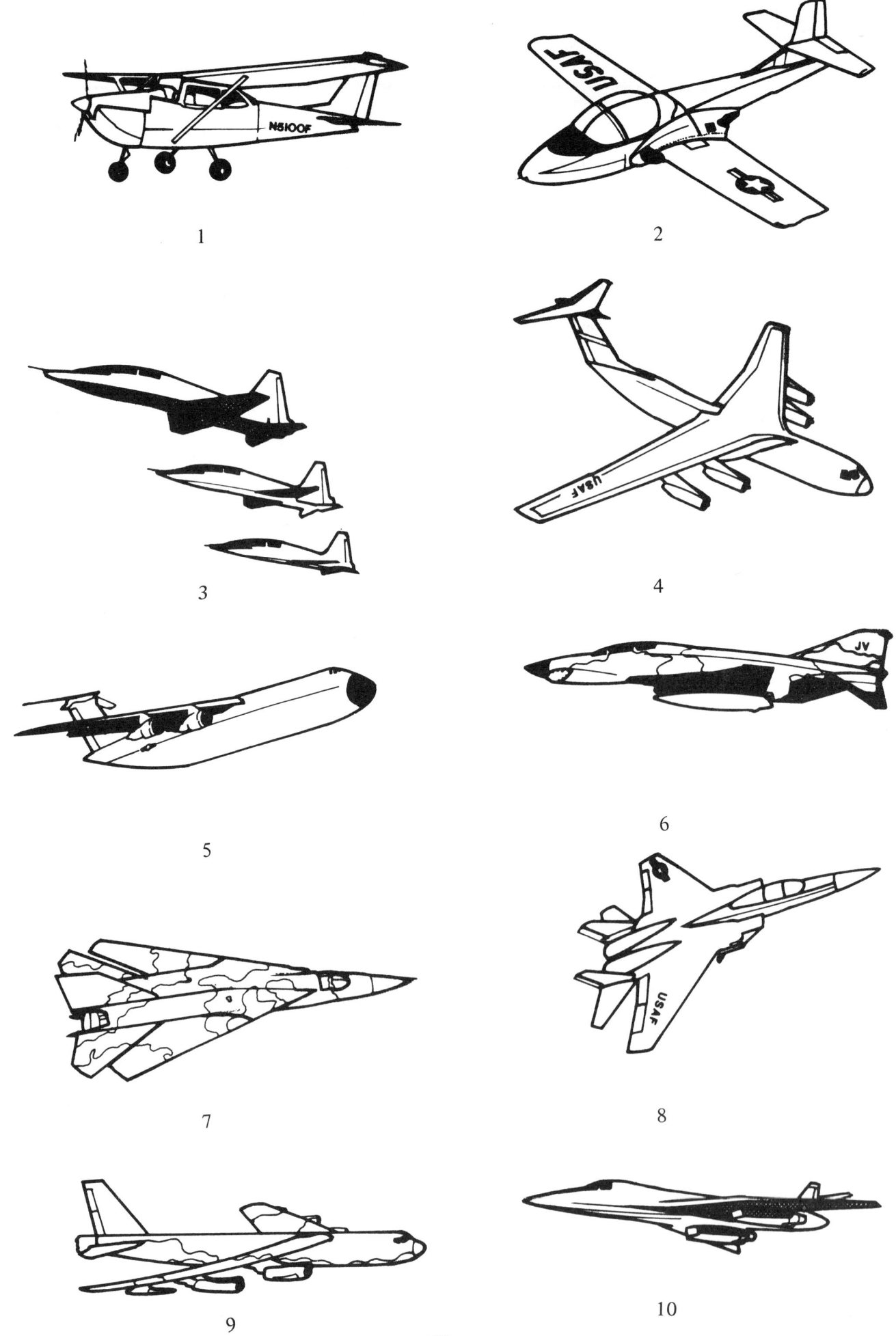

2

3

4

5

6

7

8

9

10

128

General Daniel James

1920-1978

U.S. Air Force General

General Daniel James was born in Pensacola, Florida. "Chappie" James finished high school in 1937 and graduated from the Tuskegee Institute in 1942. In 1945 James, a seasoned pilot, was commissioned as a second lieutenant in the Army Air Corps. He completed fighter pilot school in Michigan and served 6 years in fighter units in the U.S. During the Korean War James flew 101 combat missions in F-51 and F-80 fighter aircraft. He served as Deputy Commander for Operations for a Tactical Fighter Wing in Thailand and later as Deputy Assistant Secretary of Defense before his death.

Name: General Daniel James

Skill: Social studies concept development

Procedure: Invite a local member of the Tuskeegee Airmen to speak to your class.

Variation: Order a single copy (limited supply) of the learning activity pack on General "Chappie" James on school letterhead stationary from Civil Air Patrol, National Headquarters, Maxwell AFB, A1 36112.
Order Minority Contributions in the Military and Afro-Americans in World War II from Federal Aviation Administration, Washington, DC 20591 (limited supply)

August Martin

1919 - 1968

Pilot

August Martin was born in Los Angeles, California on August 31, 1919. He graduated from New York City's DeWitt Clinton High School in 1938 then returned to California to attend San Mateo Junior College and the University of California. While he was at San Mateo, he worked at the Oakland Flying Service to earn money for flying lessons. By the time he graduated from the University of California, he had achieved his Flight Instructor Rating. Employed as a civilian flight inspector in the Navy V-12 program at Cornell (New York), he joined the Army Air Corps in 1943, receiving his flight training at Tuskegee, Alabama. He became a B-25 pilot, but World War II ended before he could be sent overseas. Following the war, Martin continued his aviation career. He took a job with Willis Air Service in Teterboro, New Jersey. From 1946 to 1955 he flew part-time for Buffalo Skylines, El Al Airlines, and World Airlines. Martin holds the distinction of being the first Black captain of a scheduled U.S. airline—in 1955 he was hired by Seaboard World Airlines as a captain of a DC-3. Captain Martin felt strongly about helping emerging African nations and often used his vacation time to fly needed supplies to their struggling people. Typical of his dedication to helping others was the mercy mission that he was flying in Biafra on behalf of the Red Cross when he was tragically killed on July 1, 1968 while trying to land on a highway during a rainstorm. Martin was one of the pioneer Black pilots employed by scheduled U.S. airlines. Few people have the opportunity to be of service to others as much as August Martin who gave his life helping the starving Biafrans. Equally significant, few find that their efforts are memorialized in an institution that touches as many lives as the living memorial that honors him, the August Martin High School in Queens, New York.

Name: Captain August Martin

Skill: Career Awareness

Procedure:
1. Write Civil Air Patrol for the coloring book and personality packet on August Martin. CAP National Headquarters, Maxwell AFB, AL. 36112.
2. Write FAA for "A Model Curriculum": FAA, Office of Public Affairs, Washington, D.C.
3. Learn the Theory of Flight

Variation: Integrate aerospace concepts described in the August Martin High School curriculum into your school's curriculum.

132

THEORY OF FLIGHT

An important principle in understanding why an airfoil can produce *lift* is called *Bernoulli's law*. Daniel Bernoulli proved that where the speed of a moving gas is high, the pressure is low. Where the speed is low, the pressure is high.

A simple experiment will help you see how this principle works.

Cut a piece of paper two inches wide and seven inches long. Hold it against your chin with the narrow part under your bottom lip. Then blow hard over the top of the paper. The paper rises!

What actually happens is the "air in a hurry" on top of the paper has less pressure. The pressure under the paper is greater and lifts the paper up. If you take the same paper and just pull it through the air, it will rise again.

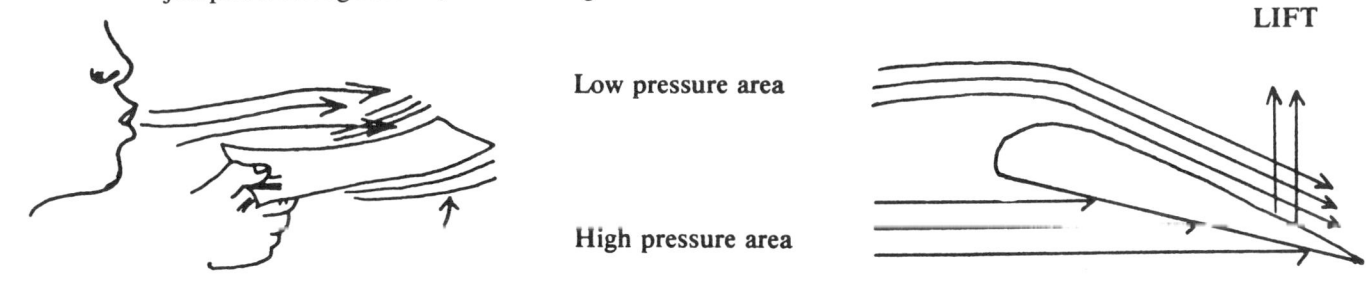

The wing of an airplane rises when it is pulled through the air by an engine just as the paper is pushed up by greater pressure below. The air moving over the curved wing on top must travel faster to reach the back of the wing. Some of the air goes under the wing also, but it reaches the trailing edge at the same time. Therefore, the air pressure on top of the wing is less than the pressure on the bottom of the wing, so the plane lifts up.

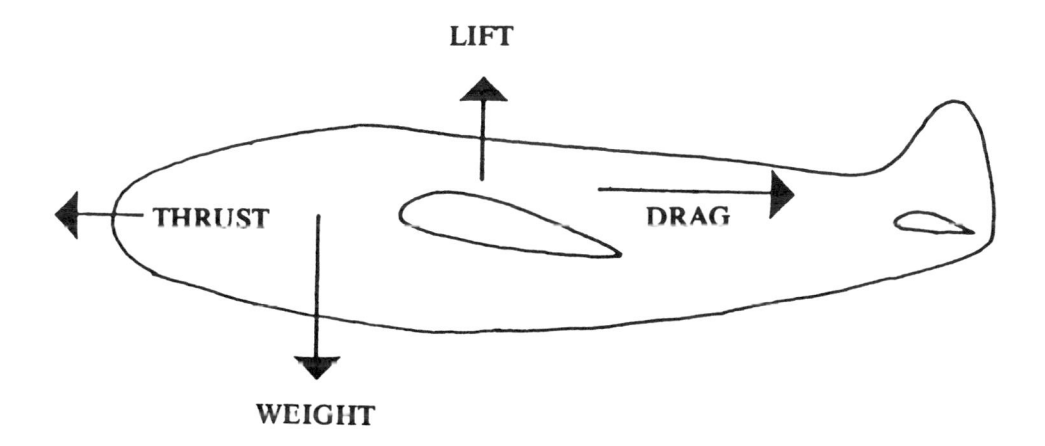

Level Flight and Constant Speed

Center of Gravity, CG, is the balance point of the aircraft. The CG must be maintained within design limits to ensure proper control of the aircraft.

Thrust is equal to the *drag* and acts below the CG to cause a slight lifting action to the nose which mostly overcomes the pitch down tendency caused by the lift acting behind the CG.

Lift is equal to weight and acts behind CG so that aircraft will nose down when power is reduced. Tail load could be up or down depending on the location of the CG and the effect of the combined forces.

Weight always acts toward earth. The direction of the other forces depends on the positions of the aircraft.

humanities

Hector Hill

1934 - 1963

Painter

Born in New York City, Hector Hill graduated from the High School of Music and Art. (This is the high school on which the T.V. show "Fame" was based.) He then volunteered for the U.S. Air Force and studied at San Bernardino Valley College in California. After serving in the Korean War, Hill studied art at the Louvre Museum in Paris and at the Brooklyn Museum of Art. His first formal show was at the Marino Gallery in New York in 1958. Thereafter, he had successful art shows at the Market Place Gallery, the Ligoa Duncan Gallery and others. The unique thing about Hector Hill's art is that he used concepts of color from the old and modern masters. He worked in figurative and abstract art. Hill traveled to Cuba in 1963 along with a group of students. It was a controversal time due to the Cuban Missile Crises in 1962. He died there in a swimming accident.

Name: Hector Hill

Skill: Art appreciation

Procedure:
1. Read books on Black art and Afro-American artists.
2. Locate the artist' work. Study their work, discuss what you think influenced their style, and compare them.

Variation:
1. Make the batik and basket weavings explained on the following page.
2. Check exhibits at local galleries to determine the displays available in your area.

Hector Hill
1934 - 1963
Painter

Born in New York City, Hector Hill graduated from the High School of Music and Art. (This is the high school on which the T.V. show "Fame" was based.) He then volunteered for the U.S. Air Force and studied at San Bernadino Valley College in California. After serving in the Korean War, Hill studied art at the Louvre Museum in Paris and at the Brooklyn Museum of Art. His first formal show was at the Marino Gallery in New York in 1958. Thereafter, he had successful art shows at the Market Place Gallery, the Ligoa Duncan Gallery and others. The unique thing about Hector Hill's art is that he used concepts of color from the old and modern masters. He worked in figurative and abstract art. Hill traveled to Cuba in 1963 along with a group of students. It was a controversial time due to the Cuban Missile Crises in 1962. He died there in a swimming accident.

AFRO-AMERICAN ARTIST

The definition of Black Art by Afro-American painters is as varied as their work. The definition used in this book is an artist that happens to be black and thus his/her work is influenced by the fact the individual is black. Afro-American art is art which has characteristics of African heritage by the American which is used in his style of art, by means for a search for identity.

Blacks' experiences in civilization have been through the expressive means of the Visual Arts. From the time of the first arrivals of Black people in North America, transplanted here from African soil, Afro-Americans have been preoccupied with the creation of objects carefully and finely formed so to possess aesthetic merit, but yet for practical purposes. Thus, there have always been Afro-American Artist, even though other aspects of the culture failed. Now it is extremely difficult to retrace the steps of the workers in wood and iron that became the population of Black painters and sculptors producing some of the strongest and most original art to be seen in contemporary America.

Many Afro-American artist today feel compelled to direct their work toward the specific interests and sensibilities of black people, toward an interpretation of the struggle for equal rights. When Afro-American artist began to receive national attention in the late 19th Century, they were considered pretentious by blacks, as well as by whites, since painting was thought to be the "ultimate expression of a civilized people."

Although Black Africans boasted a long tradition in the arts, most Afro-Americans, cut so abruptly from their culture roots, were unaware of it. In Africa, weaving, metalwork, and sculpture were the principal arts and African artistic skills were technical, rigid controlled, and disciplined. Characteristic African art expression is therefore, sober, conventionalized, and restrained. However, in isolated areas with heavy slave concentrations, elements of folk art traditions of basketry, woodcarving, and ceramics survived.

Many artists working in Paris in the early part of the 20th Century discovered African art and began to incorporate elements of it into their own paintings and sculptures. Some of these artist are, Pablo Picasso, Andre Dercan, Mauice de Vlaminck, and Henri Matisse. African art is shown in Picasso's "Head of Man" — it looks like an African head mask.

The relationship of the Afro-American artist to the American society is different from other artist, the Afro-American artist had a special relationship to American society. The Black artist faces all the hardships of an artist in addition to the acceptance as a Black into the art world. Black artists are concerned with the images and forms their work takes because they are striving for dignity and respect in a visual art world.

Afro-American Artist

The definitions of Black art by Afro-American painters are as varied as their work. The definition used in this book is art produced by an artist who happends to be Black and therefore whose work is influenced by that fact. Afro-American art has characteristics of African culture. Searching for an artistic identity separate from the white European tradition, Black Americans often use their African heritage in their work.

Blacks have always expressed their experience through the visual arts. From the time of their first arrival in North America, transplanted here from African soil, Afro-Americans have created objects so carefully and finely formed that they possess aesthetic as well as practical merit. There have always been Afro-American artists, even though other aspects of Black-American culture failed. It is extremely difficult to trace these early workers in wood and iron, the ancestors of modern Black painters and sculptors, who are currently producing some of the strongest and most original art seen in contemporary America.

Today many Afro-American artist feel compelled to direct their work toward the specific interests and sensibilities of Black people and often interpret the struggle for equal rights in their art. When Afro-American artists began to receive national attention in the late 19th century, they were considered pretentious by both blacks and whites since painting was thought to be the "ultimate expression of a civilized people."

Although Black Africans boasted a long artistic tradition, most Afro-Americans, cut so abruptly from their cultural roots, were unaware of it. In Africa weaving, metalwork and sculpture were the principal arts. Because African artistic skills were rigidly defined by religious and cultural symbols, characteristic African art was often sober, conventionalized and restrained. In isolated areas in the United States with heavy slave populations, elements of African folk art traditions of basketry, woodcarving, and ceramics survived.

Many white artists working in Paris in the early part of the 20th century discovered African art and began to incorporate elements of it into their own paintings and sculptures. Some of these artists are Pablo Picasso, Andre Derain, Maurice Vlaminck, and Henri Matisse. The influence of African influence is clear in Picasso's "Head of Man" – it looks like an African head mask.

The Afro-American artist has a special relationship to American society, different from that of other artists. The Black artist faces all the hardships of any artist as well as the struggle for acceptance as a Black in the American art world. Black artists, concerned with expressing their distinct African heritage in their art, are striving for dignity and respect in a American art world.

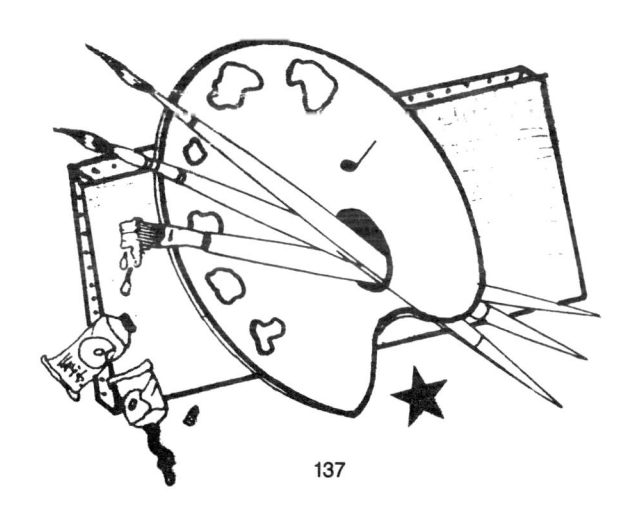

Search for books such as these on Black art and Afro-American artists in your library:

Bearden, Romare -- "The Negro Artist and Modern Art," Opportunity, XIII, Dec. 1934, Pg. 371-3

Chase, Judith W. -- Afro-American Art and Craft, Van Nostrand Reinhold, 1971, New York

Davis, Douglas -- "What is Black Art?", Newsweek, June, 1970, Pg. 89-91

Dover, Cedric -- American Negro Art, New York: New York Graphic, 1960

Dunbar, Ernest -- Black Expatriate, New York: Dutton, 1968

Fax, Elton -- Black Art through Experiences, New York: Dodd, Mead, 1971

Fine, Elsa Honig -- The Afro-American Artist, Holt, Rinehart, and Winston, Inc., New York, 1971

Lewis, Samella and Waddy, Ruth G. -- Black Artist on Art, Los Angeles: Contemporary Crafts Publishers, 1969

Paden, John N. and Soja, Edward W. -- The African Experience, Northwestern University Press, Vol. 1, 1970

Pearson, Ralph -- The Modern Renaissance in American Art, New York: Harper and Brothers, 1954

Rose, Alvin W. -- Afro-American Studies in Higher Education, University of Miami, Campus 1975

Whitten, Norman E. -- Afro-American Anthropology, New York: Free Press, 1970

See if you can locate these artists' works. Study their art to see what you think influenced their style:

"Pere Sauvage's Shop in the Rue de Rennes" - Pablo Picasso

"The Young Ladies of Avignon" - Pablo Picasso

"Henry Bibb" - Patrick Reason

"Portrait of Caroline Loguen" - William Simpson

"Two Bishops of A.M.E. Church" - Julian Hudson

"Flood Waters" - Robert Duncanson

"Little Miami River" - Edward Bannister

"John Y. Mason" - Eugene Warlourg

"Old Indian Arrow Maker & His Daughter" - Edmonia Lewis

"La Parisienne" - Annie Walker

"Disciples at the Tomb" - Henry O. Tanner

"The Artist Mother, Sarhra" - Henry O. Tanner

"The Gulfstream" - Winslow Homer

"High Yaller" - Reginald Marsh

"Evolution of Negro Dance" - Douglas Arron

"Head of a Girl" - Sargent Johnson

"Blackberry Woman" - Richard Barthe

"Trio" - Edzier Cotor

"Flowers with Red Chair" - Horace Pippin

"Shipping Out" - Jacob Lawrence

"Entrance into Jerusalem" - James Wells

"Mother & Child" - Sargent Johnson

"Landscape of City" - Lois M. Jones

"Extending Horizontal Form, Steel" - Richard Hunt

"Poultry Market" - Walter Williams

"Tenement Scene, Harlem" - Alma Thomas

"Ambulance Call" - Jacob Lawrence

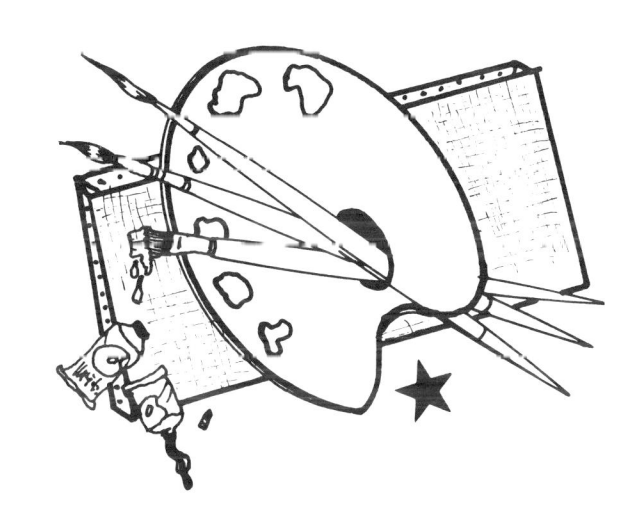

BATIK

Materials: wax, dye, fabric, brush, newspaper, iron.

Procedure:

1) Lightly pencil sketch a design on cotton fabric
2) Apply melted wax to design area. Areas not covered with wax will be dyed.
3) Let wax semi-dry then run the design under cold water
4) Put fabric into dye-bath. Dye the fabric darker than desired.
5) Take fabric out of dye and rinse in cold running water until excess dye is removed.
6) Allow fabric to dry.
7) Sandwich fabric between a newspaper with the newsprint next to the fabric. Press with medium iron to remove wax.

Repeat steps 1 - 6 if more than one color is desired, using a darker dye each time. The African batik below has a variety of color: yellow, orange, red, black.

BASKETWEAVING

Basketry is an important part of African culture. Baskets are not only functional but often are creations as well. You can purchase reeds at major hobby stores and make your own basket for the classroom. Below is a variation of the weaving process. This decorative African comb can be made by wrapping and weaving reeds then looping them together. Yarn can be wrapped around the reeds for a more decorative effect.

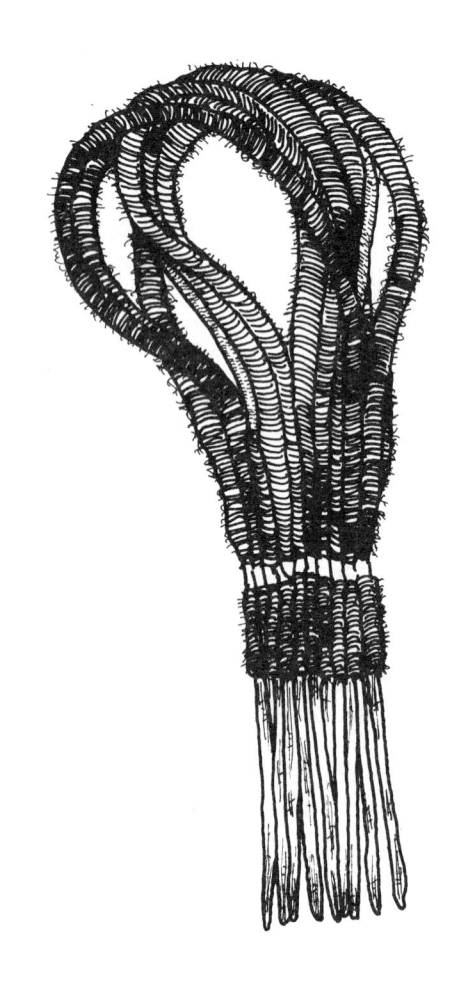

Reprinted with permission from Art Projects for Young Children, Humanics Limited.

Marian Anderson

1902 -

Singer

Marian Anderson was born in Philadelphia, Pennsylvania. Even as a young choir girl, she was able to sing nearly all the parts in the choir. She began giving recitals in Black churches, schools, and YMCA halls when she was not yet a teenager. At the age of twenty-two, she won first prize over 300 other contestants in a competition given by the New York Philharmonic Symphony. The next year she was a soloist with the New York Philharmonic Orchestra. In 1939, on Easter Sunday morning Miss Anderson made what was to become her most memorable concert. She sang on the steps of the Lincoln Memorial in Washington, D.C. after being barred from performing at Constitution Hall by the Daughters of the American Revolution. Mrs. Eleanor Roosevelt, the wife of President Franklin D. Roosevelt, arranged for the concert at the Lincoln Memorial. In 1955 Anderson made her debut in the Metropolitan Opera's presentation of the "The Masked Ball." In 1957 the U.S. State Department sent her on an around-the-world goodwill tour and then named her to the U.S. Delegation to the United Nations. Marian Anderson is considered the world's leading concert contralto of the twentieth century.

Name: Marian Anderson

Skill: Reading/Music appreciation

Procedure:
1. Find a Marian Anderson record and play it for your class.
2. Study the orchestral terms and expalin them to the class.
3. Study the history of opera. Then play Opera Trivia. Learn about various composers and listen to their works.

Variation: Have the class sing "My Country Tis of Thee" using tenors, altos, and sopranos in the class.

Marian Anderson
1902 -
Singer

Marian Anderson was born in Philadelphia, Pennsylvania. Even as a young choir girl, she was able to sing nearly all the parts in the choir. She began giving recitals in Black churches, schools, and YMCA halls when she was not yet a teenager. At the age of twenty-two, she won first prize over 300 other contestants in a competition given by the New York Philharmonic Symphony. The next year she was a soloist with the New York Philharmonic Orchestra. In 1939, on Easter Sunday morning Miss Anderson made what was to become her most memorable concert. She sang on the steps of the Lincoln Memorial in Washington, D.C. after being barred from performing at Constitution Hall by the Daughters of the American Revolution. Mrs. Eleanor Roosevelt, the wife of President Franklin D. Roosevelt, arranged for the concert at the Lincoln Memorial. In 1955 Anderson made her debut in the Metropolitan Opera's presentation of the "The Masked Ball." In 1957 the U.S. State Department sent her on an around-the-world goodwill tour and then named her to the U.S. Delegation to the United Nations. Marian Anderson is considered the world's leading concert contralto of the twentieth century.

IMPORTANT ORCHESTRAL TERMS

SONATA - originally meant piece to be played; piece of music, usually for the piano of three or four movements: (1) allegro, (2) slow movement, (3) minuet, and (4) rondo for finale.

ALLEGRO - very fast.
MINUET - a stately and deliberate dance.
RONDO - cheerful dance, round song with recurring theme.
FINALE - conclusion, usually elaborate.

CANTATA - originally meant piece to be played; now a work for chorus and solo, often with orchestral accompaniment.

OVERTURE - an elaborate prelude to an opera, oratorio, or play.

ORATORIO - a sacred work constructed like an opera, but performed now without action, costume, or scenery.

OPERA - drama set to music.

OPERETTA - a small light opera.

SYMPHONY - a sonata for orchestra.

ORCHESTRA - now means the place and its occupants, and the instruments.

BAND - composed only of woodwinds and brass.

CONCERTO - a composition for one, two or three or more solo instruments with orchestral accompaniment.

BALLET - an elaborate dance by professionals, often spectacular and narrative.

CONDUCTOR - the time-beater and director of the orchestra.

SCORE - an arrangement of the parts of a composition.

Before the era of the conductor, the first violinist was the leader of the orchestra. With the advent of the conductor it became customary to print and publish the score.

The score is compiled by the composer and is a record of all the instrumental parts.

Each instrument is in a different key which necessitates transposing. If we were to reproduce the notes we find in the score, the chord chosen would not have the sound we had heard performed by the orchestra.

Important Orchestral Terms

SONATA - originally meant piece to be played; piece of music, usually for the piano, of three or four movements; (1) allegro; (2) adajio slow movement; (3) minuet; and (4) rondo or finale.

ALLEGRO - very fast.

MINUET - a stately and deliberate dance.

RONDO - cheerful dance, round song with recurring theme.

FINALE - conclusion, usually elaborate.

CANTATA - originally meant piece to be played; now a work for chorus and solo, often with orchestral accompaniment.

OVERATURE - an elaborate prelude to an opera, oratorio, or play.

ORATORIO - a sacred work constructed like an opera, but now performed without action, costume or scenery.

OPERA - drama set to music

OPERETTA - a small light opera

SYMPHONY - a sonata for orchestra.

ORCHESTRA - now means the place and its occupants and the instruments.

BAND - composed only of woodwinds and brass.

CONCERTO - a composition for one, two or three or more solo instruments with orchestral accompaniment.

BALLET - an elaborate dance by professionals, often spectacular and narrative.

CONDUCTOR - the time-beater and director of the orchestra.

SCORE - an arrangement of the parts of a composition.

Before the era of the conductor, the first violinist was the leader of the orchestra. With the advent of the conductor it became customary to print and publish the score.

The score is compiled by the composer and is a record of all the instrumental parts.

Each instrument is in a different key which necessitates transposing. If we were to reproduce the notes we find in the score, the chord chosen would not have the sound we had heard performed by the orchestra.

TRANSPOSING - used by instruments not in the key of "C." The extent of this transposition is the interval between the key of the instrument and key of "C" major.

For example,

the French Horn is in the Key of "F"

Clarinets - "A" and "Bb"

Trumpet - "A" and "Bb"

Piccolo - "C"

Double Bass - "C"

VIRTUOSO - a performer of exceptional skill.

VIBRATION - variations in the strength of the tone; the pitch of the tone varies directly with the rapidity of the vibrations.

CONCERT MASTER - the first violinst.

BATON - stick used in beating time by the conductor.

TREMOLO - shivering sound produced by small rapid strokes.

PIZZICATO - plucking the violin with the fingers.

LIBRETTO - the text of an opera, oratorio, etc.

LIBRETTIST - a writer of such texts.

TUNING - correction of the tone-production of an instrument. The orchestra is tuned by the oboe on Concert A.

History of the Opera

Opera began as a court function toward the end of the sixteenth century. The first opera given in America was performed in English in a court room in Charleston, S.C. The Metropolitan Opera House in New York City began its first season in 1883 and continuously presented operas for eighty-three years. The first major company to employ Black singers in principle roles was the New York City Opera in 1945. In 1955, Marian Anderson was the first black artist employed by the Metropolitan Opera (Met). Even though the Black artist had been admitted into the world of grand opera, it was not until the 1960's that they had the opportunity to sing with the major companies on a regular basis. The new Metropolitan Opera House opened its doors to the public for the first time on September 16, 1966. The new House took approximately five years to build.

ACTIVITY: Opera Trivia

Divide class into two teams. This is played much like 'Trivial Pursuit.' Make cards with questions about the history of Opera above — write answers on the back of the cards. Sample questions follow:
1) Where was the first opera in America performed? A court room, Charleston, S.C.
2) What was the function of early opera? Court entertainment
3) What century did opera begin? 16th
4) The first opera performed in America was in what language? English
5) In what year was the Italian language used in opera in America? 1825
6) What was the first major company to employ Black singers in principal roles? New York City Opera
7) The first season of the Metropolitan Opera was in what year? 1833
8) The Metropolitan Opera House is located in what city? New York City
9) How many years was opera presented in the old Metropolitan Opera House? 83
10) Who was first Black artist employed by the Met? Marian Anderson
11) What year did the first Black artist make her debut at the Met? 1955
12) In what decade did Black artists have the opportunity to sing with the major companies on a regular basis? 1960
13) In what year did the new Metropolitan Opera House open its doors? 1966
14) How long did it take to build? 5 years

OPERA

Opera is a western theatrical art form consisting of a dramatic text (libretto or little book) and music that is usually singing with instrumental accompaniment. Opera is basically a play set to music. The unique characteristic of opera is that the leading people (principals) sing their lines rather than speak them. It is the culmination of fine acting, beautiful staging and art work, and choral music with ensembles, chorus numbers and solos. The accompaniment is provided by an orchestra, seated down in front of the stage. Many of the solos are called arias. These arias are used to display the vocal and technical skills of the leading singers. There are many operas from different countries. One can learn much about the customs of a people by seeing their operas.

ACTIVITY: Learn about these well known opera composers and some of their famous works. Marian Anderson made her debut at the Metrobolitan Opera in Verdi's "The Masked Ball" and Leontyne Price made hers in "II Travatore."

contributed by Beth Harris

Louis Armstrong

1900 - 1980

Trumpeter

Louis Armstrong was born in New Orleans, Louisiana on the 4th of July 1900. As a child Louis used to carry coins in his mouth, which earned him the nickname "Satchelmouth" which was shortened to "Satchmo." In 1914 Armstrong was arrested for firing a pistol and sent to the Colored Waifs Home. He learned to play the cornet in the boy's home. By the time he was released from the home he was playing well enough to earn money as a musician. Jazz great King Oliver became his mentor and taught Armstrong the skills of playing jazz that would eventually gain Armstrong world fame. When King Oliver left for Chicago in 1919, Armstrong replaced him in Kid Ory's New Orleans band. Two years later when Armstrong was 24, Fletcher Henderson hired him to play for his New York band. It was Henderson who suggested that Louis change from cornet to trumpet. Before Armstrong was 29 he had to his credit several recordings that brought him world fame. In 1929 he returned to New York to play in a revue called "Hot Chocolates" that featured his first popular song "Ain't Misbehavin'." This gave Armstrong the opportunity to lead bands and sing rather than limit himself to instrumentals. At the age of 32 he was a headliner in England at the London Palladium. Armstrong made two movies with Bing Crosby, "Pennies from Heaven" and "High Society." In "High Society" he teamed up with his former mentor Kid Ory to play several songs. Armstrong is credited with bringing jazz, the street music of New Orleans and the only contribution to music native to America, to world attention. During Louis "Satchmo" Armstrong's last years he made the transition from the status of musician to that of entertainer.

Name: Louis Armstrong

Skill: Music appreciation

Procedure:
1. Play a Louis Armstrong record for the class.
2. Talk about the difference between opera, popular, folk and jazz music.
3. Discuss jazz today: kool jazz production, jazz festivals, jazz entertainers.
4. Learn about the trumpet and participate in the activities listed on the following page.

Variation: Learn about the jazz entertainers such as Miles Davis, Wynton Marsalis and Scott Joplin.

Louis Armstrong
1900 - 1980
Trumpeter

Louis Armstrong was born in New Orleans, Louisiana on the 4th of July 1900. As a child Louis used to carry coins in his mouth, which earned him the nickname "Satchelmouth" which was shortened to "Satchmo." In 1914 Armstrong was arrested for firing a pistol and sent to the Colored Waifs Home. He learned to play the cornet in the boy's home. By the time he was released from the home he was playing well enough to earn money as a musician. Jazz great King Oliver became his mentor and taught Armstrong the skills of playing jazz that would eventually gain Armstrong world fame. When King Oliver left for Chicago in 1919, Armstrong replaced him in Kid Ory's New Orleans band. Two years later when Armstrong was 24, Fletcher Henderson hired him to play for his New York band. It was Henderson who suggested that Louis change from cornet to trumpet. Before Armstrong was 29 he had to his credit several recordings that brought him world fame. In 1929 he returned to New York to play in a revue called "Hot Chocolates" that featured his first popular song "Ain't Misbehavin'." This gave Armstrong the opportunity to lead bands and sing rather than limit himself to instrumentals. At the age of 32 he was a headliner in England and at the London Palladium. Armstrong made two movies with Bing Crosby, "Pennies from Heaven" and "High Society." In "High Society" he teamed up with his former mentor Kid Ory to play several songs. Armstrong is credited with bringing jazz, the street music of New Orleans and the only contribution to music native to America, to world attention. During Louis' "Satchmo" Armstrong's last years he made the transition from the status of musician to that of entertainer.

LOUIS ARMSTRONG

Louis Armstrong was unique as a musician not only for his 'jazz' but for his outstanding instrumental technique and creative ability. He could play in all ranges of the trumpet, both high and low registers. Known not just for beautiful tone quality, he was also a very fast trumpet player. The flexibility of his lips enabled him to make his trumpet sing. His horn was not just something exterior to him; it was a part of him. Sounding more like his own voice, it more or less gave the impression that he was singing through it not playing it.

TRUMPET

The oldest member of the brass family is probably the trumpet. Except for the addition of valves, the trumpet that is used in our orchestras and bands today is not much different from the trumpets used by the Roman armies and the trumpets mentioned in the Bible. Made of brass or silver, the modern trumpet is a tube about eight feet long with a small bell. This long tube is bent around several times to form an elongated coil. This makes the instrument easier to carry. Like other members of the brass family, the trumpet has three valves. Good jaw muscles and good lungs are needed to use this instrument.

ACTIVITY: Purchase for each student, if possible, a Kazoo. Have class take a favorite familiar song. Encourage them to visualize that they are playing a trumpet. With the concept of Louis Armstrong singing through the trumpet, have them sing through the Kazoo with expression and feeling.

LISTENING ACTIVITY: "12th Street Rag" (check out recording) Have class listen to his style. Listen for as many musical ideas and discuss the different ways he develops the theme (main idea) of the piece.
"Lawd, You Made the Night Too Long" (check out recording). This is one of his most dramatic pieces - it is a masterpiece. With their emotion, the three 'hallelujahs' absolutely stun any listener. With his deep, intense solo in the low register of the trumpet following and then the vocal, this was truly a climax in jazz music the way Louis sings in this piece. He returns to the theme on his trumpet. Have class listen to his style. Call attention to his flexibility to go back and forth from trumpet to vocal.

DID YOU KNOW???
Until the beginning of the 17th century, the trumpet was only a plain tube. Then they began to pierce holes along the tube. They were able by covering and uncovering these openings with their fingers they were able to produce a different tone. It was at the beginning of the 19th century we find that keys were used to cover these holes.

SCOTT JOPLIN

Scott Joplin was born on November 24, 1868 in Texarkana, Texas and was raised in a musical atmosphere. When he was eight years old, he became acquainted with his neighbor's piano. At the age of eleven he was improvising very well. He received few lessons in piano, harmony and sight-singing. He published his first ragtime piece "Original Rags" in 1899. That same year he performed his most famous work, "The Maple Leaf Rag", a composition that sold hundreds of thousands of copies. Scott Joplin is generally acknowledged as a genius of ragtime. He even made such an impression that a large segment of twentieth century American music derived its spirit and mood of these from Joplin's compositions.

ACTIVITY: Check out some of Scott Joplin's recordings of ragtime. Probably the most popular would be "The Entertainer" or "Maple Leaf Rag."

contributed by Beth Harris

Louis Armstrong

Louis Armstrong was unique as a musician not only for his "jazz" but for his outstanding instrumental technique and creative ability. He could play in all ranges of the trumpet, both high and low registers. He was known for both his beautiful tone quality and his agility as a trumpet player. The flexibility of his lips enabled him to make his trumpet sing. His horn was not just something exterior to him; it was a part of him. Sounding more like his own voice, his playing gave the impression that he was singing through the trumpet.

Trumpet

The oldest member of the brass family is probably the trumpet. Except for the addition of valves, the trumpet that is used in our orchestras and bands today is not much different from the trumpets used by the Roman armies and the trumpets mentioned in the Bible. Made of brass or silver, the modern trumpet is a tube about eight feet long with a small bell. This long tube is bent around several times to form an elongated coil. This makes the instrument easier to carry. Like other members of the brass family, the trumpet has three valves. Good jaw muscles and good lungs are needed to use this instrument.

ACTIVITY: Purchase a kazoo for each student, if possible. Have the class play a favorite song familiar to them. Encourage them to visualize that they are playing a trumpet. After explaining to your class the concept of Louis Armstrong singing through the trumpet, have them sing through the kazoo with expression and feeling.

LISTENING ACTIVITY: Check out the recording "12th Street Rag." Have your class listen to Armstrong's style. Listen for as many musical ideas as possible and discuss the different ways he develops the theme (main idea) of the piece.
Check out the recording "Lawd, You Made the Night Too Long." This is one of his most dramatic pieces—it is a masterpiece. The three 'hallelujahs' absolutely stun any listener by their emotional power. Following them with his deep, intense solo in the low register of the trumpet and then the vocal, this was truly a climax in jazz music. He returns to the theme on his trumpet. Have class listen to his style and to the way Louis "sings" in this piece. Call attention to his flexibility in going back and forth from trumpet to vocal.

Did you know?

Until the beginning of the 17th century, the trumpet was only a plain tube. Then holes were pierced along the tube. By covering and uncovering these openings with the fingers a full scale was produced. By the beginning of the 19th century, keys were used to cover these holes.

Scott Joplin

Scott Joplin was born on November 24, 1868 in Texarkana, Texas. Reared in a musical atmosphere, he became interested in his neighbors' piano at the age of eight years. At eleven, he was improvising his own music. He received free piano lessons, instructions in harmony and sight singing. Joplin is generally acknowledged as a genius of ragtime. He published his first ragtime piece "Original Rags" in 1899; also in that year he published his most famous piece "Maple Leaf Rag," which sold thousands of copies. His music made such an impression that a large segment of twentieth century American music derived its spirit and musical shape from his compositions.

ACTIVITY: Check out some of Scott Joplin's recordings of ragtime. The most popular are "The Entertainer" and the "Maple Leaf Rag."

contributed by Beth Harris

Diahann Carroll

1935 -

Singer, Actress

Diahann Carroll was born in the Bronx, New York, the daughter of a subway conductor and a nurse. She became a member of the Abyssinian Baptist church choir. (This was the church led by Adam Clayton Powell.) At the age of ten she won a Metropolitan Opera scholarship, but she continued her schooling at the High School of Music and Art in New York. (This is the high school on which the television show "Fame" is based.) After appearing on a television talent show, she landed a job at New York's famous Latin Quarter. She then played on Broadway in "House of Flowers" and several other musicals all of which received good reviews. Later Carroll won the lead role in a television weekly show called "Julia," the first weekly network show featuring a Black star. In the show she played a war widow, a nurse who was raising her son alone. The show ran for several seasons. After this television first she continued her night club career until she landed a major role on "Dynasty" which she has played for several seasons.

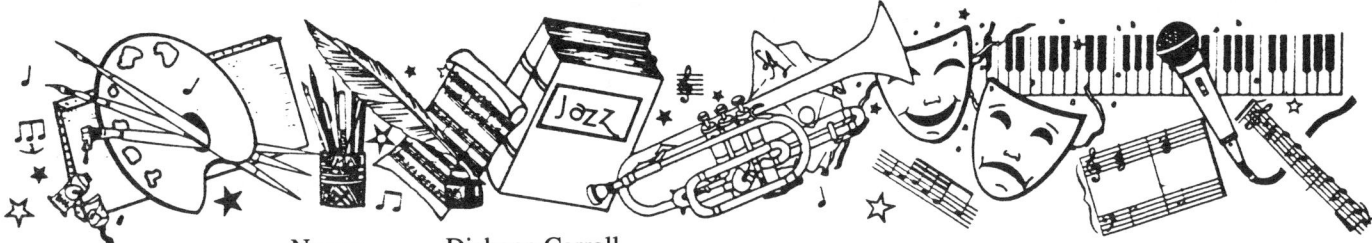

Name: Diahann Carroll

Skill: Reading

Procedure: 1. After reading the biography, complete the questions on the following page.

Variation: 1. Collect several playbills from local theatres (little theatres, etc.) and have the class read them to find specific information about the productions and players. Make your own playbills for a play.
2. Study singing. Practice according to the directions specified on the following page.
3. Watch the television shows *Fame* and *Dynasty*. Discuss the success of each show.
4. Research the lives of other stars: Cicely Tyson, Whoopi Goldberg, Oprah Winfrey (The Color Purple).

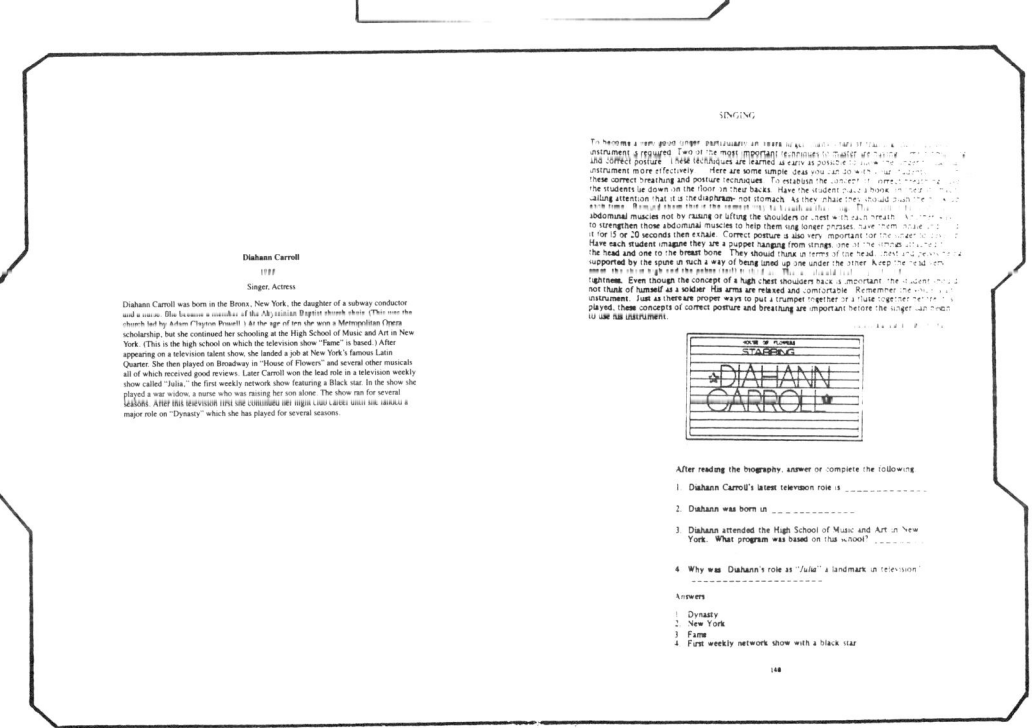

Singing

To become a very good singer, particularly an opera singer; many years of vocal training are required. Two of the most important techniques involved are correct breathing and posture. These techniques are learned as early as possible to allow the singer to use his instrument more effectively. Here are some simple ideas to use with students to teach breathing and posture techniques.

To establish the concept of correct breathing, have the students lie down on the floor on their backs. Have the students place a book on their abdomen. As they inhale, they should push the book up each time. Remind them that this is the correct way to breathe as they sing. The work of breathing is done by the abdominal muscles, not by raising or lifting the shoulders or chest with each breath. One way of strengthening the abdominal muscles, allowing one to sing longer phrases, is to inhale and hold for 15 to 20 seconds and then exhale slowly.

Correct posture is also very important for the singer to develop. Have each student imagine he is a puppet hanging from strings, one of the strings is attached to the head and one to the breast bone. He should think in terms of head, chest and pelvis being supported by the spine in such a way to be lined up one under the other. the head should be kept very erect, the chest high and the pelvis tucked in. There should be no tension or tightness in the jaw; it should be relaxed. Although the concept of chest up and shoulders back is important, the student should not think of himself as a rigid soldier, but keep his arms relaxed and comfortable. Remember to stress to the students that the voice is an instrument. Just as there are proper ways to assemble a trumpet or flute before it is played, these concepts of correct posture and breathing are important before the singer can begin to use his instrument.

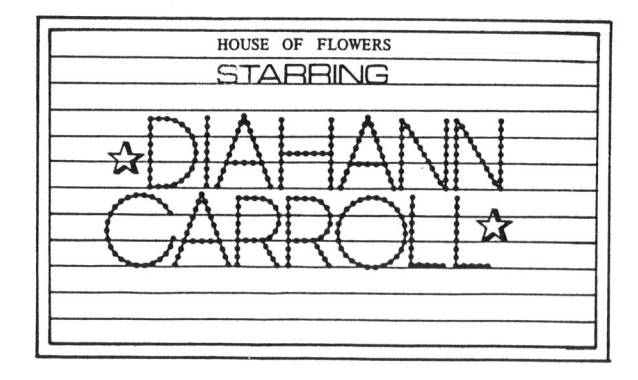

```
HOUSE OF FLOWERS
STARRING
☆ DIAHANN
   CARROLL ☆
```

WORDS WHICH DESCRIBE THE RANGES OF VOICE

Alto - The range of the second lowest female voice.
Baritone - The range of the second lowest male voice.
Bass - The range of the lowest male voice.
Contralto - The range of the lowest female voice.
Soprano - The range of the highest female voice.
Tenor - The range of the highest male voice.

contributed by Beth Harris

After reading the biography, complete the following.

1. Diahann Carroll's latest television role is in_____

2. Diahann was born in_____   _____

3. Diahann attended the High School of Music and Art in New York. What TV program was based on this school?_____

4. Why was Diahann's role as "Julia" a landmark in television?_____

Answers

1. Dynasty
2. New York
3. Fame
4. First weekly network show with a Black star

Nat "King" Cole

1919   1965

Singer

Nat Cole was born in Montgomery, Alabama. His family name was actually Coles. They moved to Chicago where Nat learned to play the piano and organ in the church where his father was the minister. Young Nat formed a band when he was still in high school. In 1936, Coles joined a touring company of 'Shuffle Along' as a pianist but the tour folded in Los Angeles. The following year Nat dropped the "s" on his name and formed the "Nat King Cole Trio." Cole was an instrumentalist; he did not sing until a customer in a club where the trio was playing insisted that he sing "Sweet Lorraine." This changed his career and he became known world-wide as a singer. After his first record in 1943, he had a string of hits that are still selling: "Paper Moon," "Route 66," "Chestnuts Roasting on an Open Fire," "Nature Boy," "Mona Lisa," "Too Young," "Smile" and "Pretend." When he died in 1965, he had sold more records than any other person in the world.

Name: Nat King Cole

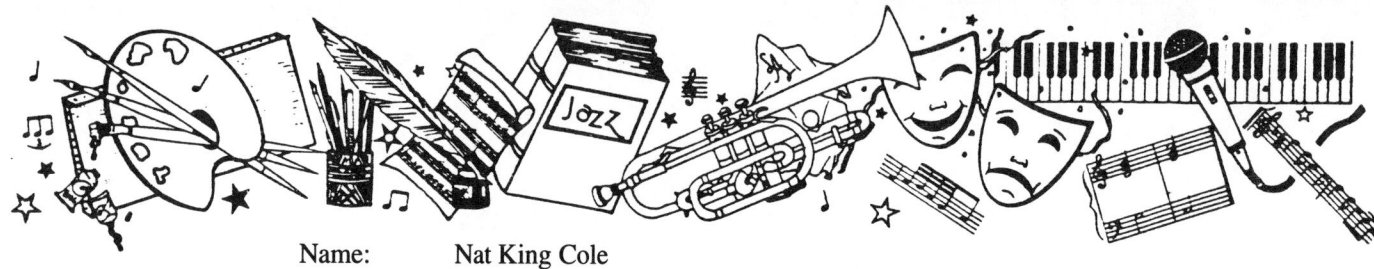

Skill: Reading/Music appreciation

Procedure:
1. Get the record, "Route 66" and play it for the class. You can use this record with a map to show them all the cities on the route and teach them how to read a road map.
2. Discuss Stevie Wonder's many contributions to pop/rhythm & blues.

Describe Motown's contributions to popular music.

Variation:
1. Play Cole's other records in class. Discuss why you feel his work was so popular.
2. Play records by Nat's daughter, Natalie Cole.

Nat "King" Cole
1919 - 1965
Singer

Nat Cole was born in Montgomery, Alabama. His family name was actually Coles. They moved to Chicago where Nat learned to play the piano and organ in the church where his father was the minister. Young Nat formed a band when he was still in high school. In 1936, Coles joined a touring company of 'Shuffle Along' as a pianist but the tour folded in Los Angeles. The following year Nat dropped the "s" on his name and formed the "Nat King Cole Trio." Cole was an instrumentalist; he did not sing until a customer in a club where the trio was playing insisted that he sing "Sweet Lorraine." This changed his career and he became known world-wide as a singer. After his first record in 1943, he had a string of hits that are still selling: "Paper Moon," "Route 66," "Chestnuts Roasting on an Open Fire," "Nature Boy," "Mona Lisa," "Too Young," "Smile" and "Pretend." When he died in 1965, he had sold more records than any other person in the world.

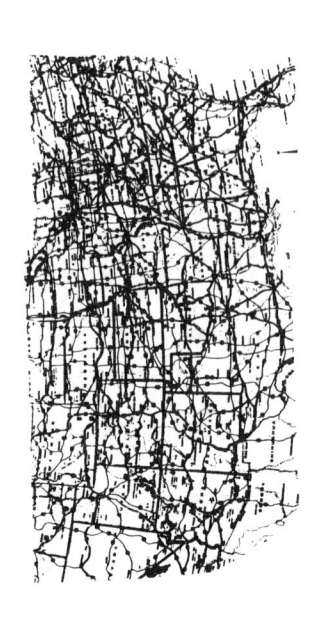

Bill Cosby

1938 -

Comedian, Actor

Bill Cosby was born in Philadelphia, Pennsylvania. He attended Temple University where he played football and ran track. Working evenings as a bartender, he began to entertain his customers with his comedy routines. He then played small clubs in Philadelphia, New York, and Greenwich Village in New York. Two years later he was playing the top clubs around the country and appearing on the Johnny Carson television show. Teamed with Robert Culp in "I Spy," Cosby became the first Black actor ever to star in a network television show. He was also the first to win an Emmy. Bill Cosby returned to school to receive his Ph.D. degree. In recent years he has put together a successful comedy show that is still running on television. The "Cosby Show," the series he developed, was the highest-rated weekly television show from 1984 to 1986.

Name: Bill Cosby

Skill: Dramatics

Procedure: 1. Discuss the cartoon, "Fat Albert" and allow students to describe their feelings about characters.
2. Have the class watch "The Cosby Show." Re-enact some of its scenes in class and discuss them.
3. Locate copies of Cosby's comedy albums. They can be located in libraries and music stores. Have the students compose an essay on what makes Bill Cosby entertaining to all age groups.

Variation: 1. Watch Cosby on television. Why is this show such a success?
2. Read the book, Fatherhood, by Bill Cosby.

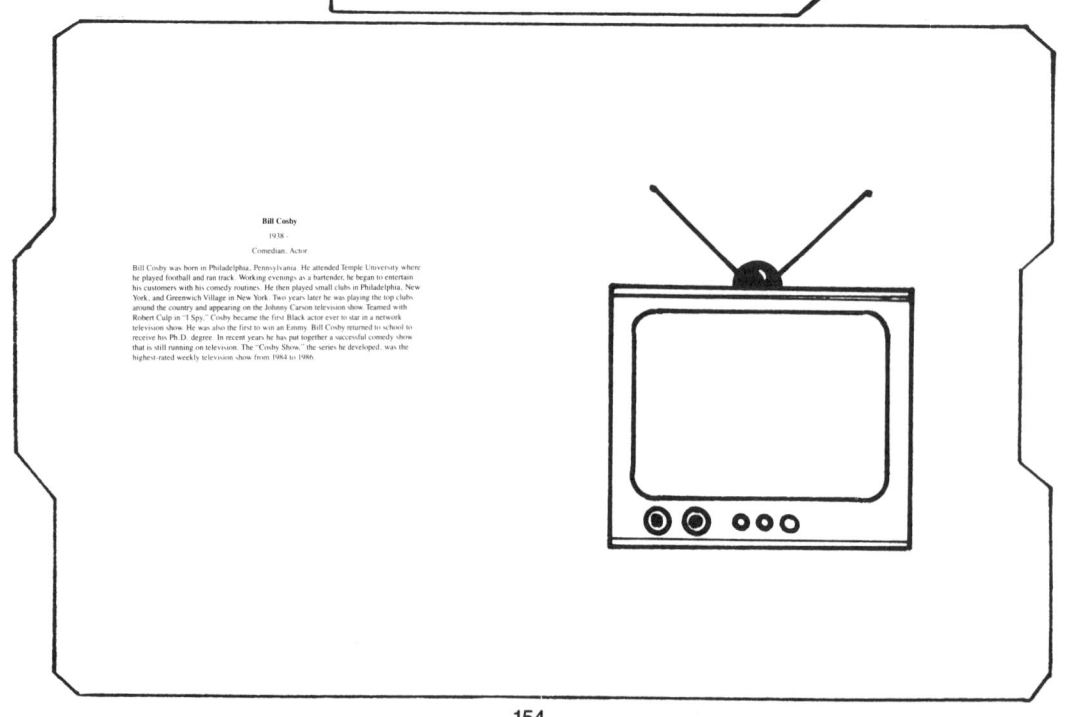

Bill Cosby
1938 -
Comedian, Actor

Bill Cosby was born in Philadelphia, Pennsylvania. He attended Temple University where he played football and ran track. Working evenings as a bartender, he began to entertain his customers with his comedy routines. He then played small clubs in Philadelphia, New York, and Greenwich Village in New York. Two years later he was playing the top clubs around the country and appearing on the Johnny Carson television show. Teamed with Robert Culp in "I Spy," Cosby became the first Black actor ever to star in a network television show. He was also the first to win an Emmy. Bill Cosby returned to school to receive his Ph.D. degree. In recent years he has put together a successful comedy show that is still running on television. The "Cosby Show," the series he developed, was the highest-rated weekly television show from 1984 to 1986.

Sammy Davis, Jr.

1925 -

Singer, Dancer, Comedian, Actor

Sammy Davis, Jr. was born in New York to a performing family. Davis was on the New York vaudeville stage at the age four, joining his father and uncle in a group called the "Will Mastin Trio." At six Davis was cast in a movie with Ethel Waters called "Rufus Jones for President." He continued performing in vaudeville with the "Will Mastin Trio" until 1943 when he entered the Army. During his two years of military service he wrote, directed and produced camp shows. After the army, Davis and the trio teamed up again and hit the big time on the club circuit in Hollywood. Davis also developed a career as a solo singer. He recorded a string of hits like "Hey There," "Mr. Wonderful," "Too Close for Comfort" and others. A nearly fatal auto accident caused him to lose an eye in 1954 but did not stop his carer. Two years later he was a hit as the star of a Broadway play called "Mr. Wonderful." This was followed by a play written especially for him called "Golden Boy." He has appeared in many movies including "Porgy and Bess," "Oceans II" and "Robin and the Seven Hoods." His autobiography "Yes, I Can" was a best-seller for many weeks. He has also starred in several of his own television shows. As a singer, dancer, actor, mimic, comedian and musician, Davis is called by many "The World's Greatest Entertainer."

Name: Sammy Davis, Jr.

Skill: Reading/Spelling

Procedure:
1. Have the class learn about tap dancing.
2. Learn the words to "The Candy Man." Have students discuss why they think this song was so popular.

Variation:
1. Read Sammy's autobiography, "Yes, I Can."
2. Have advanced students find out which performers listed in this text once played at the Cotton Club in New York.

Sammy Davis, Jr.
1925 -
Singer, Dancer, Comedian, Actor

Sammy Davis, Jr. was born in New York to a performing family. Davis was on the New York vaudeville stage at the age four, joining his father and uncle in a group called the "Will Mastin Trio." At six Davis was cast in a movie with Ethel Waters called "Rufus Jones for President." He continued performing in vaudeville with the "Will Mastin Trio" until 1943 when he entered the Army. During his two years of military service he wrote, directed and produced camp shows. After the army, Davis and the trio teamed up again and hit the big time on the club circuit in Hollywood. Davis also developed a career as a solo singer. He recorded a string of hits like "Hey There," "Mr. Wonderful," "Too Close for Comfort" and others. A nearly fatal auto accident caused him to lose an eye in 1954 but did not stop his career. Two years later he was a hit as the star of a Broadway play called "Mr. Wonderful." This was followed by a play written especially for him called "Golden Boy." He has appeared in many movies including "Porgy and Bess," "Oceans II" and "Robin and the Seven Hoods." His autobiography "Yes, I Can" was a best-seller for many weeks. He has also starred in several of his own television shows. As a singer, dancer, actor, mimic, comedian and musician, Davis is called by many "The World's Greatest Entertainer."

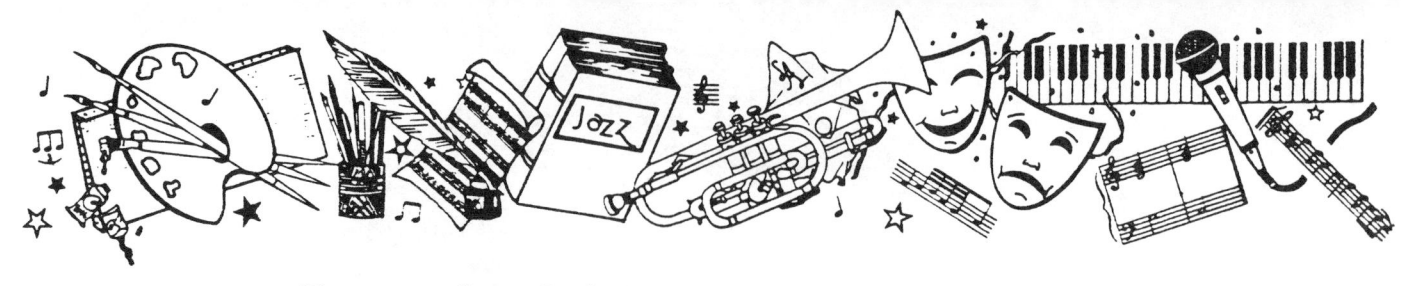

TAP DANCING

Tap dancing descended from folk steps of various countries. The sound made by the feet is of great importance in the character and style of tap dance, therefore, it is most closely related to the Irish jig. Rhythm is of primary importance in tap dancing. Keep a constant beat or pulse somewhere in the body. Tap dancing is itself up a sequence of steps without breaking the rhythm. Since most of the foot action is one of raising and lowering the foot while you swing the lower leg forward, backward and side and it is important to keep the ankle flexible. The leg as a thou is small. The tap rhythm is in the ankle and feet primarily.

Activity: "Tapping Toppers"

Materials Needed: recording of "Alexander's Ragtime Band"
2 metal tops (jelly jar lid, instant coffee lid) per student one for each shoe with avive tape

Procedure: Tape a lid to the bottom (ball of foot) to each student's shoe. Play recording. Have students tap in rhythm to the beat of the music with the tops alternating LF, RF, LF, RF and so on. Then they can tap twice on each foot in rhythm. LF tap out back together, RF out back, LF out back.

Purpose of activity: This activity will allow the students the experience of tap dancing, feeling a sense of rhythm and the pulse of the beat as they tap to the music. Remind the student to keep in mind the flexibility of the ankle as they tap. They will become more aware of their feet through this exercise. (The boys in the class may need reminding that many of the tap dancing entertainers are men!)

contributed by Beth Harris

156

TAP DANCING

Tap dancing descended from the folk steps of various countries. The sound made by the tapping feet is of great importance in the character and style of the tap dance, which is most closely related to the Irish jig. Rhythm is of primary importance in tap dancing. Keep a constant beat or pulse somewhere in the body. Tap dancing consists of making a sequence of steps without breaking the rhythm. Since most of the foot action is one of raising and lowering the foot while you swing the lower leg forward, backward and sideward, it is important to keep the ankle flexible. The leg action is small. The tap rhythm is primarily in the ankle and feet.

ACTIVITY: "Tapping Topper"

Materials needed: Recording of "Alexanders' Ragtime Band"
Two metal tops (jelly jar lid, instant coffee lid) per student (one for each shoe), adhesive tape

Procedure: Tape a lid to the bottom (ball of foot) of each student's shoe. Play the recording.
Have students tap in rhythm to the beat of the music with the tops alternating LF,RF,LF,RF and so on. Then they can tap twice on each foot in rhythm.
Lf tap out, back together, RF out back, LF out back.

Purpose of activity: This activity will give students the experience of tap dancing, feeling a sense of rhythm and the pulse of the beat as they tap to the music. Remind students to keep their ankles flexible as they tap They will become more aware of their feet through this exercise. (The boys in the class may need reminding that many of great tap dancing entertainers are men!)

Duke Ellington

1899-1974

Pianist, Band Leader, Composer

Edward Ellington was born in Washington, D.C., to a middle-class family. Edward Ellington earned the name of "Duke" because of his dapper young manner. His ability as a painter earned him a scholarship to the Pratt Institute of Fine Arts in New York, but Ellington turned down the offer to play music locally. To earn money he painted commercial signs on the side. By 1918, Ellington was earning enough as a musician to work full time with his dance band. In 1923, Fats Waller convinced Ellington to move to New York where he landed a job at the Kentucky Club. His first recordings were made under the name of "Ellington's Kentucky Club Orchestra." In 1924 he wrote his first revue, "Chocolate Kiddies," which played for two years in Germany but never made it in this country. Duke Ellington was the headliner at the famed Cotton Club in New York from 1927 to 1932. In the 1930's Ellington toured Europe, bringing the sounds of American jazz to a larger audience. By 1943, the music world had recognized that his compositions fused jazz elements with formal concert music. Ellington drew inventive sounds from his orchestra, his main instrument. He had an extraordinary gift of inspiration as he wove the individual qualities of each vocalist and instrumentalist in his orchestra together but, unlike many other band leaders, he did not insist on a uniform sound–he encouraged individuality! Because of his native artistic ability, he perceived each musician in his band as a specific color on his paint pallette. He always enjoyed mixing these sounds in beautiful combinations. Ellington copyrighted 952 compositions, including 3 concerts, 21 suites, 3 shows, 3 movie scores and 1 ballet. On his seventieth birthday, April 29, 1969, at a gala celebration at the White House, President Nixon presented Ellington with the Presidential Medal of Freedom, the nation's highest civilian honor.

Name: Duke Ellington

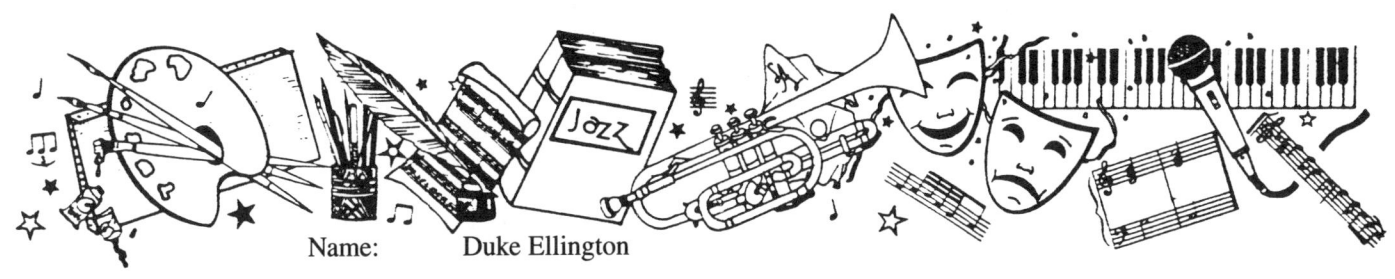

Skill: Music appreciation

Procedure:
1. Play some reggae (e.g., Bob Marley) and listen for the message of the lyrics. Compare its "beat," style, message with some of Ellington's work.
2. Listen to "Fats" Domino's "Blueberry Hill" for his piano style and skill. Can you compare Ellington's with his? What does it have in common with today's popular music?
3. Study the piano and answer the questions on the following page.
4. Learn more about being a conductor and study the basic beat patterns on the next page.
5. Study various composers and how they draft a song. The draft of the song 'I Have A Dream' by Beth Harris is included as an example of the composer's originals work. Learn the words and relate it to Martin L. King, Jr.'s speech.

Duke Ellington
1899-1974
Pianist, Band Leader, Composer

Edward Ellington was born in Washington, D.C., to a middle-class family. Edward Ellington earned the name of "Duke" because of his dapper young manner. His ability as a pianist earned him a scholarship to the Pratt Institute of Fine Arts in New York, but Ellington turned down the offer to play music locally. To earn money he painted commercial signs on the side. By 1918, Ellington was earning enough as a musician to work full time with his dance band. In 1923, Fats Waller convinced Ellington to move to New York where he landed a job at the Kentucky Club. His first recordings were made under the name of "Ellington's Kentucky Club Orchestra." In 1924 he wrote his first revue, "Chocolate Kiddies," which played for two years in Germany but never made it in this country. Duke Ellington was the headliner at the famed Cotton Club in New York from 1927 to 1932. In the 1930's Ellington toured Europe, bringing the sounds of American jazz to a larger audience. By 1943, the music world had recognized that his compositions fused jazz elements with formal concert music. Ellington drew inventive sounds from his orchestra, his main instrument. He had an extraordinary gift of inspiration as he wove the individual qualities of each vocalist and instrumentalist in his orchestra together but, unlike many other band leaders, he did not insist on a uniform sound–he encouraged individuality. Because of his native artistic ability, he perceived each musician in his band as a specific color on his paint pallette. He always enjoyed mixing these sounds in beautiful combinations. Ellington copyrighted 952 compositions, including 3 concerts, 21 suites, 3 shows, 3 movie scores and 1 ballet. On his seventieth birthday, April 29, 1969, at a gala celebration at the White House, President Nixon presented Ellington with the Presidential Medal of Freedom, the nation's highest civilian honor.

There are seven main parts to the piano – strings, keyboard, ...
... case.
There are more than 220 strings in the piano made of steel. ...
and the short strings make high sounds. There are ... in black keys and ...
octaves interval, of 9 notes. There are ... in black keys and ...
the piano are found three pedals which are used by the ... The name ...
cast iron consisting of a sheet of wood below the strings is the ... and ...
... and is strong enough to support the weight of the piano. Steinway is a well-known maker ...
Many of Steinway Grand Pianos are used by concert artists.

Answer the following questions:
1) There are ----- main parts of a piano
2) How many strings on the piano -------
3) The piano has ----- keys.
4) There are ----- black keys.
5) There are ----- white keys.
6) The ----- is made of wood and is strong enough to support the weight of piano
7) There are ----- pedals located at the bottom.
8) A ----- started when piano ... a key ... every to move a hammer
9) The strings are made of -----
10) There are ----- octaves.
11) The ----- strings make low sounds.
12) The ----- strings make high sounds.
13) ----- is a maker of pianos.

ANSWERS: 88   220   36   Steinway   52   case   7   74   short   long   action   steel

CONDUCTING ACTIVITY

Check out a recording of Duke Ellington. Duke was also a conductor. Have children use a pencil and conduct patterns, feeling the beats. Conductors use a baton because it gives a point to the beat. Also a baton can be seen better than a hand. The baton is usually held in the conductor's right hand. Here are three basic beat patterns.

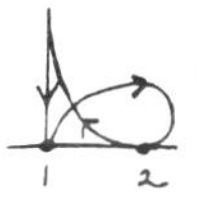

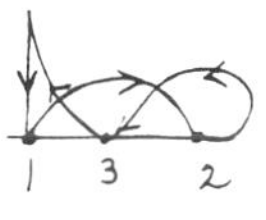

PIANO

Her are some parts of the piano: 1) strings 2) keyboard 3) pedals 4) soundboard 5) case. There are more than 220 strings made of steel in the piano. The long strings make deep low sounds and the short strings make high sounds. There are 88 keys found on the keyboard consisting of 7½ octaves (interval of 8 notes). There are 36 black keys and 52 white keys. At the bottom of the piano are three pedals used by the feet. The frame of the piano is made of cast iron. Consisting of a sheet of wood, the soundboard is below the strings. The action of the piano begins when the pianist strikes a key causing levers to move a hammer. The case is made of wood and is strong enough to support the weight of the piano. Steinway is a well-known maker of pianos. Many Steinway Grand Pianos are used by concert artists.

Match the following questions with the answers below.

1) There are _____ main parts of a piano.
2) How many strings are on the piano _____
3) The piano has _____ keys.
4) There are _____ black keys.
5) There are _____ white keys.
6) The _____ is made of wood and is strong enough to support the weight of piano.
7) There are _____ pedals located at the bottom.
8) _____ is started when a pianist strikes a key causing levers to move a hammer.
9) The strings are made of _____.
10) There are _____ octaves.
11) The _____ strings make low sounds.
12) The _____ strings make high sounds.
13) _____ is a maker of pianos.

ANSWERS: 88, 220, 36, Steinway, 52, case 3
7, 7½, short, long, action, steel

CONDUCTING ACTIVITY

Check out a recording of Duke Ellington. Duke was a conductor as well as a composer. Have children use a pencil to conduct patterns and show the beat. Conductors use a baton because it gives a point to the beat. Also a baton can be seen better than a hand. The baton is usually held in the conductor's right hand. Here are three basic beat patterns:

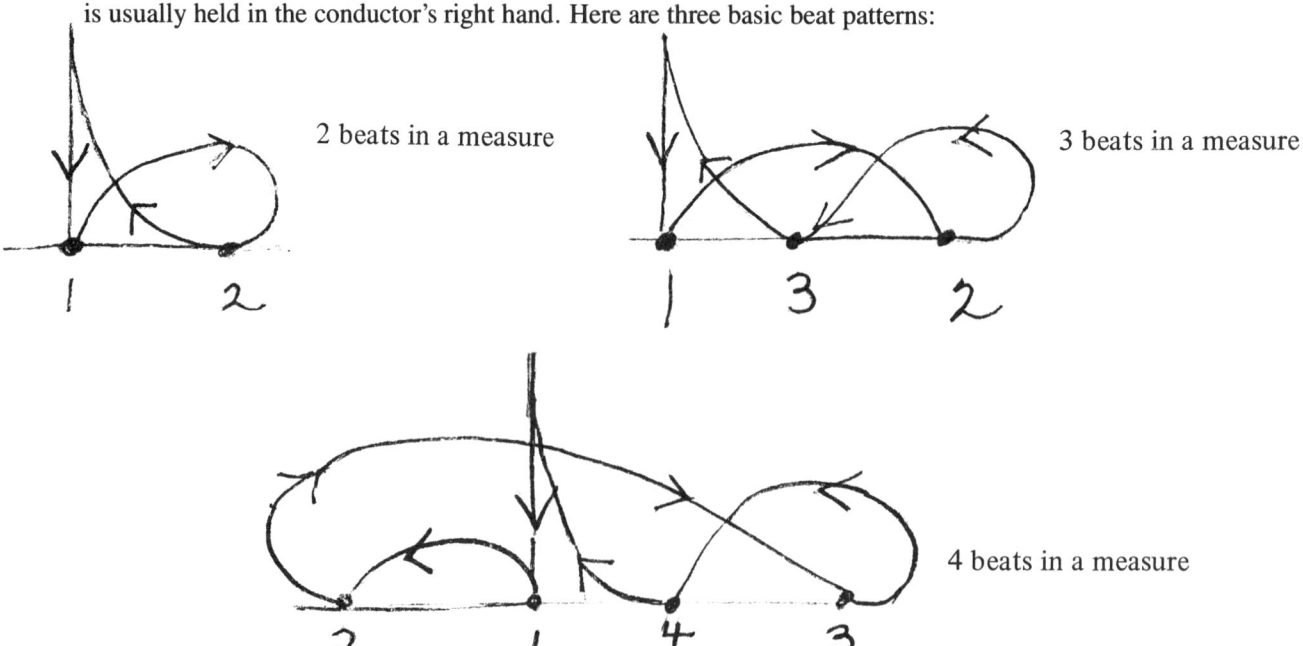

2 beats in a measure

3 beats in a measure

4 beats in a measure

contributed by Beth Harris

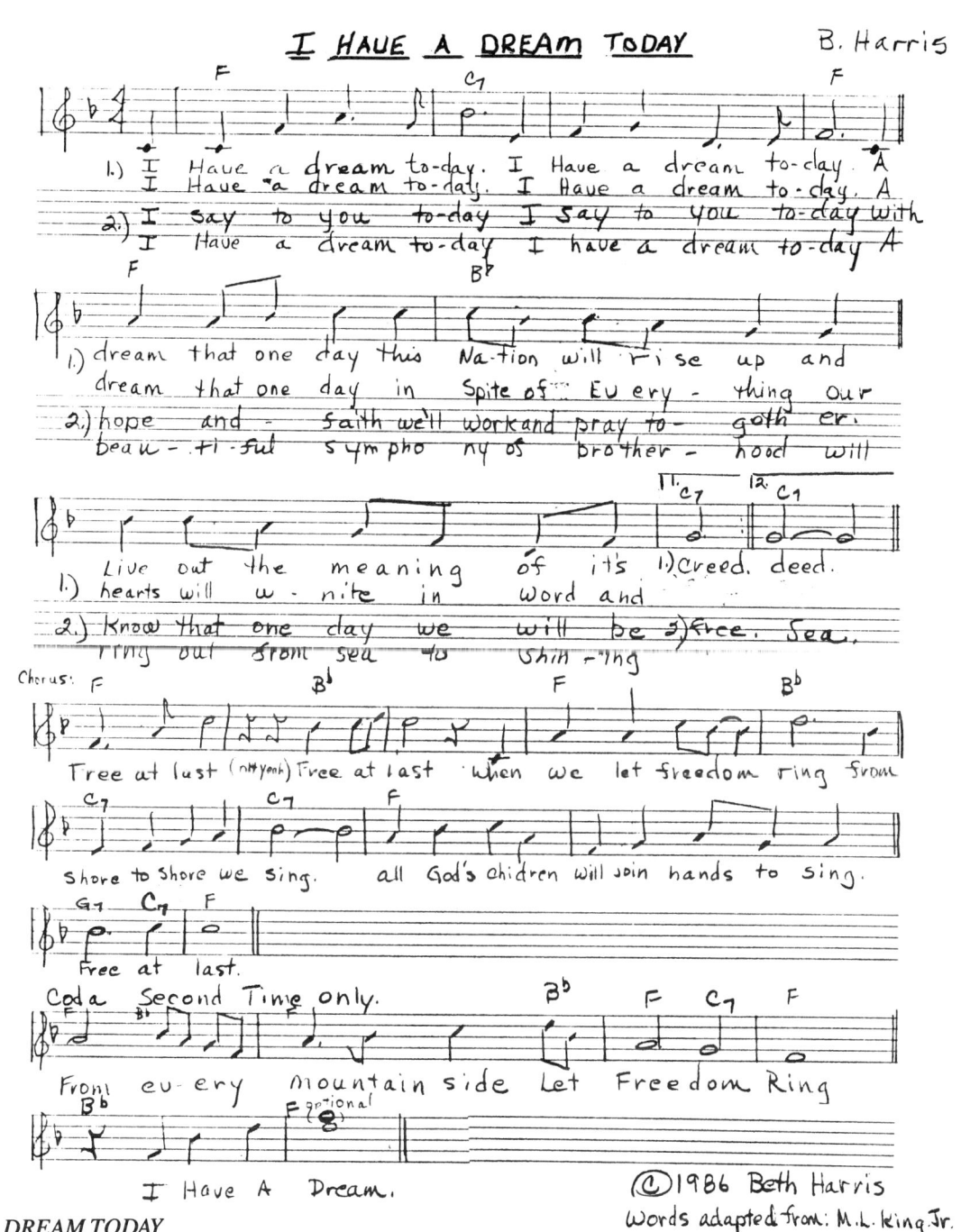

I HAVE A DREAM TODAY

Verse 1
I have a dream today
I have a dream today.
A dream that one day our nation will rise up
And live out the meaning of its creed.

I have a dream today
I have a dream today.
A dream that one day in spite of everything
Our hearts will unite in word and deed.

Refrain:
Free at last (oh yeah)
Free at last.
When we let freedom ring
From shore to shore we sing.
All God's children will join hands to sing
Free at last.

Verse 2
I say to you today
I say to you today
With hope and faith we'll work and pray together.
Know that one day we will be free.

I have a dream today
I have a dream today.
A beautiful symphony of brotherhood
Will ring out from sea to shining sea.

Refrain: 2nd ending
From every mountainside
Let freedom ring.
I have a dream.

Lena Horne

1917 -

Singer, Actress

Lena Horne was born in Brooklyn, New York, and attended school there. At the age of sixteen she was a member of the chorus line at the famed Cotton Club in New York. She toured for a short time as a dancer with the Noble Sissle Orchestra and later received her first lead role in a Broadway show called "Blackbirds." After the show closed, she joined Charlie Barnett's band as a singer. She made her first recording at that time. In the 1940's she went to Hollywood where she became the first Black woman ever to sign a term-contract with a film studio. Her film credits include "Panama Hattie," "Cabin in the Sky," "Stormy Weather" in 1943, "Meet Me in Las Vegas" and the "Wiz." Her most popular recordings include "Stormy Weather," "Blues in the Night," "The Lady is a Tramp" and "Mad About the Boy."

Name: Lena Horne

Skill: Music appreciation/Film appreciation

Procedure:
1. Watch television listings for old movies or visit a video cassette store to obtain Lena Horne's movies, e.g., Stormy Weather.
2. Read her daughter's new book about their heritage, "The Hornes: An American Family" (Gail Lumet Buckley, Knopf, 320 pgs.).
3. Learn the musical terms on the following page.

Variation:
1. Obtain copies of Lena Horne's recordings and discuss her style of singing.
2. Learn the word to "Believe in Yourself" sung by Lena in the movie "The Wiz." Talk about how believing in yourself can influence your life.

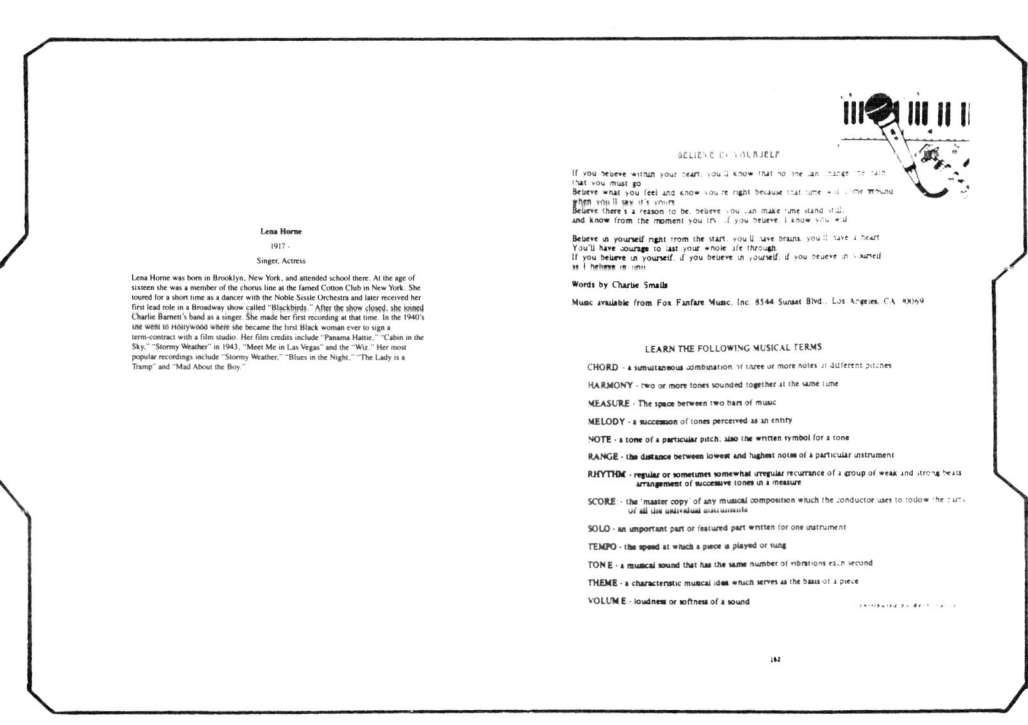

Lena Horne
1917 -
Singer, Actress

Lena Horne was born in Brooklyn, New York, and attended school there. At the age of sixteen she was a member of the chorus line at the famed Cotton Club in New York. She toured for a short time as a dancer with the Noble Sissle Orchestra and later received her first lead role in a Broadway show called "Blackbirds." After the show closed, she joined Charlie Barnett's band as a singer. She made her first recording at that time. In the 1940's she went to Hollywood where she became the first Black woman ever to sign a term-contract with a film studio. Her film credits include "Panama Hattie," "Cabin in the Sky," "Stormy Weather" in 1943, "Meet Me in Las Vegas" and the "Wiz." Her most popular recordings include "Stormy Weather," "Blues in the Night," "The Lady is a Tramp" and "Mad About the Boy."

BELIEVE IN YOURSELF

If you believe within your heart, you'll know that no one can change the path that you must go
Believe what you feel and know you're right because that time will come around when you'll say it's yours
Believe there is a reason to be, believe you can make time stand still,
and know from the moment you try ... if you believe, I know you will

Believe in yourself right from the start, you'll have brains, you'll have a heart
You'll have courage to last your whole life through
If you believe in yourself, if you believe in yourself, if you believe in yourself as I believe in you

Words by Charlie Smalls
Music available from Fox Fanfare Music, Inc. 8544 Sunset Blvd., Los Angeles, CA 90069

LEARN THE FOLLOWING MUSICAL TERMS

CHORD - a simultaneous combination of three or more notes of different pitches

HARMONY - two or more tones sounded together at the same time

MEASURE - The space between two bars of music

MELODY - a succession of tones perceived as an entity

NOTE - a tone of a particular pitch; also the written symbol for a tone

RANGE - the distance between lowest and highest notes of a particular instrument

RHYTHM - regular or sometimes somewhat irregular recurrence of a group of weak and strong beats arrangement of successive tones in a measure

SCORE - the 'master copy' of any musical composition which the conductor uses to follow the parts of all the individual instruments

SOLO - an important part or featured part written for one instrument

TEMPO - the speed at which a piece is played or sung

TONE - a musical sound that has the same number of vibrations each second

THEME - a characteristic musical idea which serves as the basis of a piece

VOLUME - loudness or softness of a sound

BELIEVE IN YOURSELF

If you believe within your heart, you'll know that no one can change the path that you must go.
Believe what you feel and know you're right because that time will come around when you'll say it's yours.
Believe there's a reason to be, believe you can make time stand still;
and know from the moment you try, if you believe, I know you will.

Believe in yourself right from the start; you'll have brains, you'll have a heart.
You'll have courage to last your whole life through.
If you believe in yourself, if you believe in yourself, if you believe in yourself
as I believe in you.

Words by Charlie Smalls

Music available from Fox Fanfare Music, Inc. 8544 Sunset Blvd., Los Angeles, CA 90069

LEARN THE FOLLOWING MUSICAL TERMS

CHORD - a simultaneous combination of three or more notes of different pitches

HARMONY - two or more tones sounded together at the same time

MEASURE - The space between two bars of music

MELODY - a succession of tones perceived as an entity

NOTE - a tone of a particular pitch; also the written symbol for a tone

RANGE - the distance between lowest and highest notes of a particular instrument

RHYTHM - regular or sometimes somewhat irregular recurrance of a group of weak and strong beats; arrangement of successive tones in a measure

SCORE: - the 'master copy' of any musical composition which the conductor uses to follow the parts of all the individual instruments

SOLO - an important part or featured part written for one instrument

TEMPO - the speed at which a piece is played or sung

TONE - a musical sound that has the same number of vibrations each second

THEME - a characteristic musical idea which serves as the basis of a piece

VOLUME - loudness or softness of a sound

contributed by Beth Harris

Ella Jenkins

1924 -

Recording Artist

Ella Jenkins is an internationally known recording artist of children's music. She was born in St. Louis, Missouri but now makes her home in Chicago, Illinois. She earned her degree from San Francisco State University in child sociology with a minor in recreation. Jenkins says her style is a call and response technique, adapted from Danny Kaye and Cob Calloway. She says the words to a song, the audience repeats them after her and soon everyone in the audience is caught up in her song and music. She says this style of music is prevalent in the Middle East and Africa. A member of the Song Writing Hall of Fame, she has recorded and preformed children's music for more than 20 years. Her songs are learning experiences. In them she depicts life here and in other countries. Through her songs she also teaches children new words and number concepts. Her munerous albums are avialable commercially through Folkway Records and Service Corporation, 43 W. 61st Street, New York City, New York 10023. She has traveled to all seven continents to seek new and fresh musical inspirations.

Name: Ella Jenkins

Skill: Appreciation of music from other cultures

Procedure:
1. Learn the notes of the staff, treble and bass clef signs.
2. Obtain records by Ella Jenkins and learn from her educational songs.
3. Play one of her records and have students participate in (1) free-style dance, (2) sea chanteys or (3) authentic dance of the culture
4. Learn the Keys to Success.
5. Read about different music styles and participate in musical activities.

Variation: Thomas Moore, educator, musician, recording artist and child advocate, has also traveled widely throughout the United States, Nigeria, and China, sharing his music to help children "want to learn." Contact Mr. Moore to obtain his children's and religious records at Suite 1000, 4600 Parks Rd., Charlotte, NC 28209

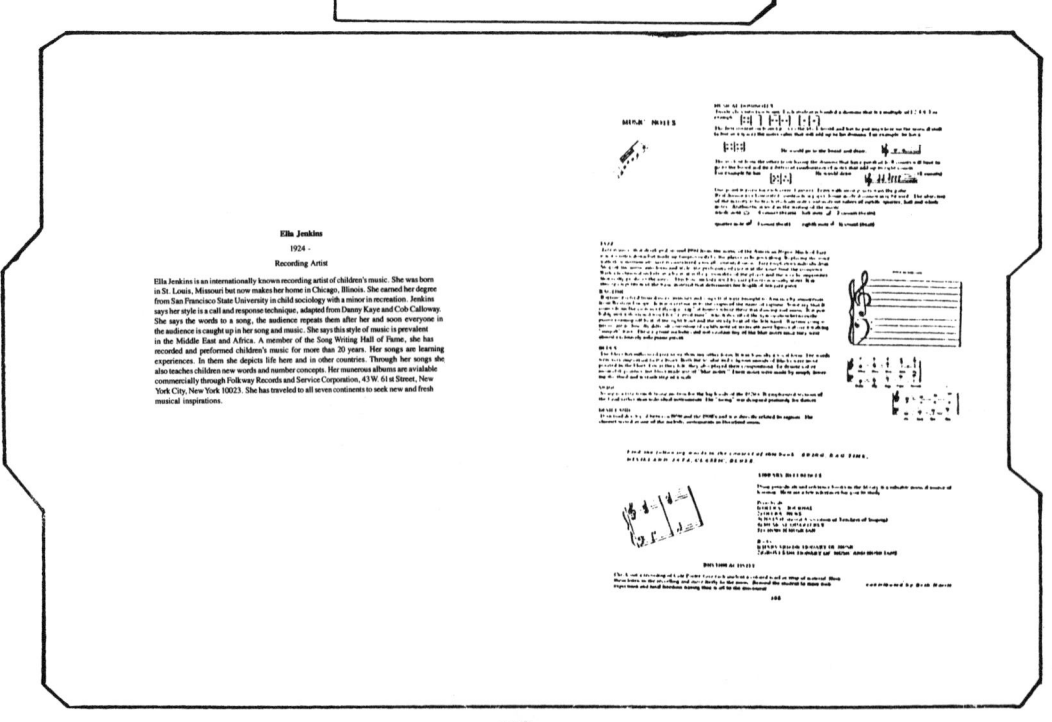

MUSIC NOTES

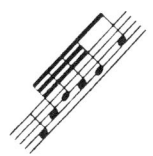

MUSICAL DOMINOTES

Divide class into two teams. Each student is handed a domino that is a multiple of 1,2,4,8. For example:

example:

The first student on team 1 goes to the black board and has to put anywhere on the musical staff (a line or a space) the notes value that will add up to his domino. For example, he has a

He would go to the board and draw:

The student from the other team who has the domino that has the equivalent of 8 counts will have to go to the board and do a different combination of notes that add up to eight counts

For example he has: He would draw: (8 counts)

One point is given for each correct answer. Team with the most points wins the game. Real dominos or home-made dominos, made of laminated construction paper, may be used. The objective of this activity is to teach students combinations of note values of eighth, quarter, half and whole notes. Arithmetic is used in the writing of the music.

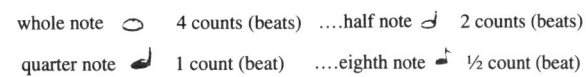

whole note ○ 4 counts (beats) ....half note ♩ 2 counts (beats)

quarter note ♩ 1 count (beat) ....eighth note ♪ ½ count (beat)

JAZZ

Jazz developed around 1900 from the music of American Blacks. Much of jazz is not written down but made up (improvised) by the player as he goes along. Though jazz musicians replaced the voice with their instruments, jazz is still considered a vocally oriented music. Jazz emphasises individualism. By shaping the music, form and style while playing, the performer of jazz is at the same time its composer. Using a traditional melody as a basis, it is the personality of the player and the way he improvises that really produces the music. The basic melody used by jazz players is usually short. It is the repetition of the basic material that determines the length of the jazz piece.

RAGTIME

Ragtime evolved from dances, marches and songs brought to America by immigrants from Western Europe. The origin of the name ragtime is not certain. Some say that it comes from the custom of flying a "rag" at a house where there was dancing and music. However, it is probably just a shortened word for "ragged time", which describes the syncopation between the pianist's roaming off beat of the right hand and the steady beat of the left hand. Ragtime compositions are technically difficult, consisting of eighth note or sixteenth note figures above a walking "umpah" bass. These ragtime melodies did not contain any of the blue notes since they were almost exclusively solo piano pieces.

BLUES

The blues influenced jazz more than any other form since it was basically a vocal form. Lyrics were very important to the blues. Both the secular and religious moods of Blacks were incorporated into the blues. Their compositions reflected their feelings, to denote sad or mournful qualities, the blues made use of "blue notes." These notes were made by simply lowering the third and seventh step of a scale.

SWING

Swing is a jazz term defining motion for the big bands of the 1920's. This music emphasized sections of the band rather than individual instruments. The "swing" was designed primarily for dances.

DIXIELAND

Dixieland developed between 1890 and the 1900's and was directly related to ragtime. The clarinet served as one of the melodic instruments in Dixieland music.

Find the following words in the context of this book; SWING, RAG TIME, DIXIELAND, JAZZ, CLASSIC, BLUES.

LIBRARY REFRENCES

Using periodicals and reference books in the library is a valuable source of musical learning. Here are a few references for you to study:

Periodicals:
1) OPERA JOURNAL
2) OPERA NEWS
3) NATS (National Association of Teachers of Singing)
4) MUSICAL QUARTERLY
5) CHURCH MUSICIAN

Books:
1) HARVARD DICTIONARY OF MUSIC
2) GROVE'S DICTIONARY OF MUSIC AND MUSICIANS

RHYTHM ACTIVITY

Check out a recording of Cole Porter. Give each student a colored scarf or strip of material. Have them listen to the recording and move freely to the music. Remind the student to move with expression and total freedom, waving their scarf to the movement.

contributed by Beth Harris

Keys to success

Many musicians believe they were born to perform and that they have something special to contribute to the music profession. Many know their talent is above average and have the confidence in themselves to make performance their livelihood. How do most performers who have made a name for themselves in music achieve success?

Communicate and establish a reputation with other musicians.
Develop skills, be versatile. Read music, master the technical skills of your instrument.
Establish an individual style.
Frequent practice sessions are necessary. Musicians are like athletes. They must keep their instrument in top form.
Get to know other musicians who do the same type of performing. Go to different places where these people are performing. Play recordings of your favorite artists and study their style. Much can be learned while listening to their technical skills.
Acquire a good stage personality. Your sincerity and warmth on stage is such a personal way of interpreting the music and making it come alive for your audience.
Be willing to become involved in other careers in addition to your music.
Classical training in theory composition, analysis and form are greatly beneficial. Borrowing these techniques from many composers is common. New combination of sounds can be created.

Review the names of the white and black piano keys. As the students draw their own keyboard, have them think about the "Keys to Success." Remind the students to become a music performer they need to believe in themselves. If a career in popular music is their dream, they should be aware that this field is extremely competitive. Their success depends on a tremendous amount of hard work and perhaps an even greater degree of luck.

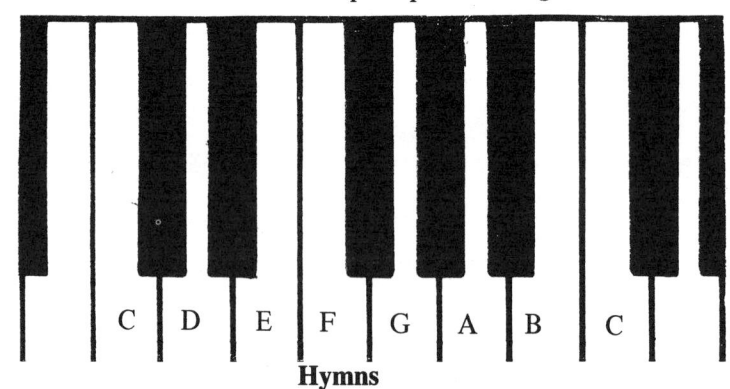

| C | D | E | F | G | A | B | C |

Hymns

Negro spirituals developed mostly from rural folk melodies. They were sung not only in worship but as work songs. The test often reflected basic tasks. The modern Negro gospel song a descendant of the spiritual is accompanied by an instrument, including the traditional clapped accompaniment. Negro gospel music often includes jazz rhythms. Black spirituals are a tribute to the creativity of Black people. Though enslaved, segregated and oppressed, their music was a way of saying that Black people affirmed their dignity through both poetry and song. Despite their oppression they professed that they are a beautiful people because God created them. In their spirituals they sang praises to Him.

ACTIVITY: Play some of the Negro spirituals, i.e. "Swing Low Sweet Chariot" and "Amen."

Have the class sing them and clap their hands as they sing.

contributed by Beth Harris

Thomas Moore, an educator, musician, recording artist and child advocate, is often referred to as the "male Ella Jenkins," has traveled throughout the United States, Nigeria, and China, sharing his music to help children "want to learn." Learn from and enjoy Mr. Moore's recordings of spirituals and children's music.

Leontyne Price

1927 -

Lyric Soprano

Leontyne Price was born in Laurel, Mississippi. She received her B.A. degree from Central State College in Wilberforce, Ohio. She then won a scholarship to the Julliard School of Music in New York. In 1952 she had a two-week run on Broadway in "Four Saints in Three Acts." Later the same year she played Bess in "Porgy and Bess," which toured the world sponsored by the U.S. State Department. She has performed with the NBC-TV Opera Company in "The Magic Flute," "Dialogues of the Carmelites" and "Don Giovanni." In 1961 she made her debut on the New York Metropolitan Opera stage in "Il Trovatore." Price is married to a noted Black bass baritone, William Warfield. In 1966 she opened the Metropolitan Opera's season in an opera written especially for her to perform. She later played Cleopatra in "Anthony and Cleopatra."

Name: Leontyne Price

Skill: Music appreciation

Procedure: Learn the different instruments and their sounds.

Variation: Get a Leontyne Price album and play some selected pieces for the class. Show them the difference between operatic music and other music they may be used to hearing.

Leontyne Price
1927 -
Lyric Soprano

Leontyne Price was born in Laurel, Mississippi. She received her B.A. degree from Central State College in Wilberforce, Ohio. She then won a scholarship to the Juilliard School of Music in New York. In 1952 she had a two-week run on Broadway in "Four Saints in Three Acts." Later the same year she played Bess in "Porgy and Bess," which toured the world sponsored by the U.S. State Department. She has performed with the NBC-TV Opera Company in "The Magic Flute," "Dialogues of the Carmelites" and "Don Giovanni." In 1961 she made her debut on the New York Metropolitan Opera stage in "Il Trovatore." Price is married to a noted Black bass baritone, William Warfield. In 1966 she opened the Metropolitan Opera's season in an opera written especially for her to perform. She later played Cleopatra in "Anthony and Cleopatra."

THE DIFFERENT INSTRUMENTS IN AN ORCHESTRA
AND THEIR SOUNDS

I. The Strings

A. Violin
1. Called the king of instruments
2. The highest voice - soprano
3. How its sound is made -
   When the stretched string is disturbed by a foreign body it vibrates. The note produced depends upon the length of the strings at a given tension.
4. Stroked by a bow
   a. Tremolo - shivering sound produced by small rapid strokes
   b. Staccato stroke produced by a succession of short separated notes
   c. Legato stroke produced by covering many notes in the one bow's length
   d. Sprung-bow stroke causing the bow to leap from the strings between the notes of a rapid passage.
   e. Pizzicato - plucking the strings
   f. Vibrato - produced by a rapid oscillation of the left hand

B. Viola
1. Physically, differs only in size from the violin.
2. Tonally its pitch is lower - tenor voice.
3. Tone quality often described as mournful.

C. Violoncello
1. Large type of violin, too large to be placed under the chin and is thus placed in a reversed position between the player's knees.
2. Tone quality more sonorous, fuller or more bell-like baritone voice.

D. Second Violins
1. Identical in structure to the first violins.
2. Alto voice, playing less melody

E. Bass
1. Largest, requiring player to stand upright.
2. Deepest-toned - bass voice
3. Main duty to keep rhythm within the orchestra

F. Harp
1. Large instrument played by plucking strings.

170

THE DIFFERENT INSTRUMENTS IN AN ORCHESTRA AND THEIR SOUNDS

1. The Strings

A. Violin

1. Called the king of instruments.
2. The highest voice - soprano.
3. How its sounds is made: When the stretched string is disturbed by a foreign body, it vibrates. The note produced depends upon the length of the strings at a given tension.
4. Bow strokes:
a. Tremolo - shivering sound produced by small rapid strokes.
b. Staccato - stroke produced by a succession of short separated notes.
c. Legato - stroke produced by covering many notes in the one bow's length.
d. Spring-bow stroke - causing the bow to leap from the strings between the notes of a rapid passage.
e. Pizzicato - plucking the strings.
f. Vibrato - produced by a rapid oscillation of the left hand.

B. Viola

1. Differs physically only in size from the violin. It is slightly larger.
2. Tonally its pitch is lower - tenor voice.
3. Tone quality often described as mournful.

C. Violoncello

1. Large type of violin, too large to be placed under the chin and is thus placed, in a reversed position, between the player's knees.
2. Tone quality more sonorous, fuller or more bell-like - baritone voice.

D. Second Violins

1. Identical in structure to the first violins.
2. Alto voice, playing less melody.

E. Bass

1. Largest, requiring player to stand upright.
2. Deepest-toned - bass voice.
3. Main duty to keep rhythm within the orchestra.

F. Harp

1. Large instrument played by plucking strings.

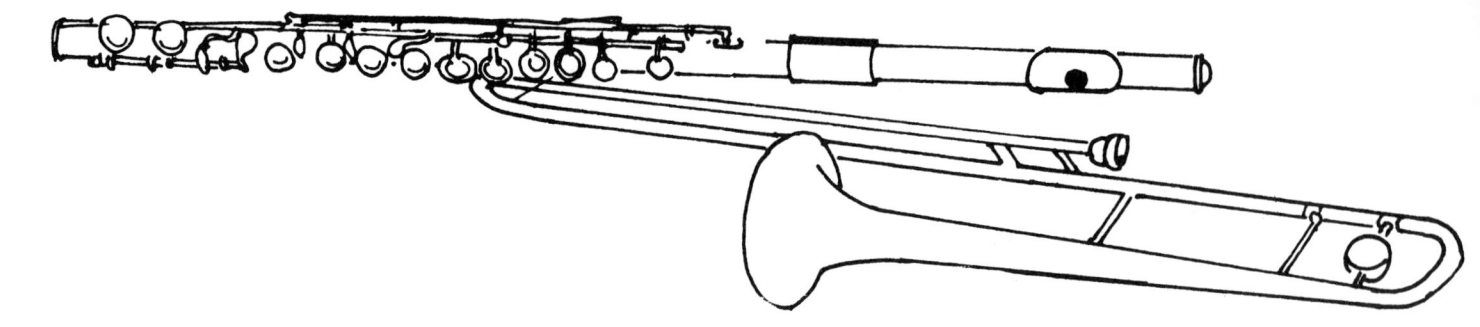

II. Woodwinds

A. Whistle type

1. Flute - high-pitched, clear, pure, velvety tone.
2. Piccolo - half the size of the flute, its tone is an octave higher.

B. Single reed

1. Clarinet - has a large range from deep rich tones to high flute-like sounds.
2. Bass clarinet - larger than a clarinet and an octave lower.
3. Saxophone - like a carved clarinet.

C. Double reed

1. Oboe - nasal tone quality that gives an oriental effect to music. Tunes the orchestra to an A. Tuning is not done until the entire orchestra ia assembled.
2. English Horn - the alto partner of the oboe. Longer than the oboe, it curves at the mouth-piece tube and has a pear shaped bell. Has a sad, dreamy voice.
3. Bassoon - produces very low tone.
4. Contra-bassoon - twice the size of bassoon and an octave lower.

III. Brass

A. Tuba - low tone. The foundation of the orchestra, it is the true bass.

B. Trombone - the baritone voice, but can also be tenor or bass voice.

C. Trumpet - loud, commanding voice; soprano of the brass family.

D. French Horn - warm, mellow tone, tenor voice which blends well with woodwinds and brass. This can also be the alto voice.

IV. Percussion

A. Instruments with indefinite pitch sounded by striking or shaking; bass drum, snare drum, triangle, tambourine, cymbals, castanets, and gong.
B. Instruments with definite pitch: tympani, glockenspiel, xylophone, celesta, and chimes.

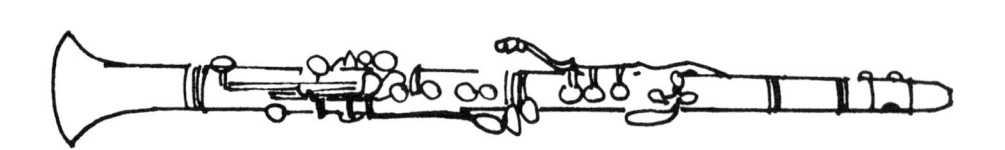

SPORTS・FIGURES

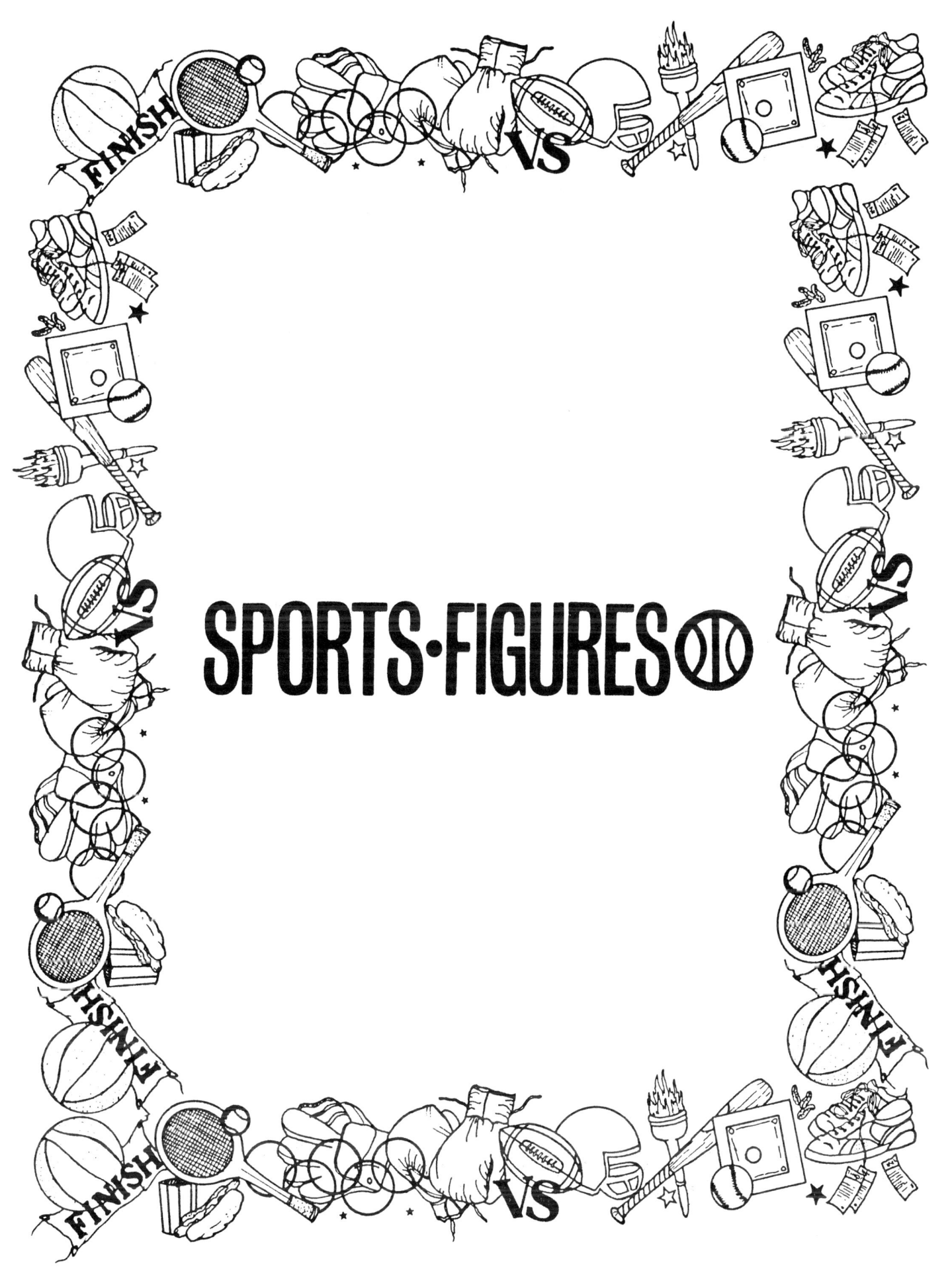

Arthur Ashe

1943 -

Arthur Ashe was born in Richmond, Virginia, and learned tennis at the Richmond Racket Club founded by Dr. R.W. Johnson, who was also the advisor and mentor to Althea Gibson. In 1958, when Ashe was only 15 years old, he reached the semifinals of the National Junior championships. In 1960, Ashe won the Junior Indoors Singles, and before finishing high school he was ranked 28th in the country. At UCLA he won the U.S. Amateur Tennis Championship. After graduating he won the U.S. Open Tennis Championship and became the first Black man ever to be named to the Davis Cup Team. Before his retirement in 1981, Ashe had won every major tennis championship in the world. He has written a book entitled "Advantage Ashe". In 1975 he crowned his great career by becoming the first Black man to win the men's single title at Wimbledon, the most prestigious tournament in tennis.

Name: Arthur Ashe

Skill: Physical Education

Procedure: Learn the rules of tennis. Arrange a tennis tournament for the class.

Variation:
1. Have a tennis player come and discuss the game with the class.
2. Discuss opportunities to participate in competition at parks and recreation departments.

Arthur Ashe
1943 -

Arthur Ashe was born in Richmond, Virginia, and learned tennis at the Richmond Racket Club founded by Dr. R. W. Johnson, who was also the advisor and mentor to Althea Gibson. In 1958, when Ashe was only 15 years old, he reached the semifinals of the National Junior championships. In 1960, Ashe won the Junior Indoors Singles, and before finishing high school he was ranked 28th in the country. At UCLA he won the U.S. Amateur Tennis Championship. After graduating he won the U.S. Open Tennis Championship and became the first Black man ever to be named to the Davis Cup Team. Before his retirement in 1981, Ashe had won every major tennis championship in the world. He has written a book entitled "Advantage Ashe". In 1975 he crowned his great career by becoming the first Black man to win the men's single title at Wimbledon, the most prestigious tournament in tennis.

TENNIS RULES SIMPLIFIED
SCORING

Points in tennis are called Love - 15, 30, 40 Deuce, Advantage, and Game.

0 (or nothing) is called Love.
1st point won by a player is called 15.
2nd point won by a player is called 30.
3rd point won by a player is called 40.
4th point won by a player gives him game, provided his opponent does not have more than 30 (which is 2 points).

If each player has won three points (40-all), the score is deuce. The next point won gives a player advantage.

If he loses the next point, the score is deuce.

When either player wins two consecutive points following the score of deuce, the game is won by that player.

The server's score is always given first.

The player who first wins six games and is leading by at lease two games wins the set.

The player who wins two out of three sets, wins the match.

RULES OF THE GAME

1. Spin for serve, winner can either serve first or take choice of courts.
2. Begin serve from right of center mark, next point served from left of center mark.
3. Allowed two serves to get the ball in play.
4. Serve which hits top of net and lands in service court is called a "let." A "let" is replayed.
5. Serve not in service court or on boundary line is a "fault." Other "faults" are as follows:
   a. Swings at, and misses the ball
   b. Hits the ball into the net
   c. "Foot fault," if foot is on the base line or in the court before the racket hits the ball on a serve.
6. A point is also lost by a player if he reaches over the net to hit the ball, or his racket, or his clothing touches the net while the ball is in play. Other reasons for losing a point are as follows:
   a. Hitting the ball more than once
   b. Ball touches player or his clothing
   c. Player throws the racket at the ball and hits it
   d. Any volley which lands outside the boundary of the court
7. Ball is in play during any of the following situations:
   a. Player hits ball outside the court before it touches the ground.
   b. A ball landing on a base line. The player in whose court the ball lands decides whether a ball is in or out.
   c. If during a rally, a player returns a ball which hits the top of the net and then lands in the proper court.

175

Tennis Rules Simplified

Scoring

Points in tennis are called Love - 15, 30, 40, Deuce, Advantage, and Game.

0 (or nothing) is called Love.
1st point won by a player is called 15.
2nd point won by a player is called 30.
3rd point won by a player is called 40.
4th point won by a player gives him or her the game, provided the opponent does not have more than 30 (which is 2 points).

If each player has won three points (40-all), the score is deuce. The next point won gives a player advantage.

If the player holding that advantage loses the next point, the score is again deuce.

When either player wins two consecutive points following the score of deuce, the game is won by that player.

The server's score is always given first.

The player who first wins six games and is leading by at least two games wins the set.

The player who wins two out of three sets wins the match.

Rules Of The Game

1. Spin for serve, winner can either serve first or take choice of courts.
2. Begin serve from right of center mark, next point served from left of center mark.
3. Player is allowed two serves to get the ball in play.
4. Serve that hits top of net and lands in service court is called a "let." A "let" is replayed.
5. Serve not in service court or on boundary line is a "fault." Other "faults" are as follows:
    a. Player swings at and misses the ball.
    b. Player hits the ball into the net.
    c. "Foot Fault," if foot is on the base line or in the court before the racket hits the ball on a serve.
6. A point is also lost by a player who reaches over the net to hit the ball, or whose racket or clothing touches the net while the ball is in play. Other reasons for losing a point are as follows:
    a. Hitting the ball more than once.
    b. Ball touches player or player's clothing.
    c. Player throws the racket at the ball and hits it.
    d. Any volley which lands outside the boundary of the court.
7. Ball is in play during any of the following situations:
    a. Player hits ball outside the court before it touches the ground.
    b. A ball lands on a base line. The player in whose court the ball lands decides whether a ball is in or out.
    c. If, during a rally, a player returns a ball which hits the top of the net and then lands in the proper court.

Wilt Chamberlain

1936 -

Basketball

Wilt Chamberlain was born in Philadelphia, Pennsylvania. He was 6'11" by the time he entered high school. He then grew two inches to be his final height of 7'1". He is the only professional basketball player to make 100 points in a single game. Besides being an outstanding basketball player, he has run a 47-second quarter mile, put a 16-pound shot 55 feet, and high-jumped 6'10". When he finished high school, 77 major colleges offered him scholarships. He attended Kansas University for three years and earned All-American honors for two of those years. After playing for the Harlem Globetrotters for a year he joined the Philadelphia Warriors in 1959. In his first year, with 14 games left in the season he had already broken the existing full-season scoring and rebounding records. He led two teams to NBA World Championships; The Philadelphia 76ers in 1967 and The Los Angeles Lakers in 1972.

Name: Wilt Chamberlain

Skill: Physical education

Procedure: 1. Learn the rules of basketball. Divide the class into two teams and play the game.

Variation: Complete the additional activities linked on the next page.

Basketball

Basketball was invented by Dr. James Naismith in 1891. Dr. Naismith was a physical education instructor in Springfield, Massachusetts where winter weather placed limits on physical activities. He was trying to design a game that would combine competition and indoor recreation. Prior to his invention, winter physical education meant gymnastics, calisthenics, and marching. The first game was played with 18 players on the court and goals made from peach baskets suspended from balconies at both ends of the gym. The first basketball was actually a soccer ball.

The new game caught on quickly in the Northeastern United States and some of its current terminology reflects its early history. The goal is referred to as a basket. In 1898, teams had to rent dance floors for their games. The playing area was enclosed in chicken wire to keep spectators off of the court. Basketball players are still referred to as "cagers."

Like football and baseball, basketball competition has several levels. There are professional, collegiate, scholastic, and intramural levels. The sport is also a popular "backyard" sport and is attracting female players to all levels.

The basketball court is 50 feet wide and from 84 to 94 feet long. The court is divided by a centerline at half-court. When the ball is put in play, the offensive team has 10 seconds to move the ball across this line by passing it between players or dribbling (bouncing). Once the line is crossed, it cannot be re-crossed during their possession. A player cannot carry the ball or dribble again after stopping. The ball may not be kicked or struck with a fist. Excessive contact between players is called a foul. The guilty player's team is penalized by turning the ball over to the other team who either takes the ball out of bounds or shoots free throws.

The goals are mounted ten feet above the playing surface at both ends of the court. When the ball is shot through the goal, two points are awarded. One point is given for free throws.

The length of a game depends on its level. Scholastic competition usually last 32 minutes, collegiate games last 40 minutes, and the professionals games even longer.

Activities

1. Define the following basketball terms:

traveling
double dribble
dunk
goal tending
jump ball
3-second violation
palming
free throw
fast break
technical foul

2. In a paragraph, describe your favorite basketball team or player.

3. If a team scored 97 points and 15 were the results of free throws, how many field goals were scored?

Ernie Davis

1940 - 1963

Football

Ernest R. Davis was born in the little town of New Salem, Pennsylvania. He attended elementary and high school in Elmira, New York, then received a scholarship to attend nearby Syracuse University. During his sophomore year at Syracuse, he led the University's undefeated football team to its very first National Championship and then on to win the Cotton Bowl. During the rest of his college career, he surpassed the rushing records of Jim Brown and became an All-American Player. In 1961, he became the first Black in history to win the Heisman Trophy. The Heisman Trophy is the most prestigious award given annually to the best college football player in the nation. By the end of his college career he was the National Football League's number one draft choice. He signed the largest contract ever signed by a rookie to play with the Cleveland Browns. During his training for the College All-Stars Exhibition Game it was reported Ernie would not play because of an illness called at the time "a blood disorder." Publicly Ernie's spirits seemed high. He never stopped signing autographs 'Ernie Davis, Cleveland Browns, 1962.' Two months later it was revealed that his disease was supposed to be in remission. The doctors said the nation's best football player had leukemia (cancer of the blood). The good news was that Ernie could play football again. However, the Browns' coach chose not to activate him for the season. By the winter of 1963 Ernie's leukemia had returned and he died on May 18, 1963. He lived 18 months after receiving the Heisman Trophy. At his funeral more than 10,000 people filed past his coffin. President John F. Kennedy said of him, "He was an outstanding man of great character who consistently served as an inspiration to the other people of the country."

Name: Ernie Davis

Skill: Physical Education

Procedure:
1. Learn the rules of football.
2. Watch your's school's games and discuss the plays.

Variation: Watch football games on television and report on plays and scores to the class.
Check out the book on Ernie Davis' life, ERNIE DAVIS: THE ELMIRA EXPRESS by Robert C. Gallagher.

Ernie Davis
1940 - 1963
Football

Ernest R. Davis was born in the little town of New Salem, Pennsylvania. He attended elementary and high school in Elmira, New York, then received a scholarship to attend nearby Syracuse University. During his sophomore year at Syracuse, he led the University's and related football teams to [illegible] [illegible] to win the Cotton Bowl. During the rest of his college career, he surpassed the rushing records of Jim Brown and became an All-American Player. In 1961, he became the first Black in history to win the Heisman Trophy. The Heisman Trophy is the most prestigious award given annually to the best college football player in the nation. By the end of his college career he was the National Football League's number one draft choice. He signed the largest contract ever signed by a rookie to play with the Cleveland Browns. During his training for the College All-Stars Exhibition Game it was reported Ernie would not play because of an illness called at the time "a blood disorder." Publicly Ernie's spirits seemed high. He never stopped signing autographs. Ernie Davis, Cleveland Browns, 1962. Two months later it was revealed that his disease was supposed to be in remission. The doctors said the nation's best football player had leukemia (cancer of the blood). The good news was that Ernie could play football again. However, the Browns' coach chose not to activate him for the season. By the winter of 1963 Ernie's leukemia had returned and he died on May 18, 1963. He lived 18 months after receiving the Heisman Trophy. At his funeral more than 10,000 people filed past his coffin. President John F. Kennedy said of him, "He was an outstanding man of great character who consistently served as an inspiration to the other people of the country."

FOOTBALL

The rules for the American variety of football were first set down in 1875. These rules were a combination of Rugby and European football, soccer. In 1880 the rules were changed to set the number of players per team at eleven. In 1882 rules were made calling for the team in possession of the ball to advance it at least five yards in three downs to retain possession. During the early 20th century, rules set the present field size, legalized the forward pass, adopted a neutral zone between the offensive and defensive lines, and changed first down yardage to ten yards.

Today's game of football is played on a field that measures 160 feet wide and 120 yards long. The two goal lines are 100 yards apart. The objective of the game is to move the ball across the opponent's goal line for a score of six points or kick the ball between the uprights of the goalpost for three points. Crossing the opponent's goal line with the ball is called a touchdown. After a touchdown the ball is placed on the 2 yard line. If the offensive team can move the ball accross the goal line again or kick it through the uprights, an extra point is added to the six already earned.

A game of football is divided into two halves of thirty minutes each. The halves are divided into fifteen minute quarters. The clock can be stopped during a game by a team calling one of its three time outs or if the ball goes out of bounds.

Violation of the rules result in penalties. For example, if a team member exhibits unsportsman-like conduct, the ball is placed fifteen yards closer to his goal for the next play.

There are several varieties of football played today. Best known to Americans are scholastic, collegiate, and professional football. However, touch football and flag football are also popular as intramural sports and backyard sports. All varieties share the basic rules of the game.

Activities

1. How many different combinations of scoring would result in a team receiving (A) 17 points (B) 28 points (C) 35 points?

2. Name the best current football player and in a paragraph, explain why he is the best.

3. Name (A) a scholastic football team, (B) a collegiate team and (C) a professional team.

4. Write a paragraph on what makes a perfect quarterback.

Football

The rules for the American variety of football were first set down in 1875. These rules were a combination of rugby and European football, called soccer. In 1880, the rules were changed to set the number of players per team at eleven. In 1882, rules were made calling for the team in possession of the ball to advance it at least five yards in three downs to retain possession. During the early 20th century, rules set the present field size, and defensive lines, and changed first down yardage to ten yards.

Today's game of football is played on a field that measures 160 feet wide and 120 yards long. The two goal lines are 100 yards apart. The objective of the game is to move the ball across the opponent's goal line for a score of six points or kick the ball between the uprights of the goalpost for three points. Crossing the opponent's goal line with the ball is called a touchdown. After a touchdown the ball is placed on the 2 yard line. If the offensive team can move the ball across the goal line again or kick it through the uprights, an extra point is added to the six already earned.

A game of football is divided into two halves of thirty minutes each. The halves are divided into fifteen-minute quarters. The clock can be stopped during a game if a team calls one of its three time outs or if the ball goes out of bounds.

Violation of the rules result in penalties. For example, if a team member exhibits unsportsman-like conduct, the ball is placed fifteen yards closer to his team's goal line for the next play.

There are several varieties of football played today. Best known to Americans are scholastic, collegiate, and professional football. However, touch football and flag football are also popular as intramural and backyard sports. All varieties of football share the same basic rules.

Activities

1. How many different combinations of scoring would result in a team receiving
   (A) 17 points   (B) 28 points   (C) 35 points?

2. Name the best current football player and explain why he is the best, in a paragraph.

3. Name (A) a scholastic football team, (B) a collegiate team and (C) a professional team.

4. Write a paragraph on what makes a perfect quarterback.

NCAA

The NCAA stands for the National Collegiate Athletic Association. In 1905, President Theodore Roosevelt called for two conferences at the White House to consider rule changes that would prevent the abolishment of football as a sport. Later sixty-two colleges met in New York to establish a football rules committee. They also decided to form a national association to set standards for several other intercollegiate sports. On March 31, 1906, this body was named the Intercollegiate Athletic Association. In 1910 the name was changed to the National Collegiate Athletic Association.

By 1921, the rules-making body was sponsoring national championships. In 1941 a new constitution set standards for membership and made provisions to expel colleges that failed to meet them.

Today the NCAA has nearly 800 members and sponsors competition leading to championships in 39 sports including football, basketball and baseball. The NCAA still serves as a rules-making body for specific sports and player eligibility. It also administers insurance programs for group travel, medical plans, and loss of revenue when games are cancelled.

Collegiate athletic competitions today would not be the same without the NCAA.

contributed by Tom Garmon

Althea Gibson

1927 -

Tennis

Althea Gibson was born in Silver, South Carolina, in 1927 and raised in Harlem in New York. Ms. Gibson became one of America's most remarkable success stories. She began playing "paddle tennis" on the streets of Harlem and went on to win the Department of Parks Manhattan Girls' Tennis Championship. She began receiving professional coaching at a New York tennis club in 1942, and then won the New York State Negro Girls Singles Championship in 1945 and 1946. In 1949, she entered Florida A & M University where she played basketball and tennis. In 1950, she was the runner-up in the National Indoor Championship and in the same year she became the first Black to play at Forest Hills. Not only was she the first Black to play at Wimbledon in England, but in 1957 she became the first to win the Wimbledon Singles Crown. Then with Darlene Hard she also won the doubles championship. She later developed a second career as a professional golfer.

Name: Althea Gibson

Skill: Reading comprehension

Procedure: Have the class play the game board on the following page. Students must answer the questions correctly to advance on the board.

Variation: Play the game of tennis referring to the rules explained in the section on Arthur Ashe.

Althea Gibson
1927-
Tennis

Althea Gibson was born in Silver, South Carolina, in 1927 and raised in Harlem in New York. Ms. Gibson became one of America's most remarkable success stories. She began playing "paddle tennis" on the streets of Harlem and went on to win the Department of Parks Manhattan Girls' Tennis Championship. She began receiving professional coaching at a New York tennis club in 1942, and then won the New York State Negro Girls Singles Championship in 1945 and 1946. In 1949, she entered Florida A & M University where she played basketball and tennis. In 1950, she was the runner-up in the National Indoor Championship and in the same year she became the first Black to play at Forest Hills. Not only was she the first Black to play at Wimbledon in England, but in 1957 she became the first to win the Wimbledon Singles Crown. Then with Darlene Hard she also won the doubles championship. She later developed a second career as a professional golfer.

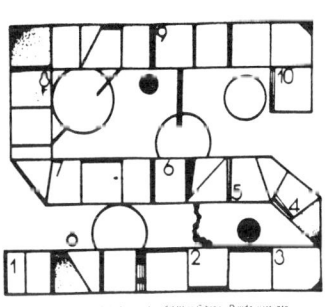

Have the class to read the biography of Althea Gibson. Divide class into groups of 4. Draw a board game with ten squares. Read the following questions to advance each student on the board.

1. Where was Miss Gibson born? _Silver, S.C._

2. In what city did she first start playing paddle tennis? _Harlem, New York_

3. In what years did she win the National Negro Girls Singles? _1945, 1946_

4. What university did she attend? _Florida A & M_

5. What other sport did she play in college? _basketball_

6. What did Miss Gibson do at Forest Hill? _first Black to play there_

7. What year did she win the Wimbledon Championship? _1957_

8. What two crowns did she win at Wimbledon? _singles and doubles_

9. Who was her teammate in the doubles? _Darlene Hard_

10. In what other sport did she become a professional? _golf_

185

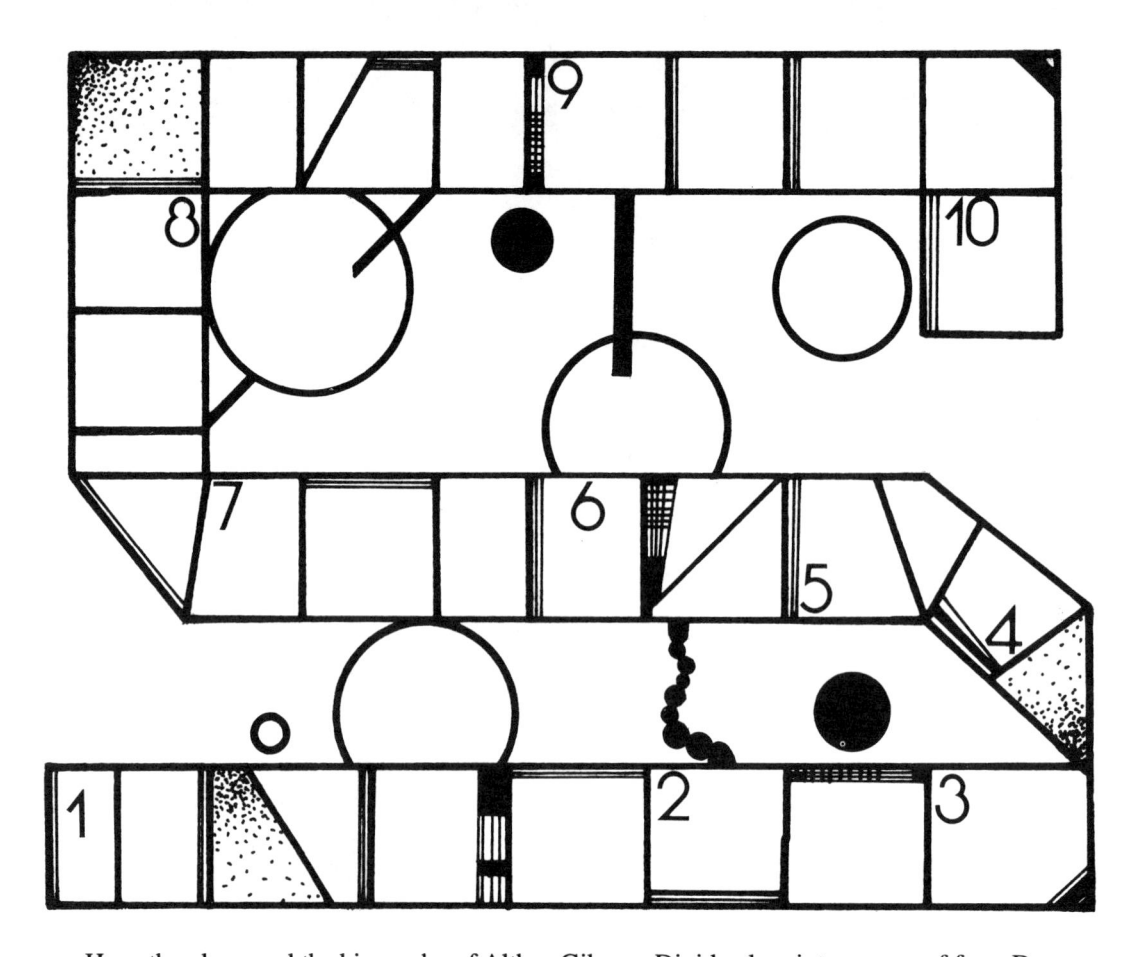

Have the class read the biography of Althea Gibson. Divide class into groups of four. Draw a board game with ten squares. Read the following questions to advance each student on the board.

1. Where was Ms. Gibson born?   Silver, S.C.

2. In what city did she first start playing paddle tennis?

    Harlem or New York

3. In what years did she win the National Negro Girls Singles?
    1945, 1946

4. What university did she attend?   Florida A & M

5. What other sport did she play in college?   Basketball

6. What did Ms. Gibson do at Forest Hills?

    She was the first Black to play there

7. What year did she win the Wimbledon Championship?   1957

8. What two crowns did she win at Wimbledon?

    Singles and doubles

9. Who was her teammate in the double?   Darlene Hard

10. In what other sport did she become a professional?   Golf

Joe Louis

1914 - 1981

Boxer

    The son of a sharecropper, Joe Louis was born in Chambers County, Alabama. As an amateur he won 50 of 59 bouts, 43 of them by knockout. He turned professional in 1934. In 1935 he fought Primo Carnera, a former champion who was staging a comeback. He knocked him out in the sixth round and earned the nickname "The Brown Bomber." After defeating Max Baer, another ex-champion, Louis suffered his first pre-championship defeat by Max Schmeling, the German titleholder. A month later Louis knocked out another ex-champion, Jack Sharkey, in the third round. After winning several other fights, he fought Jim Braddock for the title in 1937 and took him out in the eighth round. In 1941 he had 6 title fights in 6 months: in a return bout with Max Schmeling, he knocked him out in one round; he came from behind to knock out Billy Conn, later won a split decision over "Jersey" Joe Walcott and six months later knocked him out. Then Joe Louis went into retirement.

Name: Joe Louis

Skill: Reading comprehension

Procedure:
1. Copy the biography of Joe Louis and have the class read it. Question them on the facts of his life: birthplace, birthday, rounds in his title fight, etc.
2. Research current heavyweight title holders, e.g. Michael Spinks.

Variation: Obtain the video of "The Greatest" starring Muhammad Ali. The movie is about Ali's life story. The popular song, "The Greatest Love of All", performed by Whitney Houston, is from the movie.

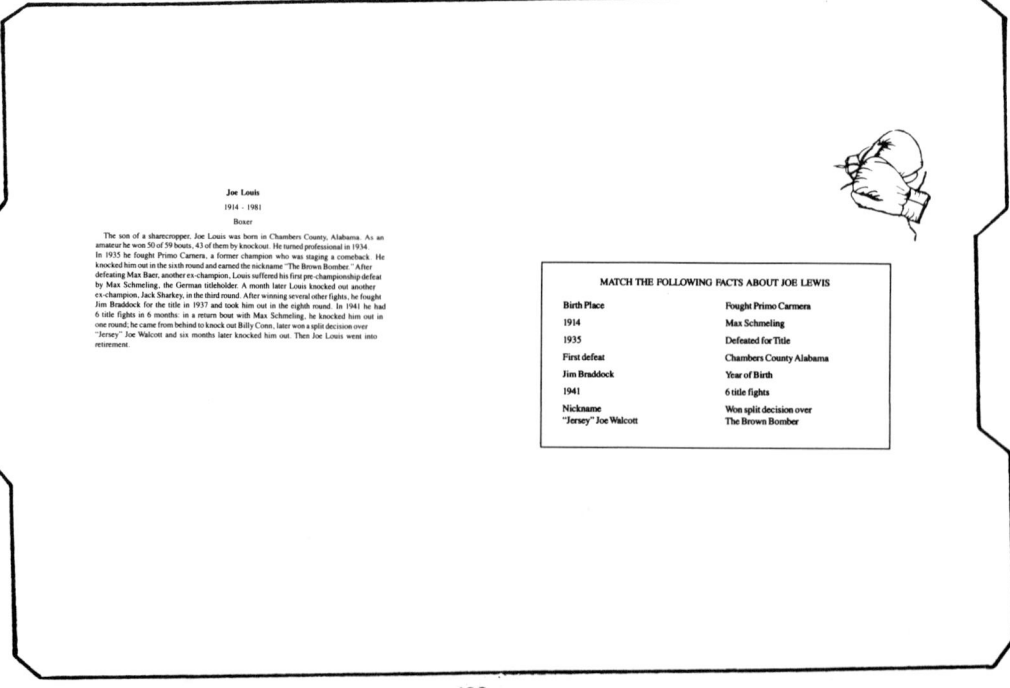

Joe Louis
1914 - 1981
Boxer

The son of a sharecropper, Joe Louis was born in Chambers County, Alabama. As an amateur he won 50 of 59 bouts, 43 of them by knockout. He turned professional in 1934. In 1935 he fought Primo Carnera, a former champion who was staging a comeback. He knocked him out in the sixth round and earned the nickname "The Brown Bomber." After defeating Max Baer, another ex-champion, Louis suffered his first pre-championship defeat by Max Schmeling, the German titleholder. A month later Louis knocked out another ex-champion, Jack Sharkey, in the third round. After winning several other fights, he fought Jim Braddock for the title in 1937 and took him out in the eighth round. In 1941 he had 6 title fights in 6 months: in a return bout with Max Schmeling, he knocked him out in one round; he came from behind to knock out Billy Conn, later won a split decision over "Jersey" Joe Walcott and six months later knocked him out. Then Joe Louis went into retirement.

MATCH THE FOLLOWING FACTS ABOUT JOE LEWIS

Birth Place	Fought Primo Carnera
1914	Max Schmeling
1935	Defeated for Title
First defeat	Chambers County Alabama
Jim Braddock	Year of Birth
1941	6 title fights
Nickname	Won split decision over
"Jersey" Joe Walcott	The Brown Bomber

MATCH THE FOLLOWING FACTS ABOUT JOE LEWIS

Birth Place	Fought Primo Carnera
1914	Max Schmeling
1935	Defeated for Title
First defeat	Chambers County Alabama
Jim Braddock	Year of Birth
1941	6 title fights
Nickname	Won split decision over
"Jersey" Joe Walcott	The Brown Bomber

Jesse Owens

1913 -

Track and Field

Jesse Owens was born in Danville, Alabama, and raised in Ohio. The name "Jesse" came from the way a teacher pronounced "J.C.", the initials for Owens' original name, John Cleveland. While still a student in a Cleveland high school he gained national fame with a record 10.3 seconds in the 100-meter dash. In 1934, Owens entered Ohio State University and made track history for four years as a college student. He was the "Ebony Antelope."
In 1935, while competing in a Big Ten Championship in Michigan, Owens had what has been called the greatest single day in the history of men's athletic achievements. In the space of an hour and ten minutes he tied the world record for the 100-yard dash as well as surpassed the world record for five other events including the broad jump, the 220-yard low hurdles and the 220-yard dash. In the 1936 Berlin Olympics he won 4 gold medals, a record not broken until 1984 by Carl Lewis. He was the hero of the games and embarrassed the Hitler regime.

Name: Jesse Owens

Skill: Physical Education

Procedure: Study the various track and field events listed on the next page. Have your class participate in a Field Day.

Variation: Study the accomplishments of Wilma Rudolph, a track and field athlete. See if you can find the video of her life story or watch TV listings for the rebroadcast of the show.

191

Track and Field Events

I. Running Events

100-meter dash
200-meter dash
400-meter dash
800-meter run
1,500-meter run
5,000-meter run
10,000-meter run

II. Hurdle Events

110-meter hurdles
400-meter intermediate hurdles
3,000-meter steeplechase

III. Jumping Events

high jump
long jump
triple jump
pole vault

IV. Throwing Events

shot put
discus
javelin
hammer throw

V. Decathlon

Field Day Events
Optional Fun Activities

Balloon toss
3-legged race
Wheelbarrow race
Raw egg in a spoon race (if you drop it, you must start over!)

To be adequately prepared to run, certain training precautions should be taken. Steadily increase your training mileage in cooler weather. On hotter days, let your body get used to the heat. This means you have to slow down so you won't risk heat injury. Wear non-restrictive clothing that allows perspiration to evaporate. Take it easy and don't push your body beyond its limits. Know the early signs of heat injury, i.e. dizziness, light-headedness, unsteadiness, nausea, chills. If you feel these signs, stop running.

Jackie Robinson

1919 - 1972

Baseball Player

Jackson Robinson was born in Cairo, Georgia, and was raised in Pasadena, California. In his junior year he left UCLA to play professional football with the Los Angeles bulldogs. After serving as a lieutenant in World War II, he returned home hoping to become a coach. Trying to make a name for himself, he decided instead to play for the Negro baseball league. In 1945 Branch Rickey, the manager of the Brooklyn Dodgers, assigned Robinson to the Montreal Royals, the team's farm club. In 1947 the Dodgers brought Robinson into the major leagues. This made him the first Black person to play in the baseball major leagues. By the time he retired in 1956, he had completed an outstanding career as a hitter, fielder and base-stealer and had won the National League's Most Valuable Player award in 1949.

Name: Jackie Robinson

Skill: Sports appreciation

Procedure:
1. Learn the field positions on page 193 of baseball.
2. Divide the class into teams and play baseball.

Variation:
1. Read the sports section of a daily newspaper to find the American and National league listings. Plot the teams on a United States map using "A" or "N" in the cities where either the American or the National League teams are.

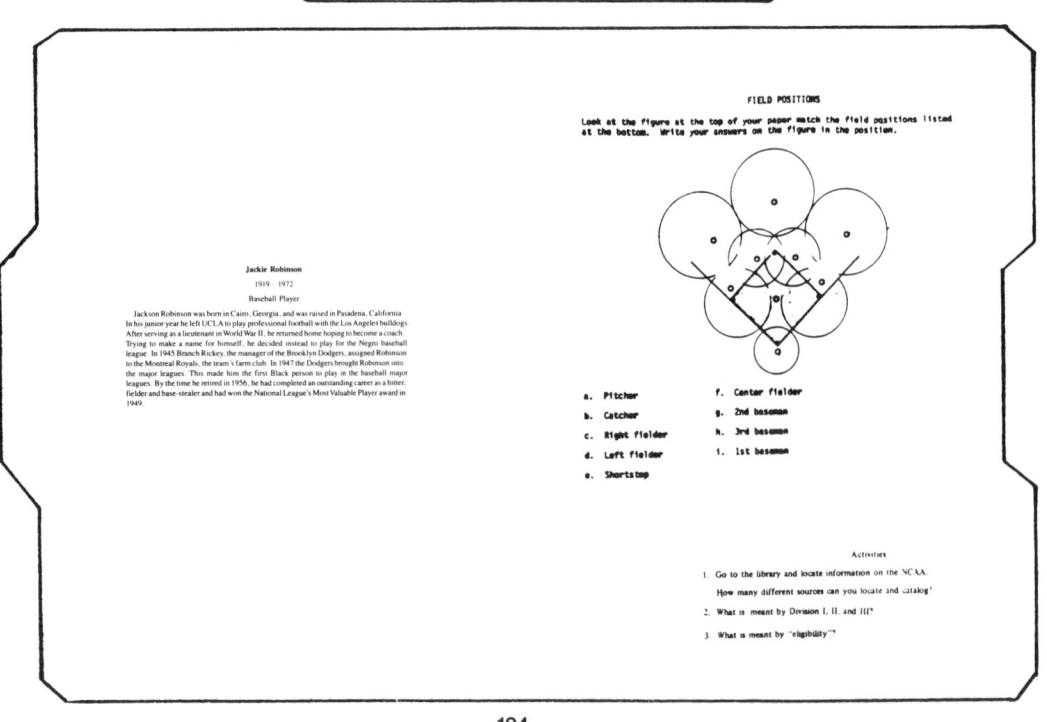

Jackie Robinson
1919 - 1972
Baseball Player

Jackson Robinson was born in Cairo, Georgia, and was raised in Pasadena, California. In his junior year he left UCLA to play professional football with the Los Angeles bulldogs. After serving as a lieutenant in World War II, he returned home hoping to become a coach. Trying to make a name for himself, he decided instead to play for the Negro baseball league. In 1945 Branch Rickey, the manager of the Brooklyn Dodgers, assigned Robinson to the Montreal Royals, the team's farm club. In 1947 the Dodgers brought Robinson into the major leagues. This made him the first Black person to play in the baseball major leagues. By the time he retired in 1956, he had completed an outstanding career as a hitter, fielder and base-stealer and had won the National League's Most Valuable Player award in 1949.

FIELD POSITIONS

Look at the figure at the top of your paper match the field positions listed at the bottom. Write your answers on the figure in the position.

a. Pitcher   f. Center fielder
b. Catcher   g. 2nd baseman
c. Right fielder h. 3rd baseman
d. Left fielder   i. 1st baseman
e. Shortstop

Activities

1. Go to the library and locate information on the NCAA. How many different sources can you locate and catalog?
2. What is meant by Division I, II, and III?
3. What is meant by "eligibility"?

194

Field Positions

Look at the figure at the top of your paper and match the field positions listed at the bottom. Write your answers on the figure for each position.

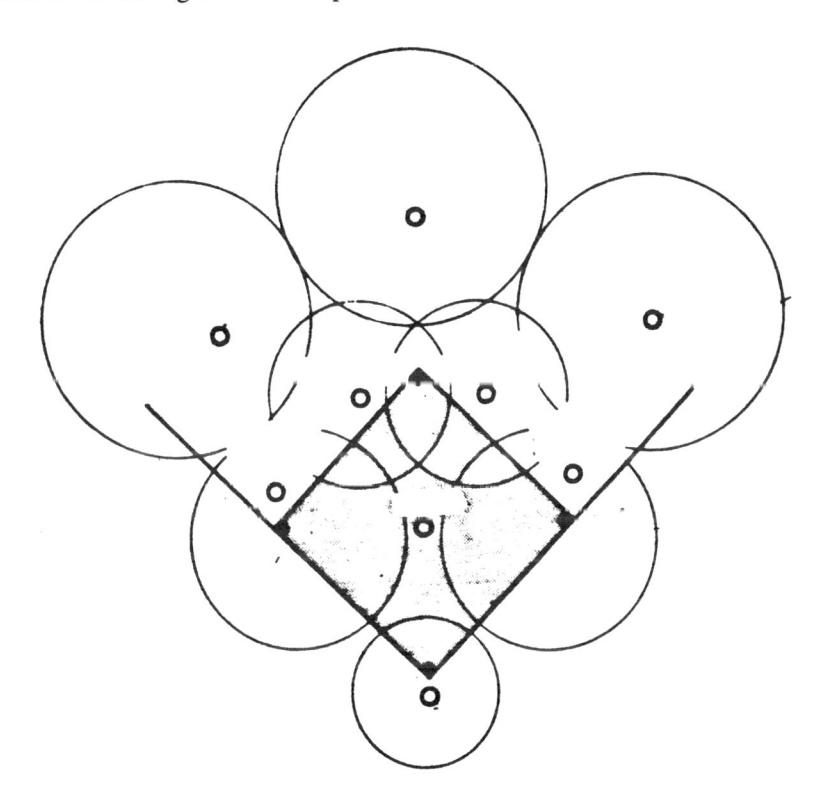

a. Pitcher
b. Catcher
c. Right fielder
d. Left fielder
e. Shortstop
f. Center fielder
g. 2nd baseman
h. 3rd baseman
i. 1st baseman

Activities

1. Go to the library and locate information on the NCAA.

    How many different sources can you locate and catalog?

2. What is meant by Division I, II, and III?

3. What is meant by "eligibility"?

The following section contains a card for each personality in this book. Two facts are given about each person. Laminate the pages, then cut on the lines. The student is to match each illustration with the facts about the personality's life.
Crossword puzzles on each chapter follow. Difficulty varies according to the number of personalities portrayed.

Jesse Owens	General Daniel James	Captain August Martin
- Injured Legs as Child - Olympic Runner in 1936, Winning 4 Gold Medals	- Nickname of "Chappie" - Four Star Air Force General	- First Black Airline Captain - Died on a Mercy Mission for the Red Cross in Biafra
Gen. Benjamin O. Davis, Jr.	Colonel Frederick Gregory	Mary McLeod Bethune
- Air Force General - Commander of the All Black 99th Fighter Squadron and the 332nd Fighter Group	- First Black Space Shuttle Astronaut Pilot - First Black Accepted to the Air Force Academy	- Started a School for Young Black Girls in 1904 - Director of the Division of Negro Affairs Under Pres. F.D. Roosevelt

Booker T. Washington	Benjamin Mays	Robert Weaver
- Founder and First President of Tuskegee Institute - Founder of the National Negro Business League	- Served 12 years on the Atlanta Board of Education in Atlanta, Georgia - Served as President of Morehouse College in Atlanta, Georgia	- Secretary of the Department of Housing and Urban Development under President Johnson - Served on Roosevelt's "Black Cabinet"
Samuel Nabrit	Ralph Bunche	Edward Brooke
- President of Texas Southern University; Commissioner of the Atomic Energy Commission - First Black to Receive Ph.D. from Brown University	- United Nations Under Secretary for Special Political Affairs - Nobel Peace Prize Winner in 1950 and 1955	- U.S. Senator from Massachusetts in 1966 - Served as Massachussetts Attorney General

W.E.B. Dubois	Frederick Douglass	Rosa Parks
- Founder of Pan African Congress (NAACP) in 1909 - Editor of "Crisis" and later "Encyclopedia Africana"	- Escaped from Slavery and Led Anti-Slavery Crusade in New York - Consul General to the Republic of Haiti	- Started Montgomery Bus Boycott - Dressmaker in Montgomery, Alabama

Sojourner Truth	Thurgood Marshall	Martin Luther King, Jr.
- Abolitionist Who Became a Traveling Preacher - Helped Runaway Slaves Settle in the North	- U.S. Supreme Court Justice - Led Team of Lawyers that Won the Supreme Court Decision on School Desegregation in 1954	- First Black Honored by a National Holiday - Nobel Peace Prize in 1964

George Washington Carver
- Agricultural Chemist
- Discovered Hundreds of Peanut By-Products

Benjamin Banneker
- Inventor of First Wooden Clock
- Surveyed Washington, D.C.

Daniel Hale Williams
- First to Perform Open Heart Surgery in 1893
- Surgeon at Howard University's Freedman's Hospital

Charles R. Drew
- Set Up First Blood Plasma Bank In England
- Surgeon at Howard University's Freedman's Hospital

Garrett A. Morgan
- Inventor of First Traffic Light, Sewing Maching Belt Fastener, and Smoke Inhaler
- Inhaler was Transformed into a Gas Mask for the Use of Combat Troops

Guion S. Bluford, Jr.
- First Black in Space, on the Eighth Shuttle Flight
- Scientific Astronaut

Adam Clayton Powell, Jr.
- Elected to U.S. Congress in 1941
- First Black to Have Legislation Pass Both Houses

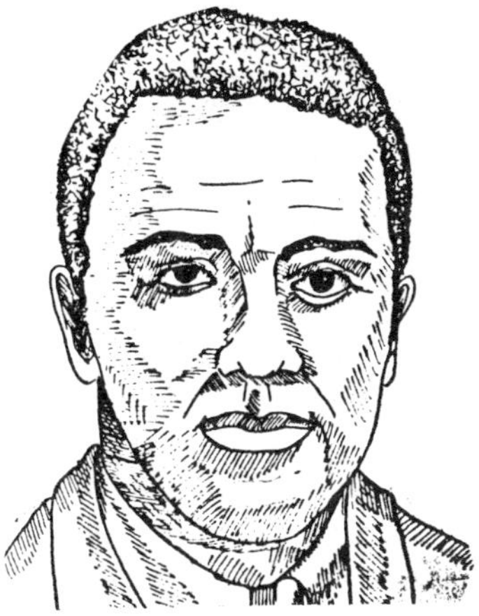

Richard Hatcher
- Mayor of Gary, Indiana
- Born in rural Georgia, the twelfth of thirteen children

Wilt Chamberlain
- Only Basketball Player to Make 100 Points in a Single Game
- Seventy-seven Major Colleges Offered Him Scholarships

Shirley Chisholm
- First Black Woman Congressman in 1969
- Ran for President in 1972

Hiram Rhoades Revels
- Led Black Regiments in Civil War
- Alcorn University President

Andrew Young
- U.N. Ambassador under President Carter
- Mayor of Atlanta, Georgia

Phillis Wheatley	Paul Lawrence Dunbar	James Baldwin
- Poet Freed to go to London to Read to the Royal Family - Published First Poem in 1770	- Published His First Book of Poems at His Own Expense in 1893. - Sold Out Books of Poems and Fiction as Soon as They Were Produced	- Novelist Whose Critically Acclaimed Works Include "Go Tell It on the Mountain" and "Nobody Knows My Name"
Langston Hughes	Richard Wright	Jackie Robinson
- Known as Negro Poet Laureate - Wrote "Ballad of the Landlord"	- Won Guggenheim Fellowship for "Uncle Tom's Children" - Dramatized the Problem of Racial Injustice to a National Audience	- Integrated Major League Baseball - A Member of the Baseball Hall of Fame

Jesse Jackson	Marcus Garvey	Ernie Davis
- 'Rainbow Coalition' Candidate for First Black President of the U.S. - Ran Operation Breadbasket in Chicago	- Founded the Universal Negro Improvement Association (UNIA) in Jamaica - Back to Africa Program Director	- All American in Football - First Black to win Heisman Trophy
Carter A. Woodson	James Weldon Johnson	Althea Gibson
- Dean at Howard University - Founded Association for the Study of Negro Life and History	- Wrote Lyrics for Black National Anthem, "Lift Every Voice and Sing"	- First Black Woman to Win Tennis Championship at Wimbledon in 1957 - Professional Golfer

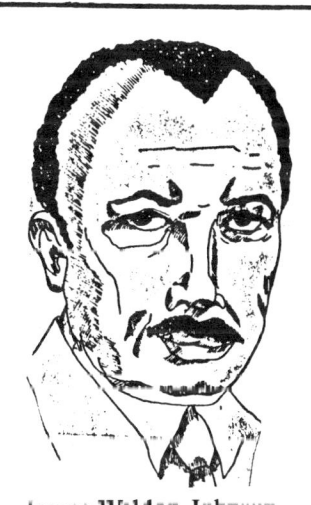

Marian Anderson	Sammy Davis, Jr.	Diahann Carroll
- Soloist with the New York Philharmonic Orchestra at the age of twenty-three - Made her debut with the Metropolitan Opera in "The Masked Ball" in 1955	- Known as "The World's Greatest Entertainer - Singer, Dancer, Actor, Mimic, Comedian, Musician, Writer	- Featured in First Weekly Network Show with a Black Star, "Julia" - Major role in Television Hit, "Dynasty"
Nat King Cole	Bill Cosby	Arthur Ashe
- Sold More Records Than Anyone in History at the Time of His Death in 1965. - Cut His First Record in 1943	- Created 'Fat Albert' - Had Highest-Rated Weekly Television Show from 1984 to 1986	- First Black to Be Named to The Davis Cup Team - Won Every Major Tennis Championship in the World

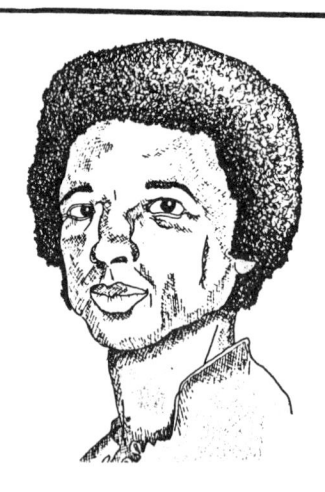

Lena Horne	Duke Ellington	Joe Louis
- Cotton Club Chorus Line Dancer - First Black Woman to Sign a Hollywood Film Contract	- Band Leader and Pianist - Jazz Composer	- Won 50 of 59 Bouts, 43 By Knockout, as an Amateur Boxer - Son of Alabama Sharecropper
Leontyne Price	Louis Armstrong	Ella Jenkins
- Soprano Opera Singer Who Made Her Debut with the New York Metropolitan Opera in 1961 Won a Scholarship to Julliard School of Music	- Acted in "High Society" and "Pennies from Heaven" - Jazz Entertainer	- Children's Song Writer and Composer - Traveled the World Giving Concerts on Children's Music, Playing the Coronet and Trumpet

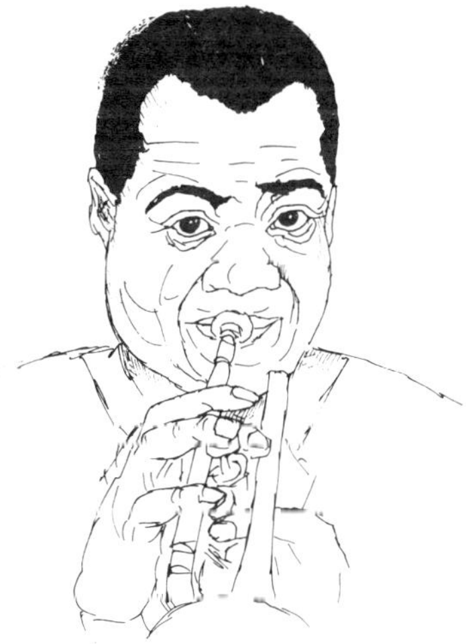

IN LITERATURE

THE CLUES

ACROSS

[1 , 6] WON GUGGENHEIM FELLOWSHIP

[4 , 9] POET IN 1700S

[6 , 6] DEAN HOWARD UNIV

[8 , 1] NOVELIST

DOWN

[1 , 10] NEGRO POET LAUREATE

[5 , 7] LYRICS FOR NEGRO NATIONAL ANTHEM

[6 , 9] PUBLISHED BOOK OF POEMS IN 1893

THE ANSWERS

ACROSS

[1 , 6] WRIGHT
[4 , 9] WHEATLEY
[6 , 6] WOODSON
[8 , 1] BALDWIN

DOWN

[1 , 10] HUGHES
[5 , 7] JOHNSON
[6 , 9] DUNBAR

IN EDUCATION

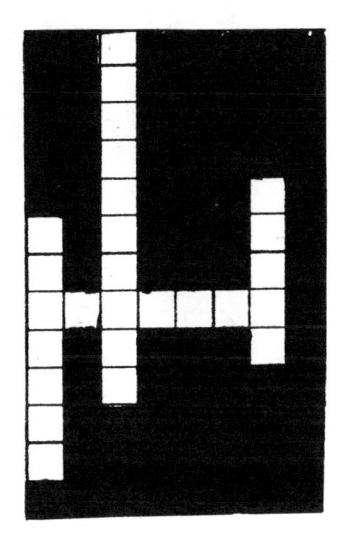

THE CLUES

ACROSS

[8 , 1]   STARTED GIRLS SCHOOL

DOWN

[1 , 3]   FOUNDER TUSKEGEE
               INSTITUTE

[5 , 7]   ATLANTA EDUCATOR

[6 , 1]   AMBASSADOR TO
               NIGERIA

THE ANSWERS

ACROSS   DOWN
------   ----

[8 , 1]   BETHUNE   [1 , 3]   WASHINGTON
                               [5 , 7]   MAYS
                               [6 , 1]   NABRIT

IN SCIENCE AND MATH

THE CLUES

ACROSS

[3 , 1]   1ST BLACK IN SPACE

[7 , 2]   INVENTED TRAFFIC
               LIGHT

[10 , 2]   AGRICULTURAL CHEMIST

DOWN

[1 , 2]   1ST OPEN HEART
               SURGERY

[6 , 6]   INVENTED WOODEN
               CLOCK

[9 , 4]   BLOOD PLASMA BANK

THE ANSWERS

ACROSS   DOWN
------   ----

[3 , 1]   BLUFORD   [1 , 2]   WILLIAMS
[7 , 2]   MORGAN   [6 , 6]   BANNEKER
[10 , 2]   CARVER   [9 , 4]   DREW

CIVIL RIGHTS LEADERS

THE CLUES

ACROSS

[2 , 6]   RAINBOW PARTY
            PRES CANDIDATE

[4 , 2]   FOUNDER NAACP

[9 , 1]   MONTGOMERY BUS
            BOYCOTT

DOWN

[1 , 7]   US SUPREME COURT
            JUSTICE

[2 , 3]   ABOLITIONIST

[2 , 9]   1ST HONORED BY
            NATIONAL HOLIDAY

[3 , 5]   ESCAPED SLAVE
            LED CRUSADE

[8 , 2]   BACK TO AFRICA
            PROG DIRECTOR

THE ANSWERS

ACROSS   DOWN
------   ----

                                [1 , 7]   MARSHALL
                                [2 , 3]   TRUTH
[2 , 6]   JACKSON   [2 , 9]   KING
[4 , 2]   DUBOIS   [3 , 5]   DOUGLASS
[9 , 1]   PARKS   [8 , 2]   GARVEY

IN POLITICS

THE CLUES

ACROSS

[1 , 6]   NOBEL PEACE PRIZE
            IN 1950

[3 , 5]   ELECTED TO CONGRESS
            IN 1941

[6 , 1]   GARY, IN

DOWN

[1 , 6]   MASS. SENATOR

[4 , 2]   ROOSEVELT'S BLACK
            CABINET

[6 , 4]   1ST BLACK
            CONGRESSWOMAN

[6 , 7]   ALCORN UNIV PRES

THE ANSWERS

ACROSS   DOWN
------   ----

                    [1 , 6]   BROOKE
[1 , 6]   BUNCH   [4 , 2]   WEAVER
[3 , 5]   POWELL [6 , 4]   CHISHOLM
[6 , 1]   HATCHER [6 , 7]   REVELS

IN THE HUMANITIES

THE CLUES

ACROSS

[1 , 5]   DEBUT IN 1961 AS
             SOPRANO OPERA STAR

[2 , 10]   JULIA

[4 , 5]   DEBUT MASKED BALL
             IN 1955

[6 , 1]   CHILDREN'S SONG
             WRITER

[7 , 12]   JAZZ ENTERTAINER

DOWN

[1 , 8]   LEADING RECORD
             SALES IN 1965

[1 , 14]   1ST TO SIGN FILM
             CONTRACT

[1 , 16]   BAND LEADER

[2 , 10]   CREATED FAT ALBERT

[3 , 5]   WORLD'S GREATEST
             ENTERTAINER

THE ANSWERS

ACROSS

[1 , 5]   PRICE
[2 , 10]   CARROLL
[4 , 5]   ANDERSON
[6 , 1]   JENKINS
[7 , 12]   ARMSTRONG

DOWN

[1 , 8]   COLE
[1 , 14]   HORNE
[1 , 16]   ELLINGTON
[2 , 10]   COSBY
[3 , 5]   DAVIS

IN THE MILITARY

THE CLUES

ACROSS

[3 , 3]   SPACE SHUTTLE PILOT

[5 , 1]   99TH FIGHTER SQUADRON

DOWN

[1 , 4]   1ST BLACK AIRLINE CAPTAIN

[4 , 2]   4 STAR AF GENERAL

THE ANSWERS

ACROSS		DOWN	
[3 , 3]	GREGORY	[1 , 4]	MARTIN
[5 , 1]	DAVIS	[4 , 2]	JAMES

IN SPORTS

THE CLUES

ACROSS

[5 , 6]   OLYMPIC RUNNER

[7 , 3]   HEISMAN TROPHY
             FOOTBALL

[10 , 1]   1ST DAVIS CUP
             TEAM

[14 , 3]   1ST WIMBLEDON
             CHAMPION-WOMAN

DOWN

[1 , 10]   PROFESSIONAL BOXER

[4 , 6]   INTEGRATED MAJOR
             LEAGUE BASEBALL

[5 , 4]   BASKETBALL CHAMP

THE ANSWERS

ACROSS

[5 , 6]   OWENS
[7 , 3]   DAVIS
[10 , 1]   ASHE
[14 , 3]   GIBSON

DOWN

[1 , 10]   LEWIS
[4 , 6]   ROBINSON
[5 , 4]   CHAMBERLAIN

213

Bibliography

Afro USA, A reference work on the Black experience. Henry A. Ploski, Ph.D. and Ernest Kaiser, Bellweather Publishing Co., 1971.

Before the Mayflower: A History of Black America. Lerone Bennett, Jr., Johnson Publishing Co., Chicago 1982.

Black Power Gary Style. Alex Poinsett, Johnson Publishing Co., Chicago 1970.

Conducting Technique. Brock McElheran. Oxford University Press, New York, 1966.

Ernie Davis: The Elmira Express. Robert C. Gallagher, Bartleby Press, Silver Spring, MD., 1983.

Jazz–A History. Frank Tirro, W.W. Norton & Co. Inc. New York, 1977.

A Junior History of the American Negro. Morris C. Goodman, Fleet Press, New York, 1969.

Meet the Orchestra. William W. Suggs, The Macmillan Co., New York, 1966.

The Negro Heritage Library. Edited By Alfred E. Cain, Educational Heritage Inc., Yonkers, N.Y., 1965.

Singing. The Mechanism & The Technique. William Vennard, Carl Fisher, 1967.

Selected Poems of Langston Hughes. Alfred A. Knopf, Borzoi Book, New York, 1959.

Index of Black Personalities

Abernathy, Ralph	109	Hughes, Langston	16,17
Ali, Muhammad	188	Jackson, Jesse	106,107,108,109
Anderson, Marian	141,142	Jackson, Maynard	72
Armstrong, Louis	145,146,147	James, Daniel	129,130
Ashe, Arthur	174,175	Jenkins, Ella	165,166,167
Baldwin, James	10,11	Johnson, James Weldon	20,21,22,23
Banneker, Benjamin	77,78	Joplin, Scott	146,147
Barry, Marion	73	King, Martin Luther, Jr.	72,106,109,110,111
Bartholomy, Sidney	73	Lewis, Carl	190
Bethune, Mary McLeod	34,35	Louis, Joe	187,188
Byrd, Manford, Jr.	37	Marley, Bob	159
Bluford, Guion S., Jr.	81,82	Marshall, Thurgood	112,113
Bolden, Charles	126	Martin, August	131,132
Bond, Julian	48	Mays, Benjamin	36,37,38
Bradley, Tom	73	Marsalis, Wynton	146
Brooke, Edward	47,48,49	McNair, Ronald	82
Brown, Jim	180	Moore, Thomas	166,167
Bunche, Ralph	50,51	Morgan, Garrett A.	90,91
Carroll, Diahann	148,149,150	Morial, Ernest "Dutch"	59
Carver, George Washington	85,86	Nabrit, Samuel	39,40
Chamberlain, Wilt	177,178	Oliver, King	145
Chisholm, Shirley	54,55,56	Ory, Kid	145
Cole, Nat King	151,152	Owens, Jesse	190,191
Cole, Natalie	152	Parks, Rosa	109,115,116,117
Cosby, Bill	153,154	Patterson, Frederick D.	40,41
Crim, Alonzo	37	Powell, Adam Clayton, Jr.	61,62,63,125,126
Davis, Benjamin O., Jr.	122,123	Price, Leontyne	169,170
Davis, Benjamin O., Sr.	122,123	Revels, Hiram Rhoades	65,66
Davis, Ernie	180,181	Robinson, Jackie	193,194
Davis, Miles	146	Rudolph, Wilma	190
Davis, Sammy, Jr.	155,156,157	Sissle, Noble	162
Domino, Fats	157	Spinks, Michael	187
Douglass, Frederick	96,97,98	Truth, Sojourner	118,119
Drew, Charles R.	88,89	Tyson, Cicely	149
Dubois, W.E.B.	99,100,101	Waller, Fats	158
Dunbar, Paul Lawrence	12,13	Warfield, William	169
Edelman, Marion Wright	55,56	Washington, Booker T.	43,44
Ellington, Duke	158,159	Waters, Ethel	155
Garvey, Marcus	102,103	Weaver, Robert C.	68,69,70,71
Gibson, Althea	174,184,185,186	Wheatley, Phillis	24,25
Goldberg, Whoopi	149	Williams, Daniel Hale	93,94
Gregory, Frederick	88,125,126,127	Winfrey, Ophrah	149
Hatcher, Richard	58,59,60	Wonder, Stevie	151
Henderson, Fletcher	145	Woodson, Carter G.	27,28
Hill, Hector	135,136	Wright, Richard	30,31,32
Horne, Lena	162,163	Young, Andrew	72,73,109,110